"There are many books chronicling an author's quest for his heritage, but how many of them begin with a bout of appendicitis, wend through Azerbaijan, Albania, and Romania, and land in Pittsburgh, with interludes of Kafka, the composer Mendelssohn, and the curious exercise known as Pilates? Adam Sobsey's *A Jewish Appendix* is unique, thrilling, and epically weird, in the very best sense."

—Mark Oppenheimer, author of *Squirrel Hill: The Tree of Life Synagogue Shooting and the Soul of a Neighborhood*

"In this unusual, understated, and brilliant memoir and travelogue, Adam Sobsey writes that he shares much with his parents, including the same area code, but 'a significant difference between us is that they were raised Jewish and I wasn't.' In trying to reconcile this lifelong difference, he journeys into geographic roots of his family tree overseas and the inner evidence of his own past. He searches for—and is searched out by—compelling and sometimes oblique traces and hints: the heaviest doors he'd ever tried to open at a museum in Albania; the oldest Jewish theater company on earth in Romania; the agonies he went through while writing a play about the antisemitic

Ezra Pound. Always musing deeply, with a subliminal pulse of comedy, Sobsey makes the most variable and memorable use of the metaphor of the appendix since Brian Eno's memoir, *A Year with Swollen Appendices*."

—Sam Stephenson, author of *Gene Smith's Sink: A Wide-Angle View*

"This is a book about travel. Travel matters as transformation. So Adam Sobsey cites in the beginning, 1 Samuel 10:16: 'And you shall turn into another man,' and writes of himself at the end. 'I shall go on becoming another man.' 'As People of the Book in permanent revolt against resignation' is how he registers the non-identical nature of Jewish presence. One of many interesting flirtations with travel and book in this work is the one Sobsey has with the philosopher Benjamin Fondane's essay 'Existential Monday and the Sunday of History': as an element of his exploration of Romania, as a work of philosophy about freedom and inevitability, and as part of his investigation of Jewish becoming in the world. Adam Sobsey remains true throughout to his journey and to his name, as man (Adam) and earthling (Adamah)."

—Leonard Schwartz, editor and co-translator of *Benjamin Fondane's Cine-Poems and Other* (New York Review Books Classics)

A JEWISH APPENDIX

Adam Sobsey

For Ruth,
Life is transformation;
life is Torah.
All The best,

SPUYTEN DUYVIL
New York City

For my family and my tribe

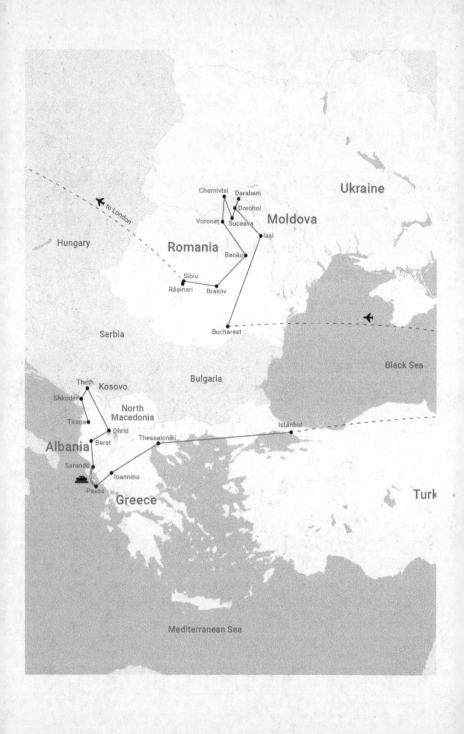

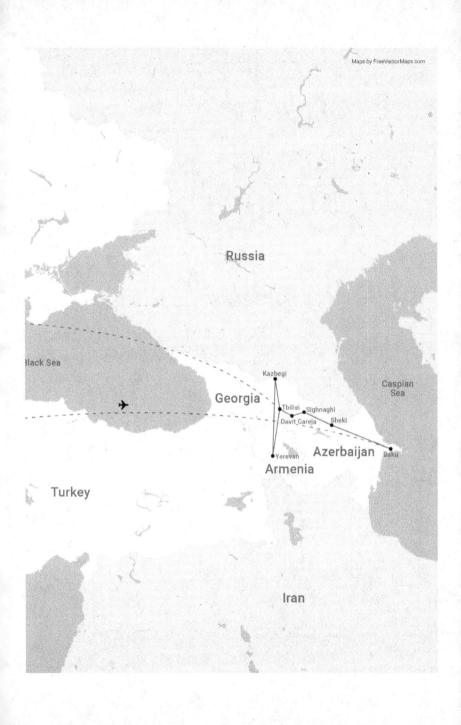

And you shall turn into another man.
1 Samuel 10:6

1.

Preparing

i.

It was an ordinary Sunday. I woke up feeling fine, but by mid-morning I had stomach cramps that worsened as the day went on. I thought through the possible causes: food poisoning, stomach flu, possibly just very bad gas or an unaccountable bout of constipation. In case it was the latter, I drank some coffee and went for a run, a reliable laxative remedy for me. I go running most days in any case.

The remedy worked but the cramps returned. By midafternoon I felt like there was a rock inside me. I went to work anyway. Partway through service I went into the bathroom and vomited into the toilet: a meager ejecta of bile and spit. A little while later I went out the kitchen door to collect myself and suddenly vomited again into a trash can. After the early dinner rush, I clocked out and left. I felt bad for cutting my shift short. I'm disposed to fight through things.

When I got home, my wife Heather was out. I texted her to tell her what was happening. I lay on the sofa, writhing around, unable to find a comfortable position or to make the pain subside. I picked up my notebook and found myself writing, in a jagged, convulsive script:

FILLED WITH REVULSION

FILLED WITH REVULSION

FILLED WITH REVULSION

I write almost every day, but this was nothing like the sort of thing I usually wrote, and I did not know why I was writing it. It occurred to me that it was in many ways an ordinary day—run, work, write—but that these ordinary activities had taken afflicted, contorted, or aborted forms.

Heather came home and assessed my symptoms. She suspected appendicitis and took me to the hospital, where her suspicion was confirmed early Monday morning. My appendix had not yet burst but it needed to come out, and an operation was scheduled for later that afternoon. While I was still in the ER awaiting transfer, a blood test came back with a suddenly elevated white blood cell count. I was moved ahead in the queue, and by late Monday morning I was in surgery.

When the surgeon came by, he said it was a good thing they hadn't waited any longer because my appendix was "very, very sick—completely necrotic."

My recovery was quick and full. I am generally a very healthy person.

I will always remember the date of that Sunday. It was October 28, 2018, which was the day after a man armed with an assault rifle entered the Tree of Life synagogue in Pittsburgh, shot and killed eleven Jews, and wounded six others.

I was raised and educated under nonviolent principles, and I am firmly opposed to capital punishment. When I first got news of the shooting, I was surprised to find myself feeling that the man who killed all those Jews should also be killed. Not denounced, sentenced, imprisoned, or even injured. Just killed. Deleted. It troubled me that I felt this way, but it was unquestionably how I felt. Cut him out of life, I thought.

I have Jewish relatives in Pittsburgh. It was years since I had been there or seen them. I had never been close to that side of my family, which was my mother's side. After I recovered from my appendectomy, I asked her whether our family members in Pittsburgh were alright. She told me that they belonged to another congregation, the same one they had belonged to for three generations.

But my strong reaction to the shooting and the shooter had nothing to do with my relatives, or Pittsburgh, or being Jewish. I was brought up non-observant and felt the way Primo Levi felt about being Jewish: "I had always considered my origins as an almost negligible but curious fact, a small amusing anomaly." Like an appendix.

My decision to go to Romania the following year, 2019, to see where the Pittsburgh side of my family came from, also had nothing to do with the Tree of Life shooting or my feelings about it. Well before my appendectomy, I had already resolved to take this trip.

I have no living relatives in Romania and wasn't interested in looking for traces of my family history, which I knew to be both ordinary and obscure. My ancestral past had been abandoned when my great-grandparents left Romania for Ellis Island in 1910, part of the large wave of immigration of Eastern European Jews in the early twentieth century. Nor was I especially interested in Romania itself.

Like my family history, my decision to go to Romania was also ordinary and obscure. Ordinary because many people, especially Americans, feel a desire to see the source of their ancestry. Obscure because I could not say why or when this desire became active in me. I simply wanted to stand where my ancestors stood. That was my habitual answer when I was asked why I had decided to go to Romania. Just to stand there.

Heather, my wife, was to turn fifty in 2019 and wanted to cross that threshold in time far from home. After much studying of the atlas and her desires, she settled on the Caucasus, particularly the Republic of Georgia, and specifically a place called Kazbegi, where there was a historic mountain monastery, a challenging trail up to that monastery and a glacier high above it, and a renowned hotel in the town. She wanted to hike to the monastery and glacier and stay in the hotel.

Laying out the map, we saw that Istanbul, where neither of us had ever been, was right between our two destinations in Romania and Georgia. Heather contacted two of her closest friends, American expats both living in Europe, and arranged for us to meet them in Istanbul and rent an apartment for a few nights. We also saw that Georgia was not very far from the Caspian Sea. Heather and I quickly discovered that we shared a desire, long harbored but never spoken, to see the Caspian. We had not known this about each other. On such hidden concordances are marriages sustained. The very first booking we made for the entire trip, even before we bought plane tickets from the United States to Europe, was a one-way flight from Istanbul to Baku, the capital of Azerbaijan, on the Caspian's western shore. This would be as far east as our trip would take us.

Heather and I would begin from two different places. She was scheduled to teach a study-abroad college course in May and June. She had also taught this course in 2015 and 2017, in France, but this time the course would be conducted in Ireland. I didn't want to go to Ireland. I gave various reasons for this, one of which was that I had already been to Ireland years earlier, but the real reason was that I wanted to travel alone for a while. I wanted to go somewhere I had never been and had never even thought of before, somewhere new and unknown to me.

I decided to go to Albania.

I had four reasons for choosing Albania. Each reason taken separately was no more substantial than my reason for wanting to go to Romania, in fact much less so. But together they seemed to add up. The first—the reason I had any notion of Albania as a real place, not just a word on a map—was that I had an Albanian colleague at the restaurant where I tended bar, and he often talked up his country to me. The second was that, while Heather was teaching in Ireland, I wanted to go somewhere that would make a good junction point between there and our planned eastward progress across southern Europe toward the Caspian. The third was that, given the length and breadth of our trip as a whole, three months and many thousands of miles, I wanted to go somewhere that felt contained and manageable. Albania is a small country, about the size of Massachusetts. The fourth was that I needed to conserve funds for our longer ensuing stint as a couple. Albania was affordable. In fact it was dirt cheap. The expenses of my entire three and a half weeks there totaled less than a thousand dollars. I made sure of that.

Three conjoined trips: first me alone in Albania; then the two of us together across Europe and the Caucasus to the Caspian, culminating in Heather's birthday at Kazbegi in Georgia; and finally, doubling back west to Romania, where I would stand where my ancestors stood. Our plan was set. It would take three months.

We were able to take so extensive a trip because of two circumstances which are often considered disadvantages but in this case were not. One was that we married too late in life to have children. The other was that neither Heather nor I had what were recognized as regular careers. We were both freelancers, and I was also a bartender. Our lives, mismatched to the world's ways, matched each other's. We could take three months off. We had the time.

We didn't have the money. But in the fall of 2018, not long before my appendectomy, I had a stroke of good fortune. A friend of mine offered me temporary work as a copywriter. I could do that job during the day in addition to the nightwork I already had as a bartender, and reserve the extra income for our trip. I felt especially lucky to have gotten the copywriting job when my appendectomy forced me to miss two weeks of work in the bar. I also felt lucky that my appendicitis had occurred more than half a year before I went to Albania. By then, the illness and surgery were distant memories and I was fully healthy.

The day we arrived in Romania, I got sick. I stayed sick until the day we left, three weeks later.

iii.

I had no substantial reason for going to Romania, but there were many possible reasons I got sick.

Our overnight flight from Tbilisi, the capital of Georgia, to Bucharest, the capital of Romania, was short, only about three hours, but it departed at 3AM, and I had barely slept on the plane. I was quite tired when we landed in the early morning. We took a bus into the city and had a light breakfast while we waited for the apartment we'd booked to be ready. After we checked in, I changed into exercise clothes and went for a run. During our two months of travel so far, I had only run three times. The last time was four weeks earlier. Now I had an excellent setting in which to run again: a warm midsummer day, a beautiful and spacious park with a lakeside loop trail. I ran longer than I probably should have, given my levels of fitness and fatigue.

Afterwards, I had only enough time to shower and change into fresh clothes so I could take a Pilates class. We had been invited to this class by Heather's American friend Julie. Julie lives a few blocks away from us in North Carolina. Coincidentally, she spends a few months each year in Bucharest. Seeing her there was an additional inducement to go to Romania.

I don't practice Pilates and I found the class quite difficult. The studio was unairconditioned and already very warm when the session began. After an hour of a dozen or so students straining and sweating in close, mat-to-mat quarters, it was sweltering and I was exhausted and very dehydrated.

The anteroom outside the studio was where the students changed their clothes. I was the only man in the class, so I went into the bathroom for mutual privacy. I turned on the faucet to splash some cold water on my face and armpits. The water ran out of the tap brown—not rust brown but dirty brown, the color of mud or worse. Against my better judgment, I splashed it on myself anyway and rinsed my hands in it. I made a point not to swallow it, but the water had already been on my lips and surely some of it got into my mouth.

After class, we went to dinner with Julie. By way of introducing us to Romania, she took us to a place that served traditional Romanian food. As a longtime restaurant person with an abiding interest in gastronomy, especially new foods, my eye landed on a dish called *crap țărănească*. It wasn't hard to deduce that *crap* meant *carp*, and our waitress explained (via Julie's translating) that *țărănească* referred to a traditional Romanian style of "sour soup." The sourness was achieved not by the usual means—lemon juice, say, or vinegar—but by fermenting wheat or barley bran in water: a unique kind of sour. She encouraged me to try it, so I ordered *crap țărănească*.

Over dinner, Julie told us something interesting about the Pilates instructor. Her name was Cécile Dumetrier. She was probably in her late fifties or early sixties, but her demeanor was that of someone a good deal younger. She was a charming and ebullient teacher and a demanding one, a former dancer who had come from Paris. Or so her official biography went. In fact, Julie told us, it had recently transpired that Cécile was not French at all but Romanian. She had Gallicized her name (originally Cecilia Dumitrescu, most likely) during the years when she had lived in France. Neither the general circumstances of her return to Romania nor the details of her resumed life in her home country were clear. There was an ex-husband in her prehistory, but she seemed to have no family in Bucharest or anywhere else, and she continued to act as though she were French.

I was enamored and even slightly envious of Cécile. To invent a life and a new name to go with it; to adopt the nationality of the place where you went to become the dancer you really were; and then to return to the land you came from, but to keep the nationality and the name: there seemed to me to be no greater act of self-invention in a lifetime. I have often thought of what Bob Dylan, who was born Robert Zimmerman in Minnesota, liked to tell interviewers when he was first becoming a star and they asked him where he was from. Gallup, New Mexico, he said. Half a century later, he told another interviewer: "Life isn't about finding yourself. Life is about *creating* yourself."

iv.

It was the first time I had ever eaten carp, although not the first time I had ever considered eating it. The first time was when I was a child. I read a children's book called *The Carp in the Bathtub*. The story, originally published in 1972, is set in a Flatbush tenement some decades earlier. A brother and sister (who has the same name as my sister) grow fond of the live carp their mother has bought and put in the family's bathtub a week in advance of making gefilte fish out of it for the Passover Seder. Keeping the carp in the bathtub was a traditional practice intended to fatten it up and, it was believed, to flush out its bottom-feeding digestive tract in clean water. Carp can survive for a number of days in a tub because it is a freshwater species.

Every year when the carp is put in the tub, the children are glad to have a weeklong reprieve from bathing. But something is different about this year's carp. It swims over to them when they go into the bathroom. They can reach the tub from their seat on the toilet and feed lettuce to the carp. They decide to save it from becoming gefilte fish.

How do the children save the carp? I recalled some ingenious, antic, and comical means, but many decades had passed since I had read *The Carp in the Bathtub* and I could not recall how the children saved the carp, nor whether or how they were punished for it, nor what their mother made for Passover instead of gefilte fish. I had forgotten the book's ending entirely.

Perhaps I had eaten carp and forgotten that, too. Or perhaps I simply didn't know I had eaten it. I had eaten gefilte fish in the past, although as with reading *The Carp in the Bathtub* it had been many years. I don't like gefilte fish, at least not the gefilte fish I had eaten, the storebought kind that comes preserved in jelly in a jar. It's one of the few foods I don't like. I'm not sure why I don't like it. I like strongly flavored foods generally, including Chinese fish balls, which are similar to gefilte fish. But I don't like gefilte fish. In fact I detest it.

I enjoyed the *crap țărănească*. It certainly tasted sour, and it made me even thirstier than I already was when we arrived at dinner. My skin and tongue were dry as paper. I drank down my water and all of Heather's, who hadn't touched hers. I ignored her sensible caution against drinking tap water in a foreign country. Julie had ordered a second carafe of wine but I declined another glass, which is unlike me. I just wanted more water. But the waitress did not bring more. On the way home, I felt headachy, very depleted, and overfull. Heather walked us into a grocery store, and we bought a lot of fluids.

V.

"Half a bubble off plumb."
    A phrase we heard from Julie the next day.

Earlier that morning, as we caught up on rest in our rental apartment, Heather and I had sat on the sofa lightly puzzling over whether there was any cause for concern. Probably not. Small stirrings in my gut, a vague headache, mild complaints from my limbs. The food in the Caucasus hadn't always agreed with our digestion. Maybe it was catching up with me again. More likely, we agreed, it was too much exercise after too little sleep, first under too much sun and then in an overwarm room, with not enough water. I had probably just overdone it.

Or possibly it was the *crap*. Heather and I laughed when I said it was possibly the crap.

I didn't tell her about the brown water that came out of the bathroom faucet after Pilates. I'm not sure why I didn't tell her. It seemed a way of protecting myself, or of not admitting to something.

But I really didn't think it was the brown water. Even if it was contaminated, I had only ingested a few drops. Nor did I think it was the tap water I drank in the restaurant after Pilates. There was really nothing wrong with me in any case. I was just half a bubble off plumb.

We met Julie for lunch. I ordered a dish of duck gizzards. Heather wondered aloud whether the restaurant's gizzards and my unsteady innards were a good match. I assured her that I was fine. Better than fine. It was another beautiful warm day in Bucharest. We were sitting in a very pleasant outdoor lunch spot which was a converted nine-teenth-century caravanserai—a reminder that the Ottoman Empire had once reached this far west and in fact much farther, all the way to Albania, where my trip had started, and as far east as the Caspian, where Heather and I had just been.

Over lunch, I asked Julie about dogs, specifically about dogs in Bucharest. In preparation for our trip, I had read numerous books about Romania. One was a recently published travelogue in which the author walked many miles across Romania. He recounted having been forewarned about Romania's abundant population of mean, aggressive, and dangerous strays. These warnings turned out to be warranted: he had to resort to walking with a stick to ward them off.

Perhaps I felt more concern about the dogs than other people might have. In my early childhood I was bitten by a dog when I went onto a neighbor's property one day and surprised their sleeping spaniel. Ever since, I have never been entirely comfortable around dogs.

I had not seen any dogs in Bucharest so far, and Julie told me there was nothing to worry about. Some years ago, although not very many, the city government had issued fair warning to its citizens: claim any dogs you want by such and such date, which was not far off. After that date passed, all remaining dogs were rounded up and euthanized.

I believe in the humane treatment of animals, as I believe in nonviolence generally. But I felt very relieved to hear this about the dogs.

vi.

The talk of Romanian dogs put me in mind of one of the only things I knew about my family's origins.

My great-grandfather and great-grandmother emigrated in 1910 from a small town in remote northeastern Romania. They sailed to America on a steamship with their young daughter, my eldest great aunt. Evidently, they also had with them a second daughter, slightly older, but she perished during the ocean crossing.

My mother tells me that my great-grandparents, when asked about their life before America, always refused to describe a single thing about it, or to explain why they had emigrated. It was as if they had thrown their entire lives in Romania wordlessly overboard along with their daughter who died at sea.

My mother told me that my great-grandfather did share one memory of his life in Romania. She remembered that when she was young, he sometimes spoke about his courtship of the woman who became his wife, my great-grandmother. In order to get from his house to hers, he told my mother, he had to walk for miles through the woods, and every time he took this walk he feared for his life because the woods, he said, were full of wolves.

This sounded like it could have come from a fairy tale. Maybe it did.

vii.

After lunch in the caravanserai, Julie invited us to join her for another Pilates session that afternoon. I was eager to be put through my paces again by Cécile. As if sensing this, she singled me out for extra effort and complimented me every time I rose to her challenge. I have an abiding interest in astrology and am an Aries—a sign disposed to persist through challenges and difficulties, as I had tried to run out the rock in my stomach before I knew it was appendicitis.

After Pilates, I made sure to skip the brown tap water, and then we skipped another dinner out with Julie. We were tired. Heather and I picked up a little eat-in food and went back to the very pleasant apartment we'd rented for three nights. It was in a handsome prewar building called Zodiac House. All twelve astrological symbols were painted onto its façade. Our comfortable and well-appointed apartment had astronomically correct constellations festooned on the walls. I felt that the trip to my ancestral land had commenced under a good sign—under all of them.

viii.

The next morning, I could barely move.

As I entered my forties, I often found my muscles feeling tight or sore, prone to bad pulls and strains: the cumulative effect of years of running and restaurant and bar work. I began stretching every morning when I woke up. Over time, I worked out a little routine: arm extensions, torso rotations, knee drops. Gentle motions, slow, loosening.

My stretches that morning in Zodiac House were excruciating. Everything hurt, and not in the ordinary and even sometimes satisfying way of muscle soreness after hard exercise. I could not do a couple of my movements at all. It was as though my joints, tendons, and muscles had been replaced with iron bars and then surrounded by a scaffolding of more iron. It was the sort of pain I imagined sufferers of rare syndromes felt. A pain that makes everything impossible.

I told Heather I needed to stay in. Not just in Zodiac House but in bed. I stayed in bed all morning and drank copious amounts of the different fluids we'd bought: electrolyte water, powdered ades, fresh juices. The liquid sloshed unpleasantly around in my stomach, as though my body was unable to absorb or release it. Yet I remained terribly thirsty no matter how much I drank. I tried to write in my notebook, as I had on the night I was diagnosed with appendicitis. But I couldn't concentrate and put the notebook down after a few minutes.

Eventually I dragged myself to the sofa, where Heather and I had a full and serious discussion about what was wrong with me. Was it food poisoning? Probably not. I wasn't vomiting, no diarrhea. On the contrary: although I felt crampy, nothing happened when I went to the bathroom. But I felt terribly bloated, knotted, gassy, backed up, and slightly queasy. Filled with something awful. My head was achy and swollen. I was sweaty, too, but clammy, not feverish. At least that probably ruled out an infection.

I told Heather how long and far I had run before the previous day's Pilates class—probably eight miles, plus four or five more miles walking back and forth to the park. I told her I knew I shouldn't have taken the class, that I was overdoing it. I told her about the brown water in the bathroom.

It felt like a confession. Even as we talked about what might be wrong with me, I started to feel still worse, as though acknowledging the problem was deepening it.

Then I burst into uncontrollable tears.

Heather extended our booking in Zodiac House.

ix.

So I had no answer to the question of why I was sick, or what I was sick with.

Another question I had not answered was this:

Why Romania?

I am only one-quarter Romanian. The other three-quarters are all Ukrainian and Russian. Or so it was said in our family, although with imprecision and uncertainty. My mother's father sometimes spoke vaguely about his parents descending from "the Ural Mountains" before coming to America, but he knew nothing else, partly because his father had died young. My father's mother was the only child of a musician from Kiev who emigrated in his twenties and eventually became a well-known cantor in New York City. The origins of his wife, my great-grandmother, were unknown. My father's father's family, the Sobseys, had come to the United States from Odessa but were believed to have merely sojourned there for some number of years or decades after arriving from somewhere else, no one was quite sure where, possibly Turkey, my grandfather thought.

Complicating these uncertainties was that places located in Ukraine on modern maps were referred to as Russian by my grandparents. To them, we were Russian. Or perhaps they meant places that really were in Russia but did not name these places. It was all very unclear.

I knew where my mother's mother's family had come from: Romania, specifically a remote northeastern region called Moldavia, a small town called Dorohoi. So I considered myself Romanian, and Romania was where I wanted to go.

But I did not really want to go to Romania because of a place. I wanted to go there because of my face.

Because of our face. I look just like my mother, who looks just like her mother, who looked just like her father, who had come from Romania. My desire to go there was that simple and straightforward. Yet to articulate it results in a complicated and awkward sentence: I wanted to go and see what the place where the people I looked like came from, looked like.

X.

What do I look like?

"Indeterminate ethnic origin" is a phrase I have often used to describe my appearance. During the five years when I lived in New York City in my twenties, I used to joke that every time I got into a taxi, the driver would start speaking to me in his language. This of course was not true, although something like it did occasionally happen.

Even when I was a child, people often asked me where I was from. I knew they did not mean where in America.

The first time I recall being asked where I was from was when I was perhaps ten or eleven years old. I was in a store in the mall. The salesclerk made a series of guesses. Was I Greek? No. Italian? No. American-Indian, Middle Eastern, Hispanic?

No, no, no. I felt like I was racking up points in a game.

There is a character in Don DeLillo's novel *White Noise* who has an unplaceable name and face, as I have. The narrator wonders: "Was he Melanesian, Polynesian, Indonesian, Nepalese, Surinamese, Dutch-Chinese? Where was Surinam?"

It pleased me that the salesclerk could not correctly guess where I was from. With each successive guess, I grew slightly more excited, anticipating the moment when she would give up and I would be able to say Romania.

There was another salesclerk at the counter. After the first clerk gave up guessing my origins, but before I could reveal them, the second clerk, who seemed to have been waiting his turn, said:

"He's Jewish."

That wasn't the answer I was looking for, but I had to tell him he was right.

But why did he guess "Jewish," instead of a place?

And how did he know I was Jewish?

I felt like I had lost the game.

xi.

About three years before we went to Romania, Heather and I were in a large food market pavilion in Florida. I was shopping for produce while Heather went in search of lunch. She stopped to read the menu of an Israeli eatery. The counterman was hanging around with a few other guys, chatting in Hebrew in the familiar and slightly insular way of countrymen who are in the same place very far from their homeland. One of them asked Heather, somewhat aggressively, how she would know anything about Israeli food. Could she describe shakshuka? She told him she knew the dish quite well. It was a fixture on the weekend brunch menu of our favorite café back home, and she often ordered it.

But she didn't supply that explanation as the reason for her familiarity with shakshuka. Instead, she told him her husband was Jewish.

Just then I approached. She pointed me out. The Israeli counterman glanced at me and shook his head. No, he corrected her, firmly, almost like an accusation. That man is not Jewish, he said. Your husband is Arab!

xii.

On the drive home from Florida to North Carolina, where we live, we stopped in southern Georgia to visit Heather's grandmother. She was 105 years old. She lived not far from Albany, which was known to me as the place to which Martin Luther King, Jr., once drove from Atlanta to make a speech. He arrived in Albany without an overnight bag or even a toothbrush. His purpose ran no deeper than to make the speech and then drive back to Atlanta. Instead he was arrested and jailed, leading to a protracted and difficult embroilment that lasted many months.

Generations of Heather's family, who are white, come from this region: "the Black Belt of Georgia," as W.E.B. DuBois once called it, and "the Egypt of the Confederacy." Heather's grandmother had once told her, with some discretion, that her late husband's family lineage had been colored by "darkening of the blood," as she delicately phrased it. This darkening, she added, accounted for her parents' objection to the marriage.

We were greeted at Heather's grandmother's house by Heather's mother, who was also visiting, and by another relative—a cousin unknown to me who lived nearby and had dropped in to greet us. The cousin was very friendly, in fact excited to meet new relatives. She loved to catalog the extended family and wanted to take a picture of us. First Heather and I went back out to the car to unload our bags. While we were out of the room, the cousin asked

Heather's mother a question about me, politely and discreetly: "What *is* he?"

Heather and I returned before it was necessary for her mother to answer, and the cousin did not ask me about my origins. She snapped a smartphone picture of Heather and me together. We later learned that as soon as she left, she drove directly to the house of another cousin, named Earline, thrust her phone before Earline's eyes so she could see the photo, and repeated the question in a more demanding tone:

"What IS he?"

Earline supplied a concise answer, which she related to us with some pride: "I told her he was *American*. Did I do right?" She laughed when she told us this. We laughed, too. We still do.

xiii.

Later that year, Heather became friendly with a woman who was half-British, half-Iranian. She was fair-skinned and naturally blonde. When she asked Heather to describe her husband, Heather showed the woman a picture of me on her phone.

You didn't tell me your husband was Iranian, she said.

He's not Iranian, Heather answered.

What's his last name, the woman asked?

Heather told her. Sobsey.

The woman threw her head back and laughed. *Sabzi!?*—she said. But that's an Iranian name!

It's a very common name, she said. *Sabzi* is the word for greens, the kind you eat. It's also slang for money.

But that's the other side of my family. My father's side, not the Romanian side.

My Romanian great-grandfather's surname was Sigel. *Sigel* means seal, the wax kind applied to a document to guarantee its authenticity, like the English *signet*—related, of course, to *signature*. My mother's maternal grandfather was not, however, a seal-maker any more than people named Cartwright build carts. His first job in America was as a cigar roller. Coincidentally, that was also the job held by my mother's paternal grandfather, the one supposedly from the Ural Mountains, whose name was Belansky and whose son I called Zaidie, the customary name Jewish children use for their eldest grandfather. Also coincidentally, Moshe Sigel's skin color was very like the color of tobacco, as mine sometimes is in summer.

My family visited Pittsburgh about once a year during my youth. I found the city very strange. It seemed impossible to navigate, with streets that suddenly changed direction or name, and a dizzying number of hulking bridges over Pittsburgh's three rivers: the Ohio, the Allegheny, and the Monongahela. My Zaidie had once been a cabdriver and navigated the routes expertly. When relatives who weren't Pittsburghers drove in to visit, rather than give them directions Zaidie would instruct them to pull off the Pennsylvania Turnpike at an exit outside the city limits and call him from a pay phone. He would then drive out to the exit and escort them into Pittsburgh. It was easier that way, he said.

When we visited, we would see plenty of aunts, uncles, cousins, and old family friends. They tended toward thin, brittle-boned women with pinched faces, suspicious dispositions and disapproving attitudes, and slumped men who wore cheap suit coats and dented hats and complained of aches and pains. I found them as confusing and difficult as Pittsburgh's streets. I navigated them with caution. Even their names were complicated. The man I called Uncle Allen turned out to be a second cousin. Another woman I considered an aunt was actually a family friend, no relation at all to the Sigels. I had a great-aunt named Blima but the older relatives called her Blanche.

All the relatives seemed older, even the younger ones, cousins my own age and younger. Old like Pittsburgh, gray, cold, decrepit. Everyone seemed to be diabetic, anorexic, hemophiliac. They ate terrible food. The women had been on prescription mood stabilizers and painkillers since Eisenhower: Valium, Prednisone, Percocet, Miltown.

The Sigels often gathered on the astroturfed porch of my grandparents' house. Despite their ailments and antipathies they laughed a lot, even though they did not seem like happy people and what they laughed about didn't seem funny to me. It usually seemed like nothing at all. But they had a knack for making something out of this nothing, something which I could clearly recognize but would have had trouble identifying. I could come closest to describing it by recalling what my mother related to me many years later, a line she sometimes heard her kinfolk

speak, with slight variations: "Once you marry a Sigel—
that's it—you're a Sigel."

Not what they said but their way of speaking was what
made the deepest impression on me. All the Pittsburghers spoke in what I came to call, privately, *mutterances*. Yiddish has its own words and phrases that constel-
late around *mutterance*, like *kvetch, tsuris*, and especially
Oy vey is mir. The Pittsburghers complained about their
health, their work, their sports teams, their general lot in
life or someone else's lot, usually that of a family member
not present, someone who was ill or ill-living. It seemed
likely that after we visited and left town, or even just left
the room, they had mutterances about us, too, in that
strange Pittsburgh accent, which to me always sounded,
with its dredged phlegmy consonants and glottal swal-
lows and distended vowels, *Monawn-gahela*, like a native
geographical speech impediment, an impoverished accent
and dialect. "You gaw'na shul?" one great uncle would say
to another. *Shul*. Nowhere else did I hear this word, and it
took me some time to understand that it meant the same
thing as *synagogue*, which was what my family called
it, although we were not observant and seldom went to
synagogue. But the word *shul* stuck in my mouth like
a swallow of medicine. It suggested something entirely
unlike the place where you went to be closer to God. It
sounded more like a nursing home where an old infirm
relative lived and you were obliged to pay regular visits.
"You gaw'na shul?" The question was asked regardless of
the day or time, it seemed, and often when the man being

asked was already down the porch steps, cupping a lit cigarette in his hand, walking away, his back to the question of whether he was going to *shul*. In response, mutterances: "*Probably.*" "*I guess so.*" "*On the way home.*" Going to *shul* sounded like an errand. At best, the Pittsburgh version of synagogue called *shul* might be a place to go if you were in a bad mood, or long downtrodden, or derelict on some duty, which may have been the very duty of going to *shul*, or if you were feeling generally impotent and full of failure and phlegm. You went there not for spiritual succor but for commiseration, or even immiseration.

It never occurred to me that maybe they went there because it was a place where they felt like they belonged.

My mother began taking dance lessons at a young age, and when this childhood passion became a career aspiration it was not supported by her family. In her late teens, she briefly ran away from home to pursue dancing, as Cécile the Pilates instructor did. At age twenty, my mother married my father and moved away for good. I often think that, had she stayed in Pittsburgh, I would not be me. *That's it—you're a Sigel.* I was relieved, every time we visited Pittsburgh, that I was not.

Except that I knew I was, because I looked just like them.

XV.

Perhaps my idea to visit the place the Sigels came from began to form in 2017, when I went with Heather to the south of France where she taught her summer-abroad college course, as I had also done when she taught the class in the summer of 2015. After both sessions, we stayed over in France for a while. In June of 2017, we rented a house in Provence for two weeks. Someone Heather knew owned a place there and gave us a good deal.

The house was not far from the village of Bonnieux. One day we walked to Bonnieux, going down into the valley between the two villages and up the other side. There were cherry orchards all along the walk, and I stopped and picked a few cherries off the trees. They were delicious. In picturesque Bonnieux we browsed, strolled, and took in the view of the Luberon from a café terrace. Heather lingered there while I went down the hill to the village bakery to buy some bread. Near the bakery, I found an entrance to a tunnel with an accompanying plaque. I texted Heather to come down and have a look. The plaque explained that, during the Middle Ages, Bonnieux's community of Jews went out during the day, circulated in public, kept shop, went to *shul*, and lived like anyone else. But at night they were locked up in this cave, by Papal decree, evidently for their own safety. The cave was called the *passage de la Juiverie*.

I found this cave and plaque very interesting. Or so Heather later told me. Although I remember Bonnieux quite well—I walked there several times during our stay in Provence in 2017, picking cherries—I had no memory whatsoever of the *passage de la Juiverie*.

xvi.

At the end of our two weeks in Provence we rented a car. I remember the car well because I so enjoyed driving it: a quick blue Peugeot with a manual transmission. We headed north so I could see Burgundy. My career in the food and wine business had cultivated in me a fondness for the wines of Burgundy. I had also long harbored a deep affection for a novel, by an American writer, whose central setting is a Burgundian town. I wanted to see the vines and visit the town.

We made our way slowly up from the south of France, stopping to see sights and an old friend of Heather's. After logging many days and miles in the Peugeot, when we finally arrived in Burgundy Heather was perplexed by my response, or rather my lack of response. I did not want to go to tastings or tour wineries. There was no particular village or appellation I wanted to visit, nor any specific thing or place I was keen to find. I seldom even stopped the car. When we passed the historic Château de Meursault, I merely pointed it out, along with signs bearing names I recognized from wine bottle labels: Mercurey, Santenay, Saint Aubin. I had an indifference, even a reluctance, to explore Burgundy more deeply, or really at all.

We happened by chance on the hallowed appellation of Le Montrachet. Some of the most famous and expensive white wine in the world comes from these eight hectares. I have never actually tasted a Montrachet. I suppose I could save up and splurge on a bottle, but it could never possibly seem worth it to me.

I stopped the car and took a few minutes to look at the vines. Each one, I thought, must be worth many thousands of dollars—although, of course, if you were to remove the vines from this small parcel and plant them somewhere else, they would be worth virtually nothing. Only the land conferred value, meaning, and identity.

Le Montrachet was surprisingly plain looking. Just a hillside. Indistinct, ordinary. After a few minutes, I told Heather I was ready to move on. We continued, tensely, to the city of Beaune and bickered over where to eat lunch. Then we loped dutifully through the crowded Hospices de Beaune museum.

The tension mounted as we drove from Beaune to the town where the novel I liked was set. I knew my side of the tension owed partly to my longstanding reluctance to speak freely about how much I love the book. It's full of graphic sex scenes. But I sensed it was something other than the sex that tended to keep me quiet about the book. Like me, the author was Jewish. Like me, he was married to a non-Jewish woman. Like my mother's father, he had changed his last name. Asked by an interviewer why he had done this, he declined to answer and was upset when the interviewer's magazine profile revealed that he had changed his name. Asked again about this choice three years later by another interviewer, the novelist answered merely, "The usual reasons."

It was late afternoon when we arrived at the town's main square. This was ground zero of the book, the gravitational center to which it returns again and again, rendered by the author with great evocative power. Yet now, fifty years later, it was a dull concrete slab ringed with cheap businesses: takeout pizzerias, mobile phone stores. This was not exactly a surprise given how long ago the book had been published, and longer still since the year in which its events unfold. Nonetheless, I was disappointed, partly in myself for underestimating the effects of time on a place, but mostly for having dragged us all the way here to this "blue, indolent town," as the novelist calls it, for nothing.

I apologized and said I had been mistaken in wanting to come here and that we could push further north, perhaps to Dijon. But Heather insisted we stay the night and give the town a chance. After we found a place to stay, I went for a walk alone up through the novel's "geography of favored streets," as the narrator calls them, and found many of the locations where its scenes take place, including the house that must have been the one, I deduced (or decided), where the narrator takes up residence—his vantage point on the book's entire narrative, and therefore central to its voice.

I discovered these places at a decisive moment in time. For example, the interior of the town's cathedral was undergoing a major renovation. I peered through rubble at the last remains of what the author must have seen, before it was all to be replaced with new objects and colors. Later, I went back to the main square where there was a tourist office and asked about a restaurant in which the novel's main characters frequently dine. The agent directed me to it but said *"fermé."* This made sense because it was not yet the dinner hour. But when I arrived, I discovered that by *fermé* she meant that the restaurant was out of business altogether: it was padlocked and there was an announcement on the door. The closure appeared to have just occurred, perhaps only days earlier. The silverware was still in its caddies on the bar, napkins ready to fold, aprons on a table.

We stayed that night in a five-room chambre d'hôte. After we explained the reason for coming to this seldom visited town, the proprietress told us that the novelist himself had come to her establishment just a few years earlier. He was by then an old man and behaved rather oddly, she said. He seemed to be looking for something very specific and insisted on standing for a while in a particular spot in the courtyard, as though this spot, which was a mere arm's length from a stone wall, was where a significant event in the novel, or perhaps in the author's real life, had occurred. He went so far as to request, even to demand, a ladder, so that he could climb up to a precise spot on the wall. The innkeeper supplied one despite her concern about a man as old as that going up a ladder. But he came back down unharmed, took a couple of pictures of the wall, seemed satisfied, and abruptly left without taking a room.

The incident was merely peculiar to the innkeeper, but I felt we had been made privy to a secret revealed only to us, a secret not even known to the woman who related it, because she was unfamiliar with the novel. And because she lived in the place. Its importance could be understood only by someone returning to it after many years. Or by a surrogate, standing on the precise spot where the original stood.

xvii.

The next summer, 2018, we went up to New York City for a party thrown by one of Heather's oldest friends on the occasion of his fiftieth birthday. He got his band back together, literally, and played a few rock songs for his hundreds of invited guests in a rented event space in one of Manhattan's trendiest neighborhoods. It was quite a good time, but afterwards Heather told me that the following summer, 2019, when she would turn fifty, she didn't want to do anything like what her friend had done for his birthday. She wanted to be somewhere far away, a place entirely new and even strange, without any large event or fanfare or reunion. That was how she eventually settled on Kazbegi in Georgia.

During that same trip to New York, we went to see the graves of three of my relatives, all Sobseys: my grandfather, my grandmother, and their son, my uncle. When my grandparents died, about a decade apart, I was very far away each time, and it wasn't practicable for me to attend their funerals. I had never gotten around to visiting their graves, which are in the large Jewish section of an even larger burial ground, a vast city of the dead about an hour's drive north of New York City.

A decade after the death of the last of these three Sobseys (my grandmother), I now felt impelled to pay respects. I told my father I was going to the family plot and asked him if he'd like me to leave flowers of any particular type. He answered that the Jewish tradition was to place a stone, not flowers, on graves. I had not known this. It

40

sometimes occurs to me that I share much with my parents—appearance, ideology, interests, an area code—but that a significant difference between us is that they were raised Jewish and I wasn't.

I had a special closeness to my father's parents, especially my grandmother, the daughter of the cantor who had come from Kiev. Like him, my grandmother was a musician, a classically trained pianist who studied at Juilliard. She was also a poet, and I was powerfully influenced by her example as a writer. She was a more than passable sculptor and painter, as well. Art in its many forms was how she lived. She was what we would now call a trauma survivor, a double-amputee who spent most of her life in a wheelchair.

It was very emotional for me to see my grandmother's grave for the first time. It was also emotional to see my uncle's grave. I never knew him. He committed suicide at age twenty-four, while my mother was pregnant with me, her firstborn. He has long held a spectral power over our family and especially over me. I have always felt that some part of his soul or spirit lives on in me. When I saw his grave there on the grass and read the dates on his headstone that verified his lifespan, I understood for the first time that he had been a real person in a real body, now buried.

It also struck me that I had been here before, at his funeral, when I was in my mother's womb. I knew this place without knowing that I knew it.

I dropped into a low crouch by his footstone and cried.

xviii.

Ⓑut it was the other side of the family, the Sigels, the Romanians, whose origins I wanted to see. Because I looked just like them.

All winter, we read maps and books and websites. We bought travel necessities, clothes to bridge two seasons in multiple climates where we would undertake many different types of activities. We got shots. I worked my two jobs, Heather planned for her study-abroad session.

Heather left for Ireland before I flew to Albania. I saw to the final preparations for our trip: holding the mail, hiring lawn care, and so on. One of my very last errands before leaving for Albania was getting an international driver's license. I did not think I would need one, because we were going to places where driving might not be comfortable, and public transportation was very cheap and seemed reliable. Still, the license seemed a valuable credential to have, just in case. It required a passport-sized photo. When the license was ready, I texted an image of it to Heather in Ireland to let her know the errand had been completed. She quickly texted back to say how excited I looked. How bright my eyes with vigor and youthfulness!

I packed very lightly and made room for three books, two of which I knew I would leave behind in Albania. One was an Albanian guidebook; another was a novel by Ismail Kadare, Albania's most revered writer, three of whose other books I had already read in preparation for visiting his country. I would read the novel, then leave it in his birth city, in both pilgrimage and homage.

The third book, the only one I kept with me through-out our trip, was called *The Portable World Bible*, which I had found that spring in a thrift store for fifty cents. I chose it as a kind of spiritual prophylaxis, a balm against any low, uncertain, or trying times I might encounter, as sometimes happens when one is a stranger in a strange land. But as an adherent of no particular faith I did not know which scripture to bring. *The Portable World Bible* offered a tidy solution. Each chapter contained excerpts of holy writings from a different religion, prefaced with a summary of the religion's tenets and history written by the book's compiler-editor.

There was another book I was planning to take but didn't because it was so thick and weighty. It was a guide-book to Romania. I should have included it. But on the day I packed, Romania was two months away, the last place we were going, and I was not thinking of it at all.

Heather is a much better packer than I am, and even though her bag was much smaller than mine, she had managed to fit into it a virtual pharmacopeia. To alleviate my gastrointestinal trouble in Bucharest, the roiling, the sloshing, she gave me a medication called Smecta, a powder that seems to grab all the microbes in your system, ball them up in plaster, and let you get rid of them. I took the Smecta and felt everything get balled up, including the liquid—so now I was even thirstier—and then the ball got stuck in my gut.

I had to get it out. Even though I felt weak, queasy, and achy, I told Heather I was going to get some coffee and go for a run to jar the ball loose, just as I had done to try to dislodge the rock in my stomach that turned out to be appendicitis. Heather did not think this was a good idea. I was very depleted. I had not eaten since the duck gizzard salad at lunch the previous day, and it was now noon the next, which meant it was also quite hot outside.

Heather also did not think running in my condition was a good idea because of what she had come to understand about me after seven years of marriage. Excessive exercise isn't a cause of unwellness for me. It's a symptom.

She did not say this, and I would not have heeded her if she had. I got a coffee and then went for a short, slow, plodding jog, deliberately landing with extra weight on each footfall. It was nothing like the light, gliding run I had been on just two days earlier in the beautiful park.

Instead I was making tight loops around the neighborhood surrounding Zodiac House to be near our bathroom in case my remedy worked. I have no memory of whether it did.

I also have no memory of an entire day in Bucharest.

Presumably, that was the day when Heather went out to visit with Julie again, and I lay in bed and found Jewish Bucharest.

Jewish Bucharest was a self-guided tour devised by a blogger. I found it online, not having packed the guidebook. I don't know why I wanted to take this tour. I had expressed no interest, even to myself, in anything Jewish in Bucharest. My great-grandparents had come from Moldavia, far off in the northeast of Romania, and I had no connection to Bucharest at all, let alone to anything Jewish about it.

I roused myself from bed to take the Jewish Bucharest tour. At the first stop, we were set upon by a Romanian dog. My reaction to it nearly got us killed.

2.

Wayfaring

i.

In December of 1933, a bright but disaffected eighteen-year-old student availed himself of a small allowance from his family, quit school, left England for the continent, and walked all the way from the Hook of Holland to Istanbul. This epic adventure took Patrick Leigh Fermor more than a year to complete: there were plenty of detours, diversions, and delays along the way, many of them welcome. "The Great Trudge," as Leigh Fermor later liked to call it, set the course for the rest of his intrepid, peripatetic life, and his subsequent memoirs of the walk stand as one of literary nonfiction's most legendary long journeys, nearly as invigorating in Leigh Fermor's vibrant retelling as the experience itself must have been.

I read Leigh Fermor's memoirs while planning our trip because he had walked through some of the regions where Heather and I were headed, including Romania. One episode finds him staying the night in a "general store-cum-inn" run by a Jewish proprietor he calls Domnul David. ("Domnul" is an honorific: "Mr. David.") The inn is in the south of the country, where the Jewish population is limited to "little isolated communities," Domnul David tells his young guest, whose occasional encounters with Jews along his walking route had interested him in their culture and history. (It's a poignant interest, as Leigh Fermor himself observes: his walk, which began less than a year after Hitler seized power in Germany, was "attached to trails of powder which were already invisibly burning, to explode during the next decade and a half, in unhappy endings.") Domnul David tells him that if he wants to find large, concentrated, thriving populations of Jews, "the place to go was High Moldavia," Leigh Fermor writes, "far away in the north, in places like Botoşani and Dorohoi—Domnul David's hometown."

Dorohoi happens to be my great-grandparents' hometown, too.

My notebooks are filled with passages from the books I read during the winter and spring preceding our trip, including many citations of Leigh Fermor's memoirs. My self-assigned syllabus ranged from the classics of antiquity to new guidebook editions, from contemporary Albanian poetry to historical novels to geopolitical analyses to articles about Georgian cuisine. But I made no note of Leigh Fermor's reference to Dorohoi. Not only did I neglect to write it down; I did not even remember that Leigh Fermor mentioned Dorohoi at all. When I re-read that part of the book more than a year later, looking for something else altogether, and happened on the passage again, I was totally startled.

ii.

In Albania, I felt like Patrick Leigh Fermor. I walked for entire days, visited hilltop shrines and castles, crossed rivers and fields and ancient bridges, was in and out of bus depots and ferry docks. I shouldered my thirty-five-pound pack up gravelly embankments and tossed it into rattletrap minibuses. One day I walked ten miles to cross an international land border when I impulsively decided to visit North Macedonia. I felt young, spry, adventurous, hungry, motile.

Yet in my interactions with people, I understood that they perceived me as older. Not because of my physical appearance or my demeanor, but through some less visible yet more powerful evidence of maturity. Although I felt a lightness of life about me in Albania, it was counterweighed by a seriousness and sobriety of purpose, the gravitas of a quest. People seemed to come more quickly to my assistance than they would have if I had been a kid backpacking blithely around Europe. When I sat down at a table over an espresso and my notebook to wait for a bus, gray-haired men would come to my table and insist on buying me midmorning shots of raki so we could discuss politics and the affairs of the world like men, in broken English or even pidgin Italian, which some Albanians speak and I could fake. They proudly showed me their old Communist Party membership cards, as though to confirm that our shared generation was waiting and ready for the heroic past to return.

The first volume of Patrick Leigh Fermor's memoirs is called *A Time of Gifts* and this quite literally described my three and a half weeks in Albania. It seemed that everywhere I went, access was granted, doors were opened, sustenance was provided, payment was waived. My Albanian colleague at the restaurant had prepared me for this hospitality to strangers, which has the force of a near moral imperative in his country. Still, it came as something of a shock to a citizen of America, where we do not tend to share our personal abundances so readily. In Albania, by contrast, there was no evidence of its history of totalitarian cruelty, scarcity, surveillance, and distrust. Perhaps the communist era, which lasted more than forty years under the strongman Enver Hoxha, was precisely what led to this abundant generosity and welcome. Strangers offered me cigarettes and raki. Shopkeepers genially refused my money for a hunk of cheese and a handful of olives, saying it was too little food to bother charging me for. Hastily handwritten signs saying FREE ADMISSION TODAY would appear on ticket windows as I approached. Whenever I needed a bus, I would stand anywhere on the side of the road, turn and face the traffic, and one invariably arrived within minutes, or even literal seconds. If it didn't, a car would pull up instead—in one unforgettable instance, a tractor—and its driver would offer to take me where I was going, always amiably declining payment. On a long walk in the outlands toward the ruins of an ancient Roman city I was determined to see, I came to a barred route with a NO TRESPASSING sign, only to have someone materialize nearby, as if out of thin air, and wave me through.

iii.

Another experience that should have cost me money but did not was a museum called the Site of Witness and Memory. It is in Shkodër, a good-sized city in the north of the country. The Site of Witness and Memory was created in the former detention center where, for years, "enemies" of Hoxha's totalitarian state—the grimly familiar roundup of dissidents, clerics, intellectuals, and so on—were imprisoned and tortured. Many died there.

Before it was used as a prison, the building had been a monastery. A roomful of explanatory displays in multiple languages gave historical context, after which I walked down a long, eerily lit corridor to the dozens of "holes," as the cells were called, where the prisoners had been kept. Each had its own steel door—the heaviest I had ever opened. In some of the holes, the museum curators had affixed old communist propaganda to the walls. One or two contained shrines. But most were empty and bare. Light struggled in through the tiny, barred window at the top of each hole, along with a faint tinkle of city life going on outside. At the end of each row of cells was a WC, itself another cell identical to the others except for a hole in the floor between the customary porcelain treads where feet were planted to squat. There was also an interrogation room with its recording devices and electrodes.

I had seen this sort of place before, in 2001, when I visited Phnom Penh's Tuol Sleng prison: another totalitarian regime's site of detention, torture, and murder in the middle of a city. Tuol Sleng had deeply affected me in 2001, but the Site of Witness and Memory left me oddly unmoved, "in stony disbelief," I wrote in my notebook afterward. In a missive to family and friends, I claimed I couldn't conceive of terror drawn out and coldly systematized under bureaucratic officialdom, which requires a long chain of complicity and participation, paperwork, formalization, taxonomy: a sort of twisted civil order maintained by large numbers of people engaged like any workforce in this daily infliction of torture and death. I mentioned something about the unimaginable Holocaust. But in fact I was not in disbelief at all. It made perfect sense to me. I actually felt like I was lying.

I had arrived at the Site of Witness and Memory just after opening hours. There was no one at the front desk, so I walked in and figured I would pay when I left. On my way out, the desk was still unattended. I picked through a group of German tourists in the lobby to see if I could find a museum employee among them, but I found only their own tour group leaders, and no one seemed to take any note of me. I left without paying.

iv.

From Shkodër I went north into the Alps, where there is a regionally famed mountain hike between two villages, Theth and Valbona. The trail is in fact the only route unless you go all the way around the range, a half-day's drive. The seventeen-kilometer mountain trail is well-traveled—there are even a couple of rustic cafes along the way—and like Patrick Leigh Fermor I was keen to walk.

I stayed the night in a farmhouse in Theth that had only one guestroom. After dinner and nightfall, a second guest arrived, and I was surprised to have to share my room. At first I chafed. The proprietress had told me the room was mine alone, and she herself acted as though she hadn't expected him. But I soon became quite interested in my roommate. He was a young Korean fellow called Lee, and he had—was I understanding his halting English correctly?—*biked* to Albania from Korea? Yes, he confirmed, he had been pedaling for a year and a half. He opened up his phone map app and showed me the route he had traveled so far, a jagged stitch across nearly the entire length of Eurasia, ten thousand kilometers from China to the Balkans by way of several Stans and the Black Sea. His final destination was Santiago de Compostela, the hallowed Christian pilgrimage site in Spain. Was he Christian? No. Why was he going there? It seemed like the right place, he said.

He was Patrick Leigh Fermor, reborn in Korea on a bike. Leigh became Lee.

Lee was twenty-eight, a decade older than Leigh Fermor had been when he set off from the Hook of Holland for Turkey, and two decades younger than me. The previous year, he dropped out of the army, planned his route, bought a bicycle, and set off. There it was outside the guesthouse, barely visible in the Albanian darkness, leaning unsecured against a tree. He had come to Theth for the same reason I had, just to walk over the mountain to Valbona. He intended to walk back the same day. He had innocent-child eyes and an open, almost feminine face, but he exuded a quiet yet prodigious inner assurance and intelligence—there was a core of iron inside his soft imprintable cloth. His quads were like cannons.

The next day I happened to catch up with him near the trailhead, and we hiked together. We did not talk much en route, owing mostly to Lee's tentative English, but we seemed to develop a camaraderie, even a bond. As I walked with him, hearing about the places he'd been on his way to Santiago de Compostela, I felt powerfully connected to my own quest to stand where my ancestors stood in Romania, for I was connected to someone so connected to his, and more powerfully still because we were both driven by reasons we could not quite articulate. A couple of other hikers joined us partway along the trail and the four of us made the descent into Valbona and had dinner in the same lodge. The next morning, Lee walked me to the main road where I intended to hitch another ride and we bid each other a warm goodbye. He sent occasional emails during the rest of his ride and finally a picture from Santiago de Compostela a few months later. I asked him what his plans were now that he had completed his pilgrimage. He said he would probably go work on a farm in Australia. I never heard from him again.

The last place I went in Albania on my own, before Heather flew down from Ireland to meet me, was Berat. After more than two weeks of vigorous travel I was ready to rest for a spell, and Berat, a pleasant and attractive small city, was a good place to put my heels up. And I knew someone there. Almost. Berat was the hometown of my restaurant colleague from Albania. His father still lived there, and he took me to lunch and gave me a bottle of his homemade raki to take back to his son. I had more than two months and thousands of miles of travel ahead of me and was indisposed to carry a bottle of booze all that way, but to say so struck me as rude so I made room in my bag and hoped the bottle would make it.

It rained a good deal while I was in Berat, which was fine with me because I was happy for the rest. When the weather allowed it, I went out for strolls through Mengalem, Berat's scenic old quarter.

That was how I found the Solomon Museum.

It was so new it wasn't in my guidebook, and it was barely even a museum. It was a tiny, almost artless repository of Berat's Jewish history. I had not known the town, or for that matter Albania, had a Jewish history. The display focused on Berat's protection during World War II of its Jews, whose population actually expanded during the Holocaust even though the Nazis occupied Albania for about a year.

I was the only visitor that afternoon, and I learned that

the Solomon Museum, though less than a year old, was already in danger of closing. The founder was an elderly Beratian Jew who financed it with nothing more than his pension and a donation box by the front door. He had died shortly after the museum opened; his widow was running it with the help of a college student who took me through its two rooms of black-and-white images, explanatory paragraphs of text, lists of names, and other memorabilia. The museum's clearly intended message was that Albania, and especially Berat, had been exemplary in its treatment of the Jews during the Holocaust. The young man gave me brief summaries of the plaques as I read their contents. This was unnecessary, as they were written bilingually, but I sensed that he was keen to practice his English. I was happy to oblige him.

He did go off script to offer one item of his own commentary. In earlier times, he told me, merchant-class Jews would buy up as much wheat as possible during harvest season. Then, in the cold and lean months of winter, they resold the wheat to hungry Beratians, including the farmers who had grown it, for more than double its original cost.

He gave me a knowing smile and laughed. I laughed, too. His laugh was easy, comfortable. Mine was uneasy and uncertain. I wasn't sure if we were laughing for the same reason.

Heather joined me in southern Albania. We visited the ancient ruins of Butrint together and then went to a Greek island for a few nights. From there, we made our way to mainland Greece and traveled overland toward Istanbul. We spent two nights in Ioannina—a place we'd never heard of until three days before we arrived. We went to Ioannina only because there was no other plausible place to get to from the mainland ferry terminal. We were happy to discover that it was a very pleasant smallish city set on a large, scenic lake, and it had plenty to interest us for a day or two.

We visited the Municipal Ethnographic Museum and were surprised when it turned out to be, in large part, a history of the city's Jews, who for centuries were a populous and prosperous community in Ioannina. There were holy scrolls, ketubahs and other documents, traditional clothing, precious metals, and much more. Nearly all of this ample collection had been donated by a single Jewish family, evidently a rather wealthy one.

Ioannina's Jews had been welcomed to the city and thrived there, but they met a gruesome end during World War II, and unlike Berat, the city had not managed, or perhaps had not opted, to protect them.

The slaughter of Jews in a place I had never heard of. Pick almost any place on the map, open any museum door, and the bones of thousands of Jews would fall out.

vii.

Another museum we visited in Ioannina was dedicated to Ali Pasha Tepelena, an Albanian-born vassal of the Ottoman Empire who in the early nineteenth century ruled over a large territory straddling southern Albania and northern Greece. As the Site of Witness and Memory had been created in the very building where the history it memorialized had occurred, so the Ali Pasha Tepelena museum was housed in the former monastery where he had taken refuge after the Ottoman sultan falsely promised him safety there. In fact, the sultan had already called for the head of Ali Pasha, whose overreach for regional power had run him afoul of the Porte. Gunmen posing as negotiators shot him through the upper-story floorboards as he tried to escape. He was eighty-two.

The monastery was on a small island in the middle of Ioannina's broad lake. We took a diminutive ferry to get there.

I already knew something about Ali Pasha Tepelena. In advance of our trip I read a historical novel by Ismail Kadare called *The Traitor's Niche*, which reconstructs the circumstances surrounding Ali Pasha's assassination and its aftermath. When I read the book, I had found it a beguiling, slightly fantastical chronicle, its characters, events, and places no more real to me than ancient myth. Now, walking through the site of Ali Pasha's death, gazing at his bejeweled sword on display in a vitrine case and down through the bullet holes preserved under plexiglass in the floor, Kadare's novel returned to my mind, but as nonfiction: an eloquent and accurate account of events whose evidence was now before me and below me. I was standing in the very place where these things had happened.

This change in my perception did not take place all at once in the monastery. I had seen Ali Pasha Tepelena's legacy all over southern Albania, from the source of his name—Tepelena, his birthplace, very near which I had stayed a few nights—to stone bridges he built, one of which I had crossed on foot, to castles he sacked and occupied, which I visited along with ancient Greco-Roman sites where he set up his own fortresses.

I was unaware that although Ali Pasha Tepelena was born in what is now Albania, he was known by the epithet "The Lion of Ioannina." It was there that he set up his seat of power in 1790, and there that he hosted an illustrious English visitor in 1809. "[He is] very fat and not tall," the visitor later wrote, "but with a fine face, light blue eyes and a white beard, his manner is very kind and at the same time he possesses that dignity which I find universal amongst the Turks. He has the appearance of anything but his real character, for he is a remorseless tyrant, guilty of the most horrible cruelties." The Englishman was Lord Byron. (Ali Pasha is briefly mentioned in both *Childe Harold's Pilgrimage* and *Don Juan*.)

Always hungry to increase his power and territory, late in his reign Ali Pasha Tepelena made overtures to both England and France, eventually playing them off one another in a scheme to detach his rule from Ottoman sponsorship and gain absolute dominion. He appears to have encouraged an insurgent Greek independence movement for the same purpose. For these disloyalties, the sultan ordered him killed.

As I peered through the bullet holes in the floor, I imagined Byron's remorseless tyrant trying to hobble to his escape on eighty-two-year-old legs, and I nearly felt pity for Ali Pasha, who was known to roast his captured enemies alive. Also preserved at the museum is his interred body—although not quite all of it. The Sultan ordered him decapitated after he was shot to death, so that his head could be delivered to Istanbul—a journey of five hundred miles on horseback—where the Sultan had it publicly and prominently displayed as a warning in the traitor's niche of Kadare's novel's title.

The Lion of Ioannina—it was so clear that this was his home, not Albania. But then, what did that mean—not Albania? The Albanians have never called themselves Albanians. They call their country *Shqiperia*, and echoes persist of Albania's ancient name, *Illyria*. That's how Herodotus refers to what was then the northernmost reach of the Hellenic realm in his *Histories*, which I had also read in advance of going to Albania. The exonym is now a common Albanian male first name, *Ilir*. Modern Albania did not gain independence until the twentieth century, after the Balkan Wars freed it from Ottoman control. During Ali Pasha Tepelena's reign, what would later become southern Albania was considered part of a now-historical region called Epirus, whose territory included Ioannina in what is now northern Greece. Epirus had previously belonged to a larger region known as Roumelia: "land of the Romans"—as *Romania*, too, refers to Rome.

These boundaries divided not nations but notions, allegiances and alliances, provisional perforations. What is a country, exactly? How many people can really say where they are from, when so many of those places were once someplace else? I felt borders redrawing themselves around me. Time asserted its authority over space. *This* was not Greece and *that* not Albania. It was the Pashalik of Ali Tepelena, and I had seen all of it, from north to south, birth to death, and now I was at its heart, at the very place where that heart stopped beating.

viii.

In Thessaloniki, we had half a day to wait for an overnight bus to Istanbul. Thessaloniki is Greece's second-largest city after Athens. So I learned while planning our trip earlier in the spring, when it emerged as a possible stopover en route to Turkey. Like Ioannina, Thessaloniki was a pleasant surprise. Larger of course, and somewhat scruffier, but a city of the sort I always enjoy discovering: not a place where tourists throng but where people live. Thessaloniki felt satisfyingly ordinary and unassuming, quite comfortable in its modest skin, proportions, and history. Here was a statue of Aristotle; here was an esplanade where old-timers sat on benches gazing out over the Aegean and young people rollerbladed—rollerbladed, like it was a quarter-century ago! Heather and I split an enormous, tasty falafel and went about Thessaloniki with our backpacks. I felt at home and at ease, much more so than I should have felt after just a few hours' strolling. I felt a little like the narrator of the novel set in the Burgundian town who, immediately on arriving there for the first time, is visited by "a strange conviction I was in a town I already knew."

Yet I didn't know it. Just as I had never heard of Ioannina before we went there, I had also never heard of Thessaloniki. When I said so to Heather, she couldn't—almost didn't—believe me. Thessaloniki, Greece's second-largest city, a major European port? I allowed it was likely that at some point I had known of it but had since forgotten it, even that it was possible to know something without knowing that one knew it, as one knows certain parts of the Bible with no conscious awareness of ever having read or been told of them. But to my knowledge, I had never heard of Thessaloniki.

I had certainly never known that it had once been one of the most Jewish cities in the world.

When the Ottomans took control of northern Greece in the sixteenth century, they began to invite Jews into the area, mostly Sephardim fleeing Spain after the 1492 expulsion. The reason for the invitation seems to have been to supplant Greeks with a population of outsiders, especially outsiders who brought commercial and trade skills with them. Persecuted Jews from all over Europe began arriving in the city, then known as Salonika. By the time my great-grandparents were leaving Romania for America, in 1910, Jews made up half of Salonika's sizable population. They became so prominent and prosperous there that they gave the city two epithets: the Jerusalem of the Balkans, and, in the native Spanish of the Sephardim, *La Madre de Israel.*

Then two disasters befell them. First, a great fire destroyed much of Salonika in 1917, effectively wiping out every livelihood available to the Jews, economically dependent as they were upon urban commerce. They scattered around the globe. After the demise of the Ottoman Empire returned Salonika to Greece (and restored the city's original name of Thessaloniki), Jews slowly trickled back in and were granted the same rights as any Greek citizen. But then came the second disaster: the Nazis. Today, there are fewer than a thousand Jews in Thessaloniki.

Much of this history is recounted in the Jewish Museum of Thessaloniki, but of course I did not know that existed, either.

I don't generally care for Jewish museums.

In 2012, Heather and I made one of our periodic trips to New York City. Many years before we knew each other, in the 1990s, she and I had both lived in New York—just a few blocks apart from each other, coincidentally. This coincidence has a deepening effect on our marriage. Because we know the same specific time and place, we sometimes feel as though we've known each other for much longer than we have.

We were staying in a hotel in lower Manhattan. Going out for a walk, we passed the Museum of Jewish Heritage, which describes itself as "A Living Memorial to the Holocaust."

Why was a museum of Jewish heritage actually a Holocaust memorial? Was Jewish heritage synonymous with Jewish slaughter? How could a museum of six million dead call itself a living memorial?

Heather wanted to go inside but I wasn't interested. In the three years we'd known each other, I had sometimes told her that I was averse to memorials and representations of the Holocaust. I never really explained why. I suppose I might have elaborated, if asked, that on the rare occasions when I visited Holocaust memorials, they had the effect of making the Holocaust seem not more real to me but less.

But I had to use the bathroom, so we went into the lobby. While Heather waited for me, the desk agent asked her if we'd like to buy tickets. Heather said she might like to come back another time—but on her own, because her husband, she explained, probably wouldn't want to visit a Holocaust memorial. The agent told her that the museum contained much more than its Holocaust exhibition, which was limited to a single floor that could be skipped. When I came out of the restroom, Heather relayed this information to me, and we bought tickets.

The ground floor was devoted to pre–World War II Jewish heritage. There was an impressive collection of objects and images that depicted daily Jewish life and culture: photographs, letters, menorahs, children's toys, textiles, musical instruments. I came upon a small gallery of published sheet music by Jewish-American composers. I stopped short at the cover page of one composition, entitled "In That Day." The composer was Pinchos Jassinowsky, who was a New York cantor and composer of some repute during the interwar period. He was born in Kiev, according to the informational plaque. I happened to know this already because Pinchos Jassinowsky was my great-grandfather. That was why I stopped short.

Pinchos Jassinowsky's daughter was the pianist who studied at Juilliard, the poet, the painter, the sculptor, the amputee, my greatest inspiration as a writer, the visit to whose grave several years later may have had something to do with my desire to go to Romania and stand where my great-grandparents stood.

Not this great-grandparent, of course. Jassinowsky was the other side of my family.

Heather and I marveled at my great-grandfather's sheet music on the wall in the Museum of Jewish Heritage. We also marveled that we would never have seen it had I not needed to find a toilet.

There seemed now no doubt that we would continue through the rest of the museum, including the entire Holocaust floor, which was quite exhaustive. But I don't remember anything about that floor except a very large flag emblazoned with a swastika.

X.

Later that year, we got married. The officiant was a rabbi.

Even though we do not practice any formal religion, Heather and I wanted our marriage to have some sort of holy consecration. A representative from the older of our linked traditions seemed the best choice.

Heather found a rabbi by searching online for candidates in our area. The one she chose was a literary scholar at a nearby university who, in midlife, had grown curious about his Jewish roots, to which he'd long been indifferent, as I was. His study of Judaism led him to become a rabbi himself.

Some weeks before the wedding we sat down with him for an hourlong interview. At no point during our interview did anyone at the table bring up the subject of baseball, a sport I was not only covering full-time as a journalist, but which was the reason Heather and I met and provided the literal grounds of the courtship.

For three years, we spent far more time together watching baseball than we spent doing anything else. For hours a night, months of the year, we sat side by side in the seats behind home plate, slowly falling in love, pitch by pitch, game by game.

In conversation with the rabbi no one so much as mentioned the word *baseball*. Therefore I was surprised during the ceremony when the rabbi's homily was an extended baseball metaphor about the ways in which spouses support and celebrate one another.

I was even more surprised—almost shocked, in fact—when, after his remarks, the various speeches, our vows, and the rest, and it was finally time to seal our union, the rabbi instructed Heather and me to join hands, raised his hands over us, and incanted in ecstatic Hebrew.

After that, with the marriage made in a language virtually no one present understood, he joined us in a toast with a glass of expensive wine from Burgundy, which I had bought especially for this purpose.

Fifteen minutes later, he left. We never heard from him again.

xi.

In 2010, I went to Pittsburgh to attend my uncle's funeral. Uncle Larry was my mother's only sibling, her older brother by about three years. He was only sixty-nine when he died, but even when I was a small child and he was a fairly young man he appeared sickly to me, prematurely old like the rest of the Pittsburghers. He walked slowly, uncomfortably, his voice toneless and creaky, and he seemed generally frail, retreating, resigned, and constitutionally unhealthy, born that way.

Uncle Larry was a hemophiliac. From early youth, he had been treated gingerly by his parents, who taught my mother that she must do the same. Uncle Larry was not permitted to play sports or do anything that might pose the threat of injury or danger. His life seemed never to have been permitted to be fully lived. In this way, he seemed much like most of the other Sigels in Pittsburgh. After he died, my mother expressed condolences to his son, my first cousin, for the loss of his father. My cousin said, "I lost my father a long time ago."

Uncle Larry did not treat himself with the same care with which his family treated him. For much of his life he smoked. The house he had with his wife and two children, who were around my age, was the first house I was ever in that smelled like cigarettes, stale ones: that ashy reek that has lived in walls and carpets for years and permeates everything in the house. It was also the first house I was ever in that was full of Tab, the diet soda, which at the time was virtually the only brand. Someone in their house was always drinking Tab, it seemed. There were six-packs of Tab in their fridge, cases of Tab next to it, and many more in their pantry. There were larger bottles of Tab, too, and empties in the trash. It was in their house that I first tried Tab. I found it undrinkable, a sort of taunt to the palate. It promised sweetness but as it washed over my tongue and down my throat it left a strange flavor that was bitter and ashy like the smell of the cigarettes.

In the den of their house were fish tanks. Keeping fish was Uncle Larry's hobby. I watched him sprinkle fish food into the tanks, which glowed ghoulishly at night, as though he was keeping something nearly dead alive. I slept in the den with the fish tanks, on a sofa, under the purplish light. When he wasn't feeding the fish, Uncle Larry seemed to spend a lot of time sitting in his easy chair, often complaining of very bad neck stiffness and pain that made it impossible for him to do very much. Or maybe, I wondered, did his not doing very much lead to the pain? The chair was rigged up with pads, some of them heated. His wife, my aunt, would tend to him chair-side. She was a pharmacy tech. Uncle Larry seemed to be on a lot of medications. It occurred to me at one point to wonder if Tab might, in their eyes, be some sort of medical drink.

My mother tells me Uncle Larry was hilariously funny.

He did once tell me a funny story. It was about his business. He was a salesman, employed by a company called Porter. I remember the name of the company because it was printed on a bottle stopper that worked by means of a rubber gasket on the underside, which formed a suction seal when you pressed down on the stopper. His parents, my grandparents, had a number of these stoppers in their house in Pittsburgh. They used them regularly, although they drank Coca-Cola, not Tab. I had never seen a bottle stopper before and I thought they were pretty neat. I also thought it was neat that Uncle Larry sold them for a living. I imagined him going door to door with them—or I tried to imagine it, since his poor health made it difficult to envision him springing up steps onto porches in neighborhood after neighborhood, demonstrating the stopper's peerless suction action to interested residents. "Have you got an open bottle of Tab in the house, ma'am?"

The bottle stoppers were not, of course, what Uncle Larry sold. They were almost surely a promotional item made by Porter for clients. To this day, I don't know what Porter produced or what Uncle Larry sold, and I never had any real idea what he did for a living. (Both of my parents were teachers. I went to school, of course, and in fact one of my parents taught at my school, so I had a very clear and firsthand understanding of their line of work.) It was hard for me to think of Uncle Larry working in any business, because he seemed too frail. But I know he held down a job because of the funny story he told me when I was either a late adolescent or a young adult.

Uncle Larry had a business meeting in Chicago, he told me, a half day's drive from his home in Fort Wayne, Indiana, where he'd moved his family from Pittsburgh during my early childhood. His clients for this business meeting were also coming to Chicago from out of town, and he asked for their preferences for dinner after their meeting. Like him, they were Midwesterners, from somewhere like Kansas City or Omaha, and they expressed a desire for fresh seafood, which they seldom got to eat, being so far from any coast.

"So I made the necessary arrangements," Uncle Larry told me. I found this an interesting and curious choice of phrase, hard to get out of my head to this day. *The necessary arrangements* was curious not only because of what an expression so oddly heightened as that implied about merely going out to dinner, a pastime I regarded as generally casual or offhand and every now and then a special treat—but never *necessary* nor requiring any *arrangements*. You simply walked into a restaurant and if you wanted seafood you found it on the menu and ordered it. Uncle Larry's choice of words surprised me because he generally said very little around me and, when he did speak, it was in mutterances. He spoke in more mutterances than any of my other Pittsburgh relatives. He did not seem like someone who would say "necessary arrangements," long words which, despite their workaday meaning, had the ring of formal idiom, cultivated vocabulary, even a touch of stylishness.

Coincidentally, the only other time I have ever come across the phrase *necessary arrangements*, well after our trip to Romania, was in a book in which the necessary arrangements were those required by Jews to flee Nazi

Germany.

Uncle Larry chose a restaurant and called to make something more than reservations: to make *arrangements*. He spoke with the manager, or the maître d', or perhaps even the owner. I don't quite remember. On the phone he described the scenario: valued clients in from out of town; the clients' desires for seafood; his desire, perhaps even the *necessity* of making *arrangements*, to satisfy their desire. He might have requested a table away from the loudest part of the restaurant. The intricacies and art of doing business: I had not known Uncle Larry to be so practiced, so thorough, so skilled.

When the party was seated that evening, their waiter came to their table to give Uncle Larry and his clients personal attention. After pleasantries were exchanged, he recommended the walleye.

Uncle Larry paused for a moment in his story, as though to anticipate its conclusion, or punchline. Then he said, "First of all, walleye isn't *seafood*."

xii.

My first memory of Pittsburgh also involves a funeral. My great-grandfather was long-lived. He was in his early nineties when he passed away. I was six years old. Our family went up from North Carolina to Pittsburgh for the service, but the children were not permitted to attend the funeral itself. I wondered if this was because we were not considered old enough to see a dead body, and I imagined what it would be like to see one. Would I find it scary, or would the person merely appear to be sleeping?

We kids spent the service in someone's basement, with toys and cookies. I remember this only vaguely. I remember wishing I was at the funeral, with the adults.

I have a memory of meeting my great-grandfather in his old age before he died, but that memory is even vaguer than my memory of his funeral. I may be remembering having met a photograph of him.

The most notable thing I remember about my great-grandfather was what I called him. The traditional epithet for him in relation to me was Great Zaidie, but as a very young boy I misheard and thought he was called *Grape* Zaidie. To this day, that is the name my mother, my sister, and I use anytime we refer to him, and it still elicits from us a brightened tone, perhaps a little chuckle, when we say it. It was an understandable mispronunciation by a young kid, but it also made sense to me because of what Grape Zaidie looked like. He had the family's darkest version of that dark pigment we all inherited from him: a deep vegetal brown that was almost purple, like a tobacco stain stained again with red wine.

Another name I mistook was my grandmother's. Her name was Bess but many of the older relatives called her Pessie, which I later learned was a diminutive of her birth name, Pessl. Pessl led to Pessie and Pessie to Bessie, which yielded her legal name, Bess. Bess was never backformed to Elizabeth. Before she became Bess Belans, her legal name, derived from the P in Pessl, was actually Pauline. It is impossible for me to think of her with this name.

Her husband, my grandfather—my Zaidie—called her by a mutterance. He called her "Beh."

I called her Bubbie, as Jewish kids traditionally call their eldest grandmother, the counterpart to Zaidie. But I did not spell it traditionally. From early youth I spelled it, for some reason, "Boiby." I have never encountered this spelling elsewhere and have never been able to explain why I spelled it that way. When I heard the word, it just sounded to me like it should be spelled "Boiby," even though I could recognize that "Boiby" suggested an entirely different pronunciation from "Bubbie," like "boy-bee." But "Bubbie" and "Bubbe" still look wrong to me, like a homely transliteration of a word only a few philologists still know how to spell properly.

After my Boiby married my Zaidie, she was no longer a Sigel. She took his surname, Belans, which he had shortened from Belansky. Another branch of the family shortened it all the way to Bell. I have never met them. They don't seem related to me, because of their name. Zaidie also legally changed his first name from Abraham to Herbert. I never asked him why he chose that name.

When my father reached legal age, he changed his middle name from Dennis to David: a more Jewish middle name, even though he was and is not observant. I've never asked him why he changed it. I don't know why I've never asked him why. The usual reasons.

xiii.

My Uncle Larry's full name was Larry M. Belans. That's how it appeared on his birth certificate and in obituaries. Larry wasn't short for Lawrence, and the M didn't stand for anything. It was just the letter M. His father, my Zaidie, Abraham Belansky cum Herbert Belans, didn't have a middle name, and thought his children should have at least a middle initial. A necessary arrangement.

I remember it taking hours for the procession to get from the funeral home to the cemetery, a garble of endless turns and steep hills that reduced the hearse to a crawl. It had snowed the night before, making the final climb to the family plot slippery and slightly treacherous. My carmates were unnerved by the conditions of the roadway, aggrieved that the cemetery administration had been too miserly to clear it. Mutterances.

Once we were finally out of the car, frigid gusts blew across the unprotected hilltop. After just a few minutes of the graveside service it was hard for me to feel or think of anything but the profound cold, although I could perceive how lovely the burial grounds were, even in the dead of winter: beautifully situated, with a panoramic view. Someone had once told me that Jews were especially well known for their discernment in choosing cemetery sites, particularly for setting them on graceful elevations.

I don't remember a single moment of the graveside service. It has always nagged at me that I have no memory of it, perhaps because I remember what followed it so well. There was another very long and tortuous drive to the reception, with so many turns in the route that we got lost despite GPS navigation, bickering in the car, which I was driving. I wished my Zaidie were alive and behind the wheel, power steering with one finger as he always did, serenely in command and in his element. He drove enormous cars, a Plymouth Gran Fury, a Chrysler Cordoba, an Oldsmobile Delta 88. After he grew too old to drive, I was once tapped to chauffeur him from Pittsburgh to Cleveland to visit his sister on her eightieth birthday. My car was an old and large Buick Regal with crushed velour seats that I had inherited from the grandparents on my father's side. As we sailed across Interstate 80, the engine humming low, Zaidie in the passenger seat, he said to me, "You can drive me any time."

The reception was well outside Pittsburgh itself in one of its surrounding townships, in a house that belonged to someone we didn't know: the cousin of my uncle's wife or some similar remove. Not the Sigel side. Most of the attendees at the reception were unknown to me, barely my family (if at all), and not Jewish—I was oddly but acutely aware of this, and somehow it bothered me, these non-Jews, hosting the reception, providing refreshments that were nothing but cookies and juice, as though this death was for children. I felt we had just buried a stranger.

Uncle Larry's wife was born Catholic. Their high-school courtship scandalized the family until a bloody hemophilic emergency landed him in the hospital, where he nearly died. My aunt-to-be, barely of age at the time, sat by his bedside for days on end until he recovered, effacing the intermarriage taboo by sheer endurance and immovability.

All the time my mother was pregnant with me, she worried that as a carrier of hemophilia like her own mother, she might pass Uncle Larry's condition down to me. I sometimes wonder what my life would have been like if I had been born a hemophiliac. Would I have been kept from my habitual actions: running, working in bars? How would I have supported myself? How would I have taken care of my body, unable to exercise? Would I have been mostly confined to my armchair, subsisting on cigarettes and Tab, in too much pain even to write? Would I have been able to take this trip to Romania to stand where our ancestors stood?

xiv.

I slept for much of the overnight bus ride from Thessaloniki to Istanbul, but I was not really rested. That was partly because I was abruptly awakened twice. The first was at around three o'clock in the morning, when we arrived at the Greece-Turkey border. We had to present our passports, of course, and while customs officials made their routine inspection of the bus and its cargo, we were all ordered into the bedraggled duty-free shop, open in the middle of the night—I imagined it had never closed since the day it opened. We reboarded the bus and continued eastward, but a few hours later, just as daylight broke, I woke up again when the bus pulled into a terminal. We still had an hour and a half until our scheduled arrival in Istanbul, so Heather and I figured we were somewhere along the route. We were wrong. Everyone else disembarked while we sat there in a double daze, at once underslept and unawares, until the conductor shooed us off the bus. This was Istanbul.

Running is a great antidote to fatigue. One of the two friends of Heather's we were meeting had arrived in Istanbul the night before and stayed at a nice hotel with a well-equipped gym. We met her there. The two of them got caught up over coffee, and I went down to the gym and ran, egged on by the readout on the treadmill to keep going faster and farther.

Meanwhile, Heather's other friend had arrived. We had a light lunch. After we checked into the apartment we had rented, I left the three friends so they could have some time to catch up. I set out alone on what turned into a long walk. I lost myself in Istanbul. It is the second-largest city in Europe, unimaginably vast, ancient, self-perpetuating, self-fulfilling. An entire universe. If the rest of the world ceased to exist, Istanbul might not even notice.

After all the running and walking, I was very hungry again. My mother's longtime partner lived in Istanbul long ago, and he is fond of recalling one of the great gastronomic delights of his life there. Down by the wharf, he told me, fishermen would haul up their day's catch for the wholesalers to buy up. There were also men there with firepits, and you could buy a mackerel from a fisherman and then pay one of the men to clean it, dress it, and plunge it into the fire. In an almost literal hot minute, the mackerel would be perfectly cooked, the skin smoky with char, the flesh tender and juicy.

By accident, I found the place.

It had changed, of course. No more firepits, and no more fishermen, at least not at that late-afternoon hour. But there were fishmongers, and there was a man standing at a hibachi grill with some mackerel already cleaned and filleted. He put all kinds of seasonings on it and grilled it, then put it on a roll with more seasonings and condiments. He slid the sandwich into a plastic bag with a third of the sandwich jutting out so it could be easily eaten. He handed it to me. I handed him ten *lira*, two dollars.

It occurred to me that I was at an urban wharf in a foreign city with its foreign microbes, buying mackerel that had been sitting out unrefrigerated in the hot sun for an unknown length of time, grilled by a randomly chosen cook and topped with mystery ingredients. I was tired, overexerted, and dehydrated. I had been made sick by street food multiple times in past travels. But the same was true of health-inspected suburban restaurant food I'd eaten in America, name-brand tortilla chips, and food I had cooked myself, so I don't consider a riverfront mackerel sandwich categorically risky. In any case, flavor cancels fear, and it was too delicious not to eat. The copious juice was all caught in the bag and when I was done, I threw it away and rinsed my hands in a fountain. It was as though it never happened—a crime whose evidence was at once discarded, hands quite literally washed.

I was hungry yet again a few hours later and stopped into a homey-looking little eatery in which the counterman put rice in a bowl and ladled over it the food of your choice from a row of steam trays: slow-cooked pole beans, stewed eggplant. It was very satisfying food, all vegetarian, subtly seasoned, and so soft and mild that a baby could almost have eaten it. I expressed surprise to the proprietor, who like his food was also gentle and mild, telling him that the Turkish fare I had seen throughout the Balkans and the Caucasus was mostly shaved meat and grilled kebabs. His demeanor became suddenly firm, stern, even slightly disdainful. "This is Turkish food," he said. "Grilled meat is Arab." When I paid, I thanked him in his language: *teşekkür ederim*. He corrected me: that is also Arab. The Turkish word for thank you is *sağol*. This word, too, like the man's food, was easy in the mouth, gently wrapping its two vowels around the soft, wide ğ. I thanked people with *sağol* instead of *teşekkür ederim* for the rest of the time we spent in Istanbul.

The next day we went to Topkapı. It was crowded and loud, even outdoors, especially when the muezzin's call to prayer blared over the vast grounds. The most crowded area was the Privy Room where the sacred relics are displayed. We stood in line for forty-five minutes to enter. Once we were inside, irate guards bellowed at the throngs of tourists that photography was prohibited and herded us as best they could past the vitrines: Abraham's saucepan, Joseph's turban, Moses's staff, David's sword. After waiting forty-five minutes, I was out in fewer than five.

That did not bother me. I found the Privy Room unpleasant. Not because of the overwhelming crowd, the noise, or the bellowing guards, but because I didn't like what I saw. These things don't belong here, I thought. They are the possessions of our patriarchs and our founding king—*ours*, my people's, not theirs, Jewish relics, not Turkish, Arab, Ottoman, Muslim, whoever they were.

But then, these objects surely weren't authentic. Assuring myself they were fakes, they no longer bothered me.

Istanbul was still called Constantinople when its inhabitants created what I saw later at the Mosaic Museum. Unlike Topkapı, there was hardly anyone in it, and what it contained purported no sacredness. Quite the opposite, in fact. The mosaics, which were discovered and unearthed by English archaeologists in the 1930s, depict scenes of hunting and game playing. Virtually nothing religious—just life as it was lived. Men hunting beasts,

beasts hunting prey, a hawk grappling with a snake, kids playing games. There were a few surprisingly fanciful images, like a trained monkey with a hod on his back, using a mischievous pole to get fruit down from the top of a palm.

The mosaics dated to the sixth century, during the reign of Justinian, when Constantinople was the easternmost reach of Rome's dominion. I went through the entire exhibition, rapt, delighted, and immediately went through it again. When these mosaics were laid, I kept telling myself, *Muhammad wasn't even born.*

In my *Portable World Bible*, I had read that Muhammad was an illiterate from "one of the world's most backward countries" whose visionary, self-aggrandizing ravings "furnished a religion which could be comprehended by other backward peoples, thus enabling them to take a single step forward out of the darkness." This religion's scripture, the editor alerts his presumably Judeo-Christian reader, contains "some conceptions which seem degrading, many which seem meaningless, and, at their best, some few things that seem to be mere reiterations of principles with which they are already familiar through their own scriptures."

What are "backward peoples"?

The unabridged version of *The Portable World Bible* was published a long time ago, in 1939.

Walking back to our apartment, I had an unpleasant encounter. On the Galata Bridge a game of Three-Card Monty was going on. A small but fanatical crowd of men had gathered. I added myself. One player, who was actually a shill, tried to interest me with the bent-corner ruse, although I was not going to play. I continued watching for a few moments until another man ordered me away. I ignored him, as though he was not talking to me, or as though words not in my language didn't apply to me. He moved closer and repeated the order. I ignored him more determinedly. He was almost certainly another shill, protecting the con in case I should expose it, or perhaps simply pegging me for a non-player (since I didn't speak the language), inert at best, meddling at worst. When I still did not leave, he put his hands on me and tried to move me bodily. I resisted and kept watching. The man kept trying to force me away, each of us snarling in our language, mutually unintelligible. I moved to another side of the circle. The man came over and apprehended me yet again. How long could this go on until it became violent? Was I in any danger—perhaps some worse peril than I understood? Was I in fact the one causing it? I knew quite well what offense I was committing, but what offense did I not know I might be committing? With this question in mind, I left under my own power.

Much of what happened while I was in Istanbul would repeat in Bucharest: fatiguing overnight travel; contact with American friends; too much exercise after a period of too little; doubtful fish; relics of Judea and non-Judea; language complications; and a hostile encounter with a local.

The difference was that in Istanbul I didn't get sick.

XV.

What little Romanian history I knew before preparing for our trip I had learned in college. But I had not learned it from a history class. I learned it from a play.

I was a Theatre Arts major, and in my junior year I was cast in a play that was set in Romania. It was a piece of docutheater (a genre popular at the time), called *Mad Forest*, about the Romanian Revolution of 1989 that overthrew the autocrat Nicolae Ceauşescu. This history was still very fresh then, barely history. Ceauşescu had been deposed and executed less than two years before we staged the play. Our college production was one of the first in America.

During rehearsals, I told my fellow cast members that I was part Romanian. Ironically, I had been cast in the role of the play's only Hungarian, whose main function was to enact the traditional antipathy between the nations: the Hungarians generally claimed cultural superiority over the Romanians, whose country had been roughly cobbled together from diverse provinces, including Transylvania, which was taken from Hungary after World War I and appended to Romania. Nonetheless, my Hungarian character had a Romanian girlfriend, and it was to her that he delivered the only line I still remember: "You're like slaves."

I also remember devoting a good deal of time and attention to developing an impersonation of Ceauşescu, which my Hungarian character delighted in giving, simultaneously entertaining and taunting his Romanian acquaintances. To study and mimic Ceaușescu, especially his distinctive slicing hand gestures, I watched his speeches. I don't remember where I found the speeches—this was before the internet—but one of them was almost surely the last speech he ever gave, from the balcony of his ruling party's Central Committee building in Bucharest, on December 21, 1989. The speech was cut short by the jeering crowd in the square, and Ceaușescu and his wife were arrested shortly afterwards. Four days later, on Christmas Day, they were tried, convicted, and executed.

Much of our rehearsal period for *Mad Forest* was dedicated not to working on the play itself but to general theatrical exercises which were meant to build a cohesive ensemble. The first forty-five minutes of each rehearsal were allotted to a prerecorded sequence of physical stretches and vocal exercises derived from a practice known as Alexander Technique. Alexander Technique was invented in the late nineteenth century by an actor who was suffering from vocal problems. It became a very popular general training praxis for performers and was later adopted outside the theater as a means of improving overall mind-body awareness and health among the general populace. Alexander Technique was also an influence on Gestalt Therapy, which was developed by Jews. Aldous Huxley studied personally with the technique's creator, Frederick Matthias Alexander.

Most of the *Mad Forest* cast seemed to enjoy the daily Alexander Technique sequence but I disliked it. In fact,

I disliked most of the rehearsal process. I felt we spent too much time on exercises and not enough on the play. There were sessions of invasive talk that sometimes felt like inappropriate psychotherapy. I regretted having auditioned and wanted the entire experience to end as soon as possible.

During tech week, our director told us there would be an optional early call an hour ahead of formal call before each performance to allow time for the Alexander Technique tape to be played in full, for anyone interested in continuing the practice as a warmup. I told fellow cast members that I did not intend to arrive at early call with them. I said Alexander wasn't for me. Also, given that my character was the play's lone Hungarian, an outsider, indeed an antagonist, it was fitting for me not to join them. It might even improve my performance. *You're like slaves.*

On opening night, I made an exception and arrived for the optional early call in a superficial show of solidarity. I felt obliged to come the next night, as well, then decided to go ahead and join in Alexander Technique for the rest of opening weekend.

I recall virtually nothing of the actual Alexander sequence itself. Mostly I remember the motherly sound and timbre of the gentle voice on the tape. The only specific exercise I remember had us lying on our sides on the floor of the empty theater—in the lightless back aisle behind the last row of seats, not on the stage—with one arm reaching up over our heads and the opposite leg reaching away behind us, stretching us in two directions like scissors that are open all the way. I remember that this particular contortion was even more uncomfortable than all the others in the sequence. Its purpose, as I understood it, was to open our air passages from throat to abdomen so that we could expand the resonance of our voices, which we expressed as we stretched by repeating the words of the prerecorded instruction of the gentle-voiced woman on the tape:

"I."

Eventually, as she directed us to stretch our limbs even farther away from one another, the phrase would repeat:

"I. I. I."

And then elongate:

"I. Ii. Iii. I am."

I ended up arriving for early-call Alexander Technique before every performance for all three weeks of production. By the final weekend, the only attendees were me and two other cast members.

xvi.

Theater was always an important part of my life.

In my early adolescence, I played Otto Frank in the stage version of *The Diary of Anne Frank*. The girl who played Mrs. Frank was from Switzerland and spoke fluent German. She taught me how to say a line of Otto Frank's that was in German in the script: *"Was ist los? Was ist passiert?"* She told me it meant "What's going on? What's happened?"

It is one of only two lines of the play that I can recall. My character said it when he was awakened in the middle of the night, but not by the arrival of the Nazis to take the hiders away. Anne Frank's parents are roused by a domestic commotion that breaks out in the house when one of the other hiders is caught stealing food while he thinks everyone else is sleeping. It is discovered that he has been doing this for some time. All along, the other hiders had thought nocturnal vermin were making off with the food. Now everyone wants to eject him from the house, except Mr. Frank, my character, who speaks in a voice of calm reason, and the thief is allowed to stay in the house.

Every night, I looked forward to saying *"Was ist los? Was ist passiert?"* I had a crush on the Swiss girl who played my wife, and we were lying next to each other in bed in the darkness before I said it. That was why I looked forward to it. I had to wait a while because the scene takes place late in the play. It is a classic theatrical device: a false alarm that prefigures a real one. In the scene that immediately follows it, the Nazis come for the hiders. Just before the door is broken down, Mr. Frank delivers the only other line of mine that I remember from the play: "Now we can live in hope."

This line made as little sense to me as the German line that the Swiss girl taught me to pronounce properly. Every night in performance, I found that I could say the German line more comfortably than I could say "Now we can live in hope."

xvii.

About fifteen years after I learned Alexander Technique, I tried another mind-body awareness practice. It was called holotropic breathwork. Deliberate, rhythmic hyperventilation awakens and liberates a deeper level of the practitioner's consciousness. Holotropic breathwork is done under the supervision of a trained instructor, partly in case the client experiences distress, which is not uncommon. The practice can be both physically and psychically demanding, and it is somewhat controversial.

The instructor I was referred to told me to bring numerous towels to lie on during sessions because holotropic breathing can cause some people to sweat profusely. It was also necessary to bring water for rehydration.

The instructor was an easygoing white woman in her late sixties or early seventies whose voice had a languorous Southern drawl and was gentle like the voice of the woman on the Alexander Technique tape. But it was a deceptive gentleness. Just a few minutes after the start of each weekly session, the experience became extremely strenuous. My clothes and towel became totally soaked. Soon after that, a pins-and-needles sensation would creep over my skin and even underneath it, as though the needles were coming up through my skin from inside me. Then my entire body would tense up, and my limbs would begin to strain either outward or inward, as if I was performing a sort of tortured, possessed sequence of Alexander Technique without the consent of my mind or will.

I could not relax my muscles and inevitably found myself in a painful cataleptic state that felt like a living rigor mortis.

The instructor reassured me in her gentle voice that this reaction was normal early in one's breathwork practice; with repetition I would experience a breakthrough. I would achieve a state so super-oxygenated that I would not need to keep breathing. In this nonbreathing state, I would enter first into a feeling of calm, then into a higher and deeper ataraxy. Finally, I would achieve complete spiritual transport. A trance. But this did not happen for me. Relaxation did not come until after each session was over, and it was mainly in the form of a wrung-out depletion, which lasted for hours afterward. I lay debilitated and dehydrated in my apartment, the catalepsy having turned into catatonia, already dreading the next week's session.

During one of these sessions, in addition to sweating profusely and suffering an agony of muscular rigidity, I felt tears welling up, but I could not open my eyes, and the tears felt trapped in their ducts, causing immense pressure in my head. I began to panic, issuing wordless moans because I could not relax my mouth to speak or my eyes to cry. My body was in its deepest agony. I felt as though I had been possessed by an evil spirit.

"Adam," the instructor said, in her soft, slow, honeyed maternal drawl. "Do you have any *Jewish* heritage?"

I nodded as best I could.

She said that some of her Jewish clients responded

similarly to the way I did. She said it came from a deep experience of being victims. That was the word she used. The word stuck, clenched, in my head as I lay there on the table. *Victims.*

Near the end of my seventh or eighth hourlong session, I finally experienced the sensation of unbreathing bliss my instructor had assured me I would eventually reach. After that, I stopped doing breathwork. This was not because I didn't want to continue, although I did feel that I had achieved the breakthrough I sought. I stopped because I went away to finish a play I had started the previous year. The play was about Ezra Pound, the famous modernist poet, and notorious antisemite.

xviii.

I had gone very far away to write it.

I had an American friend who was living and working in Jakarta, the capital of Indonesia. I had gone there and stayed with her once before, seven years earlier, and when I mentioned that I wanted to go somewhere to write, she offered me a room in her house for as long as I liked. I hadn't enjoyed Jakarta very much the first time but nonetheless I returned for a long stay. I sold my car and rented out my apartment. Still, I had to get by in Jakarta on fifty dollars a week.

In the popular understanding of Pound, he is probably as famous for his fascist-sympathizing antisemitism, and particularly his obsession with Jewish usury, as he is for his contributions to poetry. But "contributions" is a vast understatement. Pound was a visionary and a crusader who developed a radical new poetics virtually all by himself and almost forcibly advanced literature from the pastoral slowness of the nineteenth century into the violent modernity of the twentieth.

"Artists are the antennae of the race," Pound once announced in an essay, and no one had better antennae than Pound. It seemed only natural to me that they would pick up a fair amount of noise along with the signal of poetry, which to me accounted for his muddled obsessions with Jews, usury, and fascism. In any case, hadn't he later recanted his errant affection for Mussolini and his misplaced hatred of the Jews? His weekly speeches on Rome Radio during World War II praised Mussolini, heaped invective on President Roosevelt for what Pound believed was Roosevelt's thralldom to a cabal of powerful Jews, and encouraged U.S. soldiers not to fight for their commander-in-chief. The rhetoric was strongly worded and vehemently delivered, but it amounted to the ravings of a crackpot.

Within a few weeks of my arrival in Jakarta, I was already unhappy and thinking of relocating to Bali. Jakarta was crowded, polluted, and chaotic, difficult to navigate, and there was surprisingly little to do considering its gargantuan size. Unexpectedly, though, the friend hosting me had to make a trip back to the States on a work-related assignment. She asked me to keep an eye on her house while she was gone. Because she was a close friend and a generous one in putting me up indefinitely, I agreed to stay in Jakarta.

I didn't know anyone else in the city and hadn't the first clue how to meet people. Merely leaving the house at all tended to be something of an ordeal due to the traffic and the pollution. The only person I interacted with was my friend's housekeeper, but only barely. She spoke no English and tended to avoid me. I became not just lonely but also slightly paranoid, suspecting the housekeeper alternately of shirking her duties and spying on me.

My only company was Pound: his volatile life; his domineering persona; his poetry and prose, as well as the writing of others about him and his work; and above all his *Cantos*, as overwhelming, convoluted, polluted, and difficult to comprehend as Jakarta itself. I painstakingly read and reread them, usually in the late afternoon or early evening on the patio, trying to concentrate over the ferocious sound of storms beating on the roof during Java's monsoon season—it was so bad that year that flooding closed the international airport for several days. Occasionally I would lift my head up from Pound to see one or two of Jakarta's billions of rats sitting a few feet away from me, watching me read.

Mornings I sat at my desk swatting at mosquitoes and sweating for hours over my play. It was an ambitious, quixotic five-act verse drama, parts of which I took verbatim from the poet's vicious diatribes against the Jews on Rome Radio: *"Had you the sense to eliminate Roosevelt and his Jews, or the Jews and their Roosevelt, before the last election, you would not now be at war...."*

My only regular sorties out of the house were to a nearby gym I had joined, because Jakarta's lung-blackening air pollution and traffic congestion effectively prohibited outdoor exercise. After a while, I became nearly as consumed by exercising at the gym as by working on my play. I exercised so much that the expenditure of calories far exceeded my meager intake of food, which was a result of trying to conserve my money. It was also to keep from getting sick again. While my friend was away, she asked some expat friends of hers to invite me to a get-together in their home, where I ate some unpeeled fruit and had diarrhea for three days afterward. I vowed not to eat any more food I hadn't prepared myself, and soon discovered that there were street vendors who came through the neighborhood where my friend lived, rolling carts of groceries. For about ten dollars I could buy just enough food to get me through the week. My exchanges with these vendors in pidgin Bahasa Indonesia were the only interactions I had with anyone for weeks. I lost weight, and my mood fell too. I became aware that my undernourishment and my unhappiness were mutually aggravating, but the obsessive efforts on my play seemed to have penetrated everything. How much could I work and exercise, how little could I spend and speak? Yet the tighter I held myself to these demands, the more I lost my grasp on what I had come to Jakarta to do.

I ran into writer's block in the fourth act. I skipped ahead to the fifth, which without my intention unspooled into a long, piteous howl of a concluding monologue, fully seventeen pages long in its original version, delivered by the play's narrator-guide. I conceived this character as equal parts circus ringmaster and a sort of Virgil to the play's Dante, who took the form of the audience itself, descending with the narrator-guide into the Inferno and struggling up the Purgatorio of Pound's life. The end of the fourth act I could not write was where I meant to arrive at the Paradiso. This Virgil character was based mostly on Allen Ginsberg, the Jewish poet, who in real life had visited the aging Pound in 1967 to ask for his blessing, the passing of the torch of verse. Instead, Pound merely expressed general remorse for "the worst mistake I ever made," according to another person present at their meeting: "that stupid, suburban prejudice of antisemitism."

While my friend was in the States, I broke out with a terrible case of acne. Proneness to it runs in my family, the Sigel side. I became so self-conscious that I did not want to go anywhere in public even if I had a reason to do so. I limited my excursions only to my daily trips to the gym, where I could lose myself in hard exercise. I developed a radically split regard for my appearance: an athletically sculpted body topped by a terribly blemished face. I tried to grow a beard to conceal the acne, but Jakarta was too hot and humid for a beard, and the beard worsened the acne in any case.

My friend's trip back to the United States had to be extended beyond a month. My only regular communication was by email with my family and friends. I told them everything was going well, the play was coming along, the weather was warm, and the guavas were tasty. My girlfriend was planning to fly over from the States and travel around Southeast Asia with me when I was done working on my play and her grad school courses were finished for the semester.

A few days after my friend returned to Jakarta from America, I told her I had to leave. I did not feel comfortable detailing the reasons why—the deep vexations of the play and my spirit, the unrelenting misery of Jakarta, the extent of my physical difficulties—and without a full explanation from me she was resentful. As soon as I got to Bali, she stopped answering my emails. My girlfriend also went silent. Finally, after my messages reached an impasse of perplexity, she dumped me.

The same month, my grandmother on my father's side, the daughter of the cantor Pinchos Jassinowsky, died after a long physical and mental decline: my first and greatest inspiration as a writer; the poet who, I now remember, had a volume of Pound on her bookshelf. It was not possible for me to make it home for her burial, which added further grief.

In Bali, I came down with a bronchial infection that lasted the whole time I was there. Meanwhile, I hacked my way back through the thicket of the fourth act of my play, trying to drag Pound from his abstruse Purgatorio toward some semblance of the Paradiso I intended, even though that Paradiso had lost all the initial clarity in which I conceived it and was now basically unstageable. When I went home to the United States, half a year after I had left for Jakarta, the play was still unfinished.

xix.

As a high school freshman, I was cast as the title character in a musical called *The Education of H*Y*M*A*N K*A*P*L*A*N*.

The show is based on a collection of stories of the same name about a Jewish immigrant from Kiev. The stories, originally published in the 1930s, are set around the end of World War I, a few years after my great-grandparents on both sides of my family emigrated from Eastern Europe. In the musical based on these stories, Hyman Kaplan is trying to learn English in night school, where he habitually writes his name in all capital letters separated by asterisks for reasons I have forgotten. I have forgotten virtually the entire story—plots tend to escape me generally, even the plots of shows I star in—except that *The Education of H*Y*M*A*N K*A*P*L*A*N* ended happily, as nearly all musicals do. I remember only a single lyric fragment, the first lines of the song "Anything Is Possible":

Anything is possible
When a man is free.

It was a coincidence that I, the great-grandson of an immigrant musician from Kiev, was cast in a musical about an immigrant from Kiev. Not only was it a coincidence, it never occurred to me that this was the case.

It was also a coincidence that the director who cast me in this role was my mother.

She was teaching in my school at the time and had selected *The Education of H*Y*M*A*N K*A*P*L*A*N* for production. Early in our first cast meeting, she made a point of announcing that she had given me the title role not because I was her son but because I had given the best audition and had earned it on merit. She said anyone was welcome to bring up with her, publicly or in private, any concerns, questions, resentments, or objections they might have to this casting choice. To my knowledge, no one did.

She did not address the curious coincidence that she had cast the great-grandson of an immigrant from Kiev as an immigrant from Kiev. It may not have occurred to her, as it had not occurred to me. She may not even have known where Pinchos Jassinowsky came from. He died well before she met my father, and the Jassinowskys were not her family in any case, especially now that she had been divorced from my father for nearly a decade and had changed her last name back to Belans from Sobsey.

Before Pinchos settled in New York, his first assignment in America after immigrating was at a synagogue in Tulsa, Oklahoma. I have never been to Tulsa. It has never occurred to me to go there and stand in the place where my ancestor stood.

XX.

The first time I had gone to Jakarta and stayed with my friend was seven years before I went there to write my Ezra Pound play. After spending a few weeks in Jakarta, I went to mainland Southeast Asia and traveled around. For a while, in Laos, I was with a few other tourists I met along the way. A few of them were Israeli. I noticed almost immediately how pushy they acted: demanding of the locals; making tour groups wait around for them for an impolitely long time while they attended to their own personal business; and insisting on leading hikes even when we were on remote jungle paths in a country that was known still to be laced with unexploded land mines.

I was walking one of these paths with one of the Israelis, picking the occasional leech off my leg. I suppose I told him I was Jewish at some point, or perhaps he could simply tell. He was talking to me about Israel, although I don't remember whether I had asked him about it or what he was saying. I just walked and listened over the furious screeching of insects as loud as whistling tea kettles. After a while he said—insisted, in fact, as though objecting to something I had said, although I had not said anything— that I should go to Israel and connect with my roots.

I said something anodyne, noncommittal. Or maybe I said nothing at all. To myself I thought, *I have no roots in Israel. My people came from Romania.*

Later, in Cambodia, I visited the Killing Fields and the notorious Tuol Sleng prison in Phnom Penh where the

Khmer Rouge tortured and killed Cambodians they identified as "traitors": teachers, writers, doctors—the same
groups targeted by Enver Hoxha's regime in Albania. As
at the Site of Witness and Memory, one could go into the
cells where the prisoners were held. Some cells contained
the original bed frames, with the manacles still attached
to them.

Just outside the windows of Tuol Sleng, which is in
an ordinary residential neighborhood, people in adjacent
buildings were leaning out of their own windows and
hanging their laundry out on lines. This too resembled
the Site of Witness and Memory. A difference, though,
was that there would have been very few urban sounds
drifting into Tuol Sleng when it was active as a prison.
The surrounding buildings were mostly empty during the
occupation by the Khmer Rouge, which force-marched
most of Phnom Penh's citizens out to work camps in the
countryside, where many perished of starvation, exhaus-
tion, disease, and more killing. Perhaps as many as three
million Cambodians, about a quarter of the population,
died between 1975 and 1979.

It was the first time I had seen anything like this, and
I withdrew into mute disbelief and horror that lasted
for hours afterwards. I was touring Phnom Penh with a
Dutchwoman I had met just a few days earlier in another
part of Cambodia. Later in the day, after I had recovered,
she asked me gently if I thought my Jewishness had intensified my response to Tuol Sleng.

No, I said. Nothing like that.

Then I asked myself, silently: *I told her I was Jewish?*

A couple of years later I visited her in Amsterdam. I had a lot of time on my hands each day while she was at work and did plenty of sightseeing on my own. I went to many museums and intended to go to the Anne Frank House, but every time I went by it, the line was too long and I never did.

xxi.

In my freshman year of college, I was cast in the lead role of another musical: Seymour Krelborn in *Little Shop of Horrors*. The story is set in a New York florist shop run by one Mr. Mushnik, whose assistant (Seymour, me) raises an odd little seedling that turns out to be carnivorous. Under Seymour's care, it eventually grows so large that it feeds on human beings. In the 1980s, *Little Shop of Horrors* was made into a very popular movie, which I had already seen when I auditioned. That probably helped me get the role.

One day, during a break in rehearsal, I was sitting with the cast member who played Mushnik. The part had been given to a woman, so the character became Mrs. Mushnik. Her lines included "mumbling something that resembles Yiddish," according to the stage directions: *"Aron, grvorn grvoxen, akebebble, mit tzibeleh."*

The actress must have been Jewish, because she pointed out that *mit tzibeleh* meant "with onions." Her name was Pebble. When she said *"akebebble,"* it sounded a little like she was saying her own name, "AkePebble," so I began to think of Pebble as a Yiddish name even though it was known to me from childhood in the *Flintstones* cartoons.

Other than "with onions," Pebble didn't know what the rest of Mushnik's Yiddish line meant. After some investigation into the matter, we discovered that it was mostly just Yiddish-sounding gibberish. During subsequent breaks in rehearsal, she and I often drove ourselves into fits of uncontrollable laughter by saying *grvorn grvoxen, akebebble, mit tzibeleh* over and over again.

Little Shop of Horrors is responsible for a lexical coinage: "Krelboyne," a slightly revocalized form of Krelborn. "Krelboyne" means "geek/nerd/dweeb" or "someone who is gifted." Academically.

Pebble is now a doctor.

xxii.

After my second trip to Jakarta, when I wrote my Ezra Pound play, I returned to the U.S. and my job as a bartender in a popular and locally venerated restaurant that had spawned a number of cooks who had gone on to become successful local restaurateurs themselves. On their nights off, many of these chefs would hang around our bar, their old stomping grounds. One of them owned a thriving catering business. He often came in to talk football with one of my coworkers.

I didn't know the caterer well but one night he asked me, after I gave him his usual drink, if I would be interested in "co-captaining" a catering event. The event was evidently so large and important that he had already arranged to fly his former event manager down from New York, where she now lived, to serve as the other captain.

I told him I had little catering experience and had certainly never captained an event. He assured me that there was not much actual labor involved. I wouldn't even have to do any food service. Captaining mostly meant standing by, making sure everything was going smoothly—which it would be, he said—and mainly just being the face of the catering company for the client. It was this latter purpose for which he wanted me. He thought I had the right presence.

I was supposed to tend bar that night, but he was offering much more money than what I stood to make at the restaurant. I told him I could arrange for a sub and work his event instead. Then I asked him what the event was.

A bar mitzvah, he said.

I had never told him I was Jewish. I had never told my own manager at the restaurant—and she was Jewish. She was surprised when someone else told her that I was Jewish, too.

The caterer asked me if I had a nice suit. I told him I did and that I would be glad for the rare opportunity to wear it.

The catering event started with a post-ceremony lunch at my town's Reform synagogue. I had never been in it. Along with my co-captain, bagels had been flown in from New York. A local, Jewish restaurateur had been engaged to make smoked fish spreads and other traditional Jewish delicacies to accompany these bagels. Cleanup at the end of the lunch took longer than I had been told to expect, and instead of having a break afterwards I had to go directly from the synagogue to the site of the evening reception, which was the family's sizable and well-appointed house in a wealthy neighborhood built around a golf course. The dinner was to be served under a rented event tent down by the property's swimming pool. There I met my New York co-captain. She was also Jewish.

I could tell.

I could also tell she wasn't attracted to men. I'm not sure how I could tell. Nonetheless I was attracted to her.

The bar mitzvah's parents did not seem to have a clear sense of the evening's overall service plan regarding dinner and how it interacted with scheduled events (toasts, speeches, music, and so forth). They kept asking for things to be done differently than I understood them to have been fairly meticulously organized to be done, or for things to be done that did not appear anywhere on the clipboard I had in hand—changes to the necessary arrangements.

I found myself going back and forth, back and forth, between the house and the tent, communicating the family's requests one by one to the caterer and my co-captain, who was better apprised of the plan than I was, having signed on to the event well before I did and with much more general experience than I had in any case. Then I would return to the house to relay their responses back to the family. These trips grew in frequency and haste until they took on an antic, almost vaudevillian feel. Up and down, back and forth I went, at one point breaking into a near sprint simply to procure a ginger ale requested by the bar mitzvah's grandmother. With each commute over grass wet from a sprinkler system, I was aware that my dress shoes were getting soiled, and the bottoms of my suit pant legs were taking on mud worked loose from the watered lawn. There was nothing I could do about it. I felt duty-bound.

The dinner hour was drawing near. Owing to the numerous unexpected trips between family and caterer, I had not had time to check on preparations by the food service staff. I had not really thought this was necessary, since many of the staff were regular event workers for the caterer and had a practiced and habitual understanding of their duties. But when I did finally go down to the reception tent, I discovered that they were behind in setup and had questions for me. I did not have answers. Nor had my co-captain been available to help them. She was working alongside the caterer himself. With dinner only a few minutes away and several loose ends still untied, I asked her for guidance on one of them. She scolded me for my dereliction, turned on her heel, and walked away.

Dinner commenced. The caterer kept barking "I need runners!"—people to carry food from the mobile kitchen to the dining tent—but frequently no runners appeared. I had to help run food even though I had been assured I wouldn't have to do any service. And this was "Russian service," in which the server stands tableside with a platter and, using large utensils, serves a portion onto each guest's plate—which also means asking each guest if they'd like a helping of the particular dish, explaining what it is, answering questions about whether it contains gluten, dairy, etc. Russian service is time-consuming and rather difficult, a relic of an earlier era that has gone almost entirely out of practice, and I had never done it. The platters were large and heavy, and the caterer had piled them high with food drenched in heavy sauce, some of which ran off the platter onto the sleeve of my suit coat. Guests, mostly the kids, kept asking me to bring them drinks. There was a drinks station staffed by a bartender but for the most part I went and got them their cherry cokes, ordered to and fro by grade schoolers. The vaudevillian character of the afternoon cocktail hour had transformed into a waking iteration of the classic waiter's nightmare, familiar to nearly all restaurant service professionals: dining rooms the size of football fields; enormous sections that suddenly fill up while the waiter is in the kitchen, the guests now irate at the waiter's absence; orders that make no sense; plates of writhing, neon-purple jellyfish.

Almost the very instant service ended, around nine o'clock, the caterer bid me goodbye. I thought that meant I could leave, too, but it became clear that someone needed to stay and supervise cleanup. It also became clear that this supervisor wasn't going to be my co-captain from New York, who was leaving with the caterer. She was much nicer to me now that service and her work were done. She told me she had enjoyed working with me.

"*Mazel tov*," she concluded, and they left.

Cleanup took until two-thirty in the morning.

The caterer had already paid me, in hundred-dollar bills. I could have simply gotten in my car and gone home, but I felt I had to stay until the very end.

The following day, I divided the fee I was paid by the number of hours I worked and discovered that I had made much less money per hour than I would have made at the restaurant.

I took the suit to the dry cleaner. The next time I wore it was to the wedding of the coworker at the restaurant who often talked football with the caterer—who catered my coworker's wedding, entirely for free, as a wedding gift.

xxiii.

I had an agreement with a local theater company to produce my Ezra Pound play, but I knew its four-hour length had to be radically shortened. Although I was eager to cut it down, I could not make any progress. Deleting something here always seemed to require adding something there; or I discovered that a scene I had regarded as superfluous was in fact essential; or I would have a sudden inspiration and find myself typing an entirely new scene in a frenetic burst of energy.

While I was attempting to finish the script, I also did some initial work on another play about a pair of chefs, one Chinese and one Jewish. I had gotten the idea for the play from a book called *Essential Outsiders*, which was a collection of essays about the social, economic, and political affinities of the Chinese and Jews in their respective environments throughout the world and its history. I found this book after my expat friend in Jakarta told me that the Chinese population there, who controlled much of the city's commerce and trade, were known as "the Jews of Asia."

One essay principally attributed the Jews' maintenance of "some semblance of common identity," despite being "a homeless, vulnerable diaspora," to "a heroic tradition of learning."

The essay did not trace the Jews' longstanding success in business matters to a single source: "For whatever combination of reasons, Europe's Jews have produced an astounding number of success stories in business [...] Much of this success is owing to a high degree of adaptability."

For whatever combination of reasons.

The usual reasons.

Adaptability to what?

After another month of arduous work on the Ezra Pound play, I had trimmed the concluding seventeen-page monologue down to three and made many other deletions, but the script somehow remained the same length. Finally, I told the director of the theater company that I was withdrawing it from production.

It was a coincidence when, one year later, in 2010, a university art museum just a few miles from my house mounted a traveling exhibition of the Vorticists. Vorticism was a short-lived, early-modernist art movement with a strong literary component. The movement was founded and centered in London and produced a remarkable amount of exciting work despite its brevity. It lasted only a few years, from about 1910 to 1914, when World War I scattered its members. Two died at the front.

The cofounder of Vorticism was Ezra Pound.

In conjunction with the exhibition, the museum commissioned a performance piece to be staged in the museum as a site-specific production. By another coincidence, the theater company selected to create this piece was the same one that was to have produced my play about Pound. The director asked me if I'd like to try reworking my play, which contained a small amount of material about the Vorticists, for the museum exhibition. I was quick to say yes. But rather than rework the script I had spent three years developing, I wrote a completely new one—or rather, I assembled a new one from the writings of Pound and some of his associates, most notably the irascible writer-painter Wyndham Lewis, whom Auden had once called the "lonely old volcano of the Right." I marshaled these writings into an hourlong found-text narrative that incorporated elements of Dada-style cabaret and vaude-villian slapstick, along with musical numbers. The lyrics to these numbers were the only original writing I did for the piece. I set them to tunes by Bob Dylan.

The showstopping moment of the production came when the actor playing Pound lip-synced, with perfect bravura mimicry, one of Pound's antisemitic rants on Rome Radio, which concluded:

"I think it might be a good thing to hang Roosevelt and a few hundred Yidds – IF you can do it by due legal process. The USA will be of no use to itself or to anyone else until it gets rid of the KIKES who started this war and Mr. Roosevelt. Kikenfeldt, Finkelstein, Oozenstink. You let in the Jew, and the Jew rotted your empire, and you yourselves out-Jewed the Jew."

"This is 'suburban anti-Semitism'?," objected the critic Alfred Kazin, citing Pound's apology to Ginsberg for his prejudice. "Of the kind used to keep Jews out of country clubs?"

After the actor mimicked Pound's Rome Radio speech, the audience was instructed to change locations in the museum and find the next act of the play out in the rotunda. At this point in each performance, the theatergoers filed out of the auditorium in total silence. Some of them simply left the museum altogether without staying for the end, which was a performance of Dylan's "Desolation Row" with my rewritten lyrics except for one line from Dylan's original: "Ezra Pound and T. S. Eliot, fighting the captain's tower." That single line was why I had chosen Dylan's music. I also chose it because Allen Ginsberg was associated with both Pound and Dylan, the acolyte of the former, the occasional colleague of the other.

I didn't choose Dylan because he was Jewish.

xxiv.

My junior-year housemate in college was the daughter of a very famous classical violinist (father) and a highly regarded flautist (mother). This was a coincidence that had nothing to do with my own semi-famous cantor-composer great-grandfather. I don't think I even told my housemate about Pinchos Jassinowsky. She went on to become a professional opera singer.

Another of my friends was a gifted composer who is now an illustrious film scorer in Hollywood. Both he and my housemate were Jewish. Once I was present while they were discussing classical music, which I didn't know very much about. Although I was also a musician, my background was limited to pop, rock, and jazz.

My housemate made a reference to Felix Mendelssohn's Wedding March. I didn't know Mendelssohn had written the Wedding March. I don't think it had ever occurred to me to wonder who wrote it, or even that it had been written. It seemed like a piece of music that had just always been there, like Happy Birthday.

When my housemate mentioned Mendelssohn, the film scorer brightened perceptibly and added: "Jewish composer."

Felix Mendelssohn was the grandson of Moses Mendelssohn, arguably the most famous Jewish philosopher of the Enlightenment. But I had never heard of Moses Mendelssohn and did not know that Felix Mendelssohn's parents converted to Protestant Christianity and had him baptized. He was not raised Jewish and there has been much scholarly writing about his inconclusive relationship to his Jewishness. To call Mendelssohn a "Jewish composer" may not be correct.

Nonetheless, at the words "Jewish composer," my housemate brightened, too, although without saying anything else. It was as though a beam had suddenly lit up between them. I was aware that this beam might well have included me, because I was both Jewish and a musician, even if I wasn't their caliber of musician or an observant Jew; but I was also aware that the beam did not include me. It seemed to pass right over my head.

XXV.

In my senior year of college I took a Music Department course called Writing about Music. One of the assignments was to listen to and write about the "Liebestod" from Wagner's *Tristan und Isolde*. My familiarity with Wagner was limited at the time to "Ride of the Valkyries" from its use as "Kill the Wabbit" in a famous Bugs Bunny cartoon. I did not know the music was actually Wagner's.

I was quickly smitten with the "Liebestod" and started listening to it over and over again. I related my enthusiasm for the piece to my grandmother, the daughter of Pinchos Jassinowsky, the famous cantor.

My grandmother was not an observant Jew. I never even heard her talk about being Jewish. She replied that Wagner was an anti-Semite, she never listened to his music, and would never play it.

For the assignment to write about Wagner, I wrote a personal essay about obsessively listening to the "Liebestod" that ended with the sentence: "Don't tell grandma."

My professor, who I assumed from her name was Jewish, wrote, "Incredibly brilliant ending." She gave me an A+.

Krelboyne: Geek/nerd/dweeb.

xxvi.

A year or so after I graduated from college, I got a job
as an arts administrator for an esteemed avant-garde
theater company in New York City. The company's artistic
director, who wasn't Jewish, complimented me one day
for having done something well, or for having been right
about something—I don't remember. I do remember what
she attributed it to, though.

"It's because you're an Ashkenazi Jew," she said, with
a bright smile.

She added that because she was good at what she did—
she won a MacArthur Fellowship, the so-called "Genius
Grant," while I was working for her—she must have been
an Ashkenazi Jew, too.

I didn't know if she was serious about that.

I didn't know if I had ever said I was Jewish.

Another day in the office, we were scheduling something, and somebody wondered aloud whether the pro-
posed date would conflict with one of the Jewish holidays.
No one was sure what date the holiday would fall on that
year.

While we looked for a calendar, the company's graphic designer, who was German, looked up at me from his
computer and said: "Adam, do you know?"

I said no, I didn't, why would I know?

xxvii.

Numerous places make claims to the title Where East Meets West (Istanbul is one of them) but Azerbaijan seemed to have the best case. Europe with Asia, the caravanserai and the cosmopolis, Aladdin's Lamp with Big Oil. On the bus into the city from Heydar Aliyev International Airport, the city was slung out before us in the summer haze, and we saw the rigs at work out in the bay, as though crude was being pumped directly from the Caspian into the capital, extracting the city from its deep incrustation in the past and powering it into a future for which it—for which the entire world—seemed not quite prepared. Massive construction projects were underway everywhere. Beautiful recreational areas would abruptly end in a chaos of rubble and work long abandoned, as though civilization had simply ended halfway up an uncompleted flight of marble steps.

But mostly I was interested in Baku because of the Caspian Sea.

When I was in grade school, probably nine or ten years old, my favorite class was called Around the World. This was essentially Geography class, but it was taught as a fun competition. Teams of student trios raced to complete a circuit of the globe. Each team advanced from one place to the next by demonstrating our learnings of locations and associated facts—population figures, languages spoken, and so on. Tegucigalpa, Addis Ababa, Copenhagen…

Not all the destinations were national capitals. They

were not all even cities or countries. One place we had to learn about was the Caspian Sea. I was especially captivated by the Caspian: the largest inland body of water in the world, I learned, landlocked yet saline, standing powerfully upright on the map between countries whose names mostly ended in -an: Turkmenistan, Iran, Azerbaijan. (Caspi-an.) An inland sea—what could it mean? Where did its salt come from if it was landlocked? Would it have beaches, like the coast we went to every summer in North Carolina? Would there be waves? What kind of fish would be in it? Would there be fish in it at all or did its oil make it uninhabitable for wildlife?

The sea's very name, the word *Caspian*, was a vast thrilling whisper that had echoed in my mind ever since, as an emblem of unfathomable depth and immeasurable farness. From then on, I had dreamed of going there and standing at its edge, as I later wanted to stand in the vineyards of Burgundy and to stand where my ancestors stood in Romania. This desire, so uncomplicated and inarticulate, this secret so cherished and so tightly kept that I was almost ashamed to carry it inside me—this was really why I wanted to go to Azerbaijan. I couldn't even bear to say that this was my reason. I almost felt ashamed of it. When Heather suggested it, I simply agreed with enthusiasm.

We booked a hotel right in Baku's Old Town, whose historic architecture was so well maintained by modern means that it looked almost like a reenactment, an ethnographic preserve, even a theme park. No cars were allowed within Old Town's walls. We checked in, dropped our bags in our room, and immediately walked out toward the waterfront. Within a few minutes we were sitting on a bench looking out at the Caspian Sea. It looked like a lake. Heather and I both cried a little. Then we walked to the oily water and dipped our hands in it. I felt that my youth had finally made decisive landfall on the banks of my adulthood, where I had met again with the child I had been and found him to have been justified.

xxviii.

The enthusiasm for geography sparked in me by Around the World class also fueled an interest in numismatics. I collected coins with a very specific purpose: I wanted specimens from as many of the world's countries as possible, especially countries that no longer existed, like Rhodesia. I was very serious, almost obsessive, about this collection and even subscribed to a mail order catalog whose quarterly issues I scrutinized intently. But because I could seldom afford the catalog's merchandise on my small weekly allowance, I usually bought my coins at the mall from a shop just a few doors down from the store where one of the two clerks had correctly guessed I was Jewish. The coins in the shop in the mall were much cheaper than the ones in the quarterly catalog, which specialized in old, rare, and uncirculated specimens. I went to the mall coin shop often enough that the shopkeeper became familiar with me and my collecting habits and would sometimes alert me to the recent arrival of a coin from a country that was new to me. He was the person from whom I learned that Rhodesia and Zimbabwe were the same place. I had coins from both countries.

His store was also where I bought my "flips": square cardboard holders with round, clear-plastic insets. You centered the coin in the plastic circle, folded the flip over, stapled it shut, and labeled it: country, denomination, year, condition, price. I also bought plastic sleeves with pockets designed to hold the flips, and a large binder to hold the sleeves. Eventually, my coin collection grew large enough to require three binders, whose contents were arranged alphabetically by country. That meant a lot of removing flips from their slots in the sleeves and moving them down to make room for coins from new countries as I acquired them. This periodic rearranging of flips was one of the most satisfying activities of my numismatic hobby.

I began to learn more new words related to coin collecting, along with new definitions of old words, as I had learned new names for old countries. For example, I learned that the term *obverse* meant a coin's front, even though to me it sounded like it should refer to the back, but the back was called the *reverse*. Many coins conformed to the same obverse/reverse design. Usually, the name of the country and the coin's monetary denomination appeared on the reverse, a monarch or national leader on the obverse. It was curious to me, though, that the same woman who appeared on the obverse of coins from the Netherlands (the queen, I deduced) also appeared on the obverse of coins from Surinam. Was she also the Queen of Surinam? Where was Surinam? Why were the Netherlands also called Holland, and why were people from that country called not "Netherlandian" or "Hollandaise" but "Dutch"? Especially when the word *Deutschland* appeared not on coins from the Netherlands but on coins from Germany? And did the relationship between the Netherlands/Holland and Surinam have something to do with the relationship between Germany and another country from which I had a coin, German East Africa? Why were there Germans in East Africa, and why did they have their own coins there?

A few years ago, my mother told me that of all the artefacts of my youth only my coin collection remained in her possession. I presumed this was in case the collection should turn out to be valuable, which given its juvenile Around the World geographical quality is unlikely. For as devoted as I was to it, I have little memory of the collection's contents. I remember the coin I was fondest of. I was sure it was very rare, because it came from a place that could not possibly have been a country, now or ever. In fact I had thought it might even be a fictional place. I regarded the coin as an almost illicit piece of currency, never meant to escape the place it came from. It was from Palestine.

xxix.

A popular Baku attraction is the ancient Ateshgah Fire
Temple. Its date of construction is unknown. It was
built atop a natural flame issuing from gas vapors that
emanated from the oil-rich earth below. Long ago, visitors to the temple discovered people there whom they
called "fire worshipers." These were probably Zoroastrians, whose religion is often symbolized by an altar of fire.

During my trip, I had become unusually interested in
the chapter in *The Portable World Bible* about Zoroastrianism. Just a couple of months before I left for Albania, I
had read Herodotus's account of the Greek-Persian battle
of Salamis in 480 BCE. When the editor of *The Portable
World Bible* introduced Zoroastrianism with a reference
to the very same battle, I perked up with recognition. The
editor made the compelling claim that, had the Greeks
not defeated the Persians, a defeat that marked the turning point in the Greco-Persian War, the Western world
would likely be dominated by Zoroastrianism today.
That world, the editor qualified, might not be radically
different from ours, for the tenets of Zoroastrianism and
Judeo-Christianity have much in common: a universal,
omnipotent "Father-God" (Ahura Mazda rather than Yah-
weh) in whose kingdom our souls shall dwell eternally;
this deity's human incarnation (Zarathustra/Jesus); an-
gels and demons, among them an arch-adversary (Angra
Mainyu/Satan); and other theological affinities. This is no
surprise: there is evidence that the Old Testament bor-

rows substantially from Zoroastrian scripture, ethics, and codes of social behavior. "Perhaps the chief differences," the editor suggests, between our world and a Zoroastrian world, "would be in matters of emphasis."

There are two stark differences in emphasis. One is that, among all the animals, Zoroastrian scripture holds the dog in the highest regard; conversely, the Bible, especially the Old Testament, considers the dog a contemptible, pestiferous creature, the lowest of the low, and to call someone a dog is to deal a very harsh insult. Another is that the ancient Zoroastrians, unlike Jews and Christians, proscribed burying their dead, a practice the Zoroastrians considered sinful: we must not desecrate Ahura Mazda's creation by filling the earth with corpses. Instead, dead bodies were covered with fragrant flora, and time and scavengers took their course. I decided that I preferred that way of disposing of the dead to burying them.

The flame of the Ateshgah Fire Temple died out in 1969, probably due to overextraction of petroleum resources by the Azerbaijani oil industry. (The temple fire is now supplied by gas from a pipeline.) A quarter century later, the president of Azerbaijan, Heydar Aliyev, announced the construction of an "Eternal Flame" monument in another location in Baku. The monument, completed in 1998, commemorates "Black January," the name given to a 1990 massacre of about 150 Azerbaijanis by the Russian military, the last and most violent result of Russia's effort to thwart Azerbaijan's move toward independence after the Soviet Union dissolved. While Azerbaijan was an SSR, Aliyev rose to power first as a KGB director, then as a politburo minister. Shortly after Azerbaijan gained its independence, he became its president, in 1995. He died in 2003 (not long before that, he passed the presidency down to his son, who still holds it), but he still looms over the country. Quite literally. Aliyev's image is ubiquitous on billboards and signs, and we got used to seeing his face wherever we went. Sometimes his gaze down on us felt warmly paternal, at other times menacing—the surveillance of a KGB strongman.

In all official representations, Aliyev is characterized not as the country's founding president but as "the leader of the Azerbaijani people." Not only Baku's airport but much else in Azerbaijan is named for him, including the famous Heydar Aliyev Center, which Heather and I toured. It took most of a day because the Heydar Aliyev Center is massive. It is also dazzling, designed by the great Iraqi-British architect Zaha Hadid. The building contains, among many attractions, a museum devoted to the life and importance of Heydar Aliyev. We went through this museum, as we had gone through the museum in Ioannina devoted to Ali Pasha Tepelena.

We did not go to the Ateshgah Fire Temple. It's well out of the city center and we had limited time in Baku. We did go to the Eternal Flame monument, which stands on a grand prospect overlooking the Caspian, not far from Old Town. The monument is at the end of a long row of plaques bearing rather macabre images of every Azerbaijani who was martyred in the Black January massacre.

These plaques made for an eerie passage toward the flame, rather like a deathly gauntlet that had to be run. The row of plaques put me in mind of a Holocaust memorial.

XXX.

From Baku we went to Sheki, in the mountainous northwest of Azerbaijan. On the way, our bus, an old, rundown heap with a groaning undercarriage and feckless air conditioning, broke down. We were many miles from any settled area. It felt even hotter inside the bus than it did outside, so we waited in the sun while the driver and his onboard mechanic worked on repairs. This took quite some time. Heather checked her phone and reported to me that it was 109 degrees.

Some Azerbaijani soldiers were on the bus with us. We chatted with them while we waited. They were nice fellows, very young, barely out of their teens from the looks of them. They were no help at all to the driver and his mechanic. I had the sense that if danger were to befall us, the soldiers would be the first to flee.

Heather looked up our location on her phone's map app and showed it to me. We were only a few dozen miles from Iran.

Just then, Heather received a text message from her brother back in the U.S. It was the only unsolicited message she received from him during our entire three-month trip. He used to work in the U.S. Department of Homeland Security and now works in the private sector in a security-adjacent industry.

His message said: "I hope you're not planning to cross the Iranian border."

We wondered if he still had security clearances that

allowed him to know where we were. We also wondered if something was happening at the Iranian border that he knew about and wanted to keep us clear of without telling us what it was. In any case we had no intention of going near Iran. Until Heather looked at the phone's map, we had no idea we were so close to it.

I'd have liked to go to Iran, ever since Heather's British-Iranian friend threw her head back and laughed and said Sabzi means greens. But it was almost impossible for U.S. citizens to travel safely in Iran. Even she, a citizen, could not go there. Not because she wasn't allowed in, she had told Heather, but because the Iranian government was known to arrest and detain visiting nationals with British or U.S. passports, as a reaction to unfavorable U.S. policies that had been backed by Great Britain.

Heather's brother insists that he had no idea where we were when he told us not to go near Iran.

xxxi.

Sightseeing in Sheki, we passed a sign for a pediatrician's office:

PEDİATRİYA

ŞÖBƏSİ

I stopped short.

Adam ŞÖBƏSİ?

The translation app on Heather's phone informed us that *Şöbəsi* meant branch or department. PEDİATRİYA ŞÖBƏSİ: pediatric department. She wondered aloud whether the Azerbaijani *söbəsi* (branch) and the Persian *sabzi* (greens) shared a plant-based etymological root.

Later, we visited Sheki's historic "Albanian church." When I had told my Albanian coworker back home that I had learned about the curious existence of an Albanian church in Azerbaijan, he said it was likely that Alexander the Great had led a detachment of soldiers two thousand miles east from Albania across the forty-first parallel, and they settled in Sheki. He said this with some pride.

Alexander the Great is actually considered Greek or Macedonian, not Albanian.

It turned out that the Albanian church in Sheki had nothing to do with Albania, the country. Caucasian Albania is an entirely distinct place from Balkan Albania. Caucasian Albania's most famous figure from antiquity is not Alexander the Great but none other than Zoroaster, who is said to have been born in Caucasian Albania.

Outside Sheki's Albanian church were a number of

ancient graves. We could look right down into two of them through plexiglass, just as we could look through the bullet holes in the floor of Ali Pasha Tepelena's monastery hideout. There were the original skeletons which had been exhumed from these graves, studied, reassembled, and put back in. According to the accompanying text display, the bones dated to the Bronze Age, and their measurements indicated a person who would have stood about eight feet tall.

The skeletons did look quite large. They could very well have been the remains of people who were eight feet tall—giants. Still, we could scarcely bring ourselves to believe our eyes. Of everything we saw on our three-month trip to ten different countries, the skeletons buried in front of the Caucasian Albanian church were the hardest for me to accept.

xxxii.

We were about to leave Sheki and cross the land border with Georgia. But before we did, Heather suggested we go to Quba. This would have meant a rather arduous backtrack. Quba is in the northeast of Azerbaijan. It's not very far from Sheki by air, only about seventy-five miles, but there are no direct flights and no roads between them over the mountain range. We would have had to go all the way back to Baku and then most of the way up the coast road from there. It would have taken at least two days to get to Quba from where we were. Heather's birthday was still five days off, so we had time to make this backtrack and she was eager for us to do it because she had discovered the existence of a Jewish enclave in Quba. For 2,500 years, it is said, the Jews have lived in this "oasis of tolerance." Not only lived but thrived. Azerbaijan, especially its farther reaches, is an unwealthy country, but if you cross the river from Quba's city center into the Jewish quarter, called Qırmızı Qəsəbə (Red Village), you will see Jews living in marked prosperity compared to the rest of Quba on the opposite bank.

The community of Jews in Qırmızı Qəsəbə are known as "Mountain Jews," as though this is another strain, a subspecies of Jew, like the Ashkenazim and the Sephardim. Qırmızı Qəsəbə may be the only settlement outside Israel whose population is nothing but Jews. They number about four thousand. The village has two active synagogues.

At no point had Heather or I said that our trip had anything whatsoever to do with Jews, Jewish communities, Jewish history, or my being Jewish. The Jewish museums in Berat and Ioannina were accidents. We had not even known they existed. Now it seemed we were on some sort of search. When had this search begun? And why?

I said Quba was too far out of the way.

xxxiii.

My parents left it up to me whether to have a bar mitzvah. I told them I didn't want to, and they said that was fine with them. Not long after that, my Boiby and Zaidie visited us from Pittsburgh. My Boiby was gravely disappointed that I did not want to have a bar mitzvah. She gave me a few reasons why I should change my mind. I don't remember what the reasons were, nor the reasons I gave in return for why I didn't want to have a bar mitzvah, or whether I gave her any at all, or if I even had any that I might have given. All I remember about the exchange was the look on Boiby's face, that pinched Pittsburgh Sigel face, which grew even more pinched as the exchange went on—and then, surprisingly, after it became clear that I could not be convinced to change my mind, softened, along with her brittle, arthritic figure. But not with compassion or understanding. She looked resigned and terribly sad, like she had lost me.

To avoid further discussions, I spent most of the rest of Boiby and Zaidie's visit in my room, which was downstairs in the basement, working diligently on my coin collection. The year after I turned thirteen, I got my first job, scooping ice cream, and had my own money to spend on coins. But by then I had stopped collecting them.

xxxiv.

The drive from Sheki to Azerbaijan's border with Georgia was brown, hot, dusty. A nearly barren land. This was our only border crossing on foot. The moment we walked through the checkpoint into Georgia, everything turned green. Vines everywhere, on hillsides, in fields, in front yards, heavy with grapes. Pastures of fat cows and fields of abundant crops. Vegetables growing extravagantly in front yards. It was still very hot, but the air felt moister, fecund, breathable. No difference between two places had ever seemed so stark.

Our first outing was to one of Georgia's holiest religious and cultural sites. Davit Gareja is a monastery complex built into both sides of a mountain ridge along a remote stretch of the Georgia-Azerbaijan border. Its most famous attraction is the series of ancient cave paintings found in the Udabno monastery. The Udabno cave lies just on the other side of the ridge which forms the boundary between Georgia and Azerbaijan, although of course the monastery was constructed long before either nation existed. In fact the border is still not clearly demarcated, as we discovered. Tourists are customarily permitted to cross the border and see the cave paintings under the watch of an Azerbaijani patrol force, but when we reached the top of the ridge it transpired that access was not being granted. Georgia and Azerbaijan were engaged in a minor political dispute. The most recent flare-up of the border dispute had been triggered by the Georgian president's call for a renewed effort to clarify where the border was. It was inferred that she thought the cave paintings should belong in Georgian territory. Her tone was, we gathered, somewhat undiplomatic, and Azerbaijan responded by enforcing its border and by barring access to the parts of the monastery situated on Azerbaijan's side of the ridge. I wondered briefly why Azerbaijan, a Muslim country, should insist on claiming Christian shrines for itself.

On the way back from Davit Gareja, our driver pulled over at a roadside restaurant so we could have lunch. There was nothing else around for miles. A German tour group occupied most of the tables inside, so Heather and I went up to the outdoor dining area on the roof. A patio umbrella gave us shade. Our food took quite a while to arrive—the Germans' order was ahead of ours—and at one point the waiter emerged from below to apologize, although we weren't in a hurry. We were enjoying the pleasantly warm day, our local wine, for which Georgia is famous, and the ample time to take in the view. A dirt track led into the steppe from the rear of the restaurant, disappearing into the horizon.

Not long after our food was served, a funeral party appeared below us.

They had not been in or anywhere around the restaurant when we arrived. The rooftop dining area faced the rear, so we hadn't seen them drive up, or whether they had driven up at all.

The pallbearers hoisted the casket. It was open, and from our vantage we could see the corpse inside it.

She was a very old woman—ancient, it seemed, as though summoned from an earlier epoch. As the procession set off down the dirt track into the steppe, she joggled about inside the box. Her dead face was the same color as the dry dirt. Her jowls quivered in disturbance, almost in annoyance, it seemed to me, while her body jounced from side to side, limbs loose, as she was borne away.

It occurred to me that I had never seen a dead body before.

I had never been to a funeral with an open casket. I did not know until many years later that open caskets are proscribed by Jewish law. It is forbidden to see the face of the dead.

Later, when we paid our bill, we could still see the procession moving down the track, like ants.

XXXV.

We had planned to stay two nights in Tbilisi, the Georgian capital, and then head north to Kazbegi, up near the Russian border, in time for Heather's birthday. But there was a problem. Rain, and even snow, looked likely. We decided with some regret to postpone. We extended our stay in Tbilisi, a city we immediately loved.

It was a lively, cultured, and vigorous place but also anodyne and easygoing. Its atmospheric old quarters, with its wrought-iron balconies draped with grapevines, put me in mind of a beguiling cross between Marseille and Savannah. We visited museums, galleries, and a few of the city's dark and warm old Orthodox churches. We attended a hip avant-garde performance piece one night, a traditional Georgian opera another. We browsed antique Georgian rugs and funky, modish Tbilisian couture. The hippest shop we found sold nothing but Soviet-era vintage kitsch, now a trendy collectible.

One day as we were walking around, Heather said— out of the blue, apropos of nothing— "There's nothing to do here but enjoy it."

We especially enjoyed the traditional Georgian food. It was even better than its considerable reputation, and although Heather and I tend to travel with fairly light stomachs, we ate quite a lot, including a splurge on Heather's birthday at one of the country's most admired restaurants.

To make room for all the food, we went for long walks.

There were many stray dogs, but they were docile beasts, mostly loping or lolling around—many were ear-tagged, and we heard they were programmatically tranquilized under a municipal initiative. One of them even joined me companionably on a long solo walk early one morning.

The only jarring incident in Tbilisi—really only a wrinkle—was when a small gang of young men burst into a sprint on a sidewalk, as though they were under sudden pursuit by authorities. But there was no one chasing them. As though discarding evidence, one of the gang hastily tossed something behind him as he ran off with the others. I picked it up. It was a cigarette lighter. It worked, and you never know when fire might come in handy. I kept it.

xxxvi.

For a while in my childhood I went to Sunday School in the basement of a synagogue my family did not attend. My parents did not belong to a congregation and were not regular shulgoers. It surprises me that my word-processing dictionary accepts *shulgoer*, as it also surprises me that I went to Sunday School at all since we were not observant. The only other semblance of a habitual Jewish experience I had as a child was when my father would take my sister and me to the campus Hillel House on occasional Friday nights because they had food that reminded him of his childhood. He always ordered the tongue sandwich. I thought that sounded disgusting. I liked pastrami on seeded rye, with a lot of mustard on it, and Dr. Brown's Cel-Ray soda.

On Friday nights at Hillel House I had to wear a yarmulke, which was pronounced in such a way that I thought it was spelled *yamaca*. *Yarmulke* still doesn't look right to me, like *Bubbie*. Another reason *yamaca* looks right is that my Boiby, who ate a lot of canned food when she ate anything at all, had a surprising taste for jicama. She said she liked the crunch. *Jicama, yamaca.*

I have no memory of anything I learned in Sunday School, but I do remember my teacher's name, which was Frances Oppenheimer. She was from South Africa and had that country's accent, which I had never heard before. I was interested in her accent not only because of the way it sounded, a sort of funny version of British, but also because I had assumed all South Africans to be black.

147

Mrs. Oppenheimer was white—and Jewish, I must have supposed, although at that age I could not really understand how a Jewish person could also be South African. I thought a Jewish person was somehow just *Jewish*, and that being American didn't really change that because no one was really "American." Most everyone, not just Jews, had come here from somewhere else. But I didn't quite know how to reconcile being Jewish with being Romanian either. I had not yet had the guessing game with the clerks in the mall.

It was all too complicated for me to understand. But Mrs. Oppenheimer's accent was pretty neat.

Nonetheless, I paid little attention to her, and when I did, it was often to disrupt her class. I suppose my bouts of misbehavior were acting-out expressions of inner turmoil over my parents' impending split. They separated when I was seven years old and were divorced the following year, after which they stopped taking me to Sunday School. No reasons were supplied. It probably owed to the logistics of their divorce. They had joint custody, and every Sunday my sister and I were transferred from one parent to the other. The necessary arrangements.

I must have kept going to Sunday School at least for a short while after my parents split up. Once my father was late in retrieving me and explained amiably to Mrs. Oppenheimer that there had been confusion over whether he was to pick me up or "my girlfriend," as he referred to the woman whose house he had moved into, and we with him for the part of each week when we weren't at my mother's.

I also thought it was neat that my father was someone who had a "girlfriend."

I don't remember whether it was at Sunday School or from my Boiby that I learned the dreidel game. When you spun the dreidel, you could win money if one of the right letters came up after it fell. I remember the letters: *aleph, gimel, shin, nun*. Actually, in writing this paragraph, I only remembered the first three of them and had to look up *nun*, which means "faithfulness." I had probably forgotten *nun* because if the dreidel came up *nun* you got no gelt. *Nun*, none.

The money you could win was called gelt and took the form of chocolate discs in shiny gold-colored foil wrappers. The dreidel game may have been played to a song that went, *"Pennies, nickels, dimes, and quarters / Hear the merry clink-clink-clink."* I remember those lines and their melody, but I'm not sure where I learned them.

Mrs. Oppenheimer's name was close enough to the name of Charlie Brown's teacher, Mrs. Othmar, that even though Mrs. Oppenheimer spoke in her elegantly clipped South African accent, I mostly heard what Charlie Brown and his classmates heard when Mrs. Othmar spoke in those *Peanuts* television specials I liked to watch as a child: *Wah-wah-wah, wah-wah, wah wah, wah wah. Alef, nickels, pennies, gimel, hear the merry wah wah wah.*

The only other thing I may have learned in Sunday School was an easy way to draw a Star of David: you made a triangle and then you overlaid another triangle upside-down on top of it. My sister and I didn't call it a Star of David, though. We called it a Jewish Star.

One of the museums we visited in Tbilisi had an extensive temporary exhibit about false messiahs from around the world. I was interested in this exhibit because of a rumor that had long circulated on my father's side of the family, the Sobsey side, that there had once been an errant Sobsey who declared himself the messiah and led a band of followers around the Caucasus. This legend was offered as evidence that we had not originally come from Odessa.

Most of the false messiahs in the exhibit did not look, act, or dress at all like our general picture of Jesus, although one of them did and was still active: a beatific Russian in flowing robes and hair who presided over a devout sect living in apparently untroubled communal harmony in remotest Siberia. In 2020, a year after our trip, he was arrested on a couple of vague charges, as though the Russian authorities suddenly decided to apprehend him after years of benign neglect. Maybe they just wanted his money. His followers were distraught.

After visiting this exhibition, thinking of the supposed false messiah in the Sobsey lineage, I discovered that there is a long and colorful history of Jewish false messiahs, from the revolutionary Bar Kokhba of Roman antiquity all the way through Menachem Mendel Schneerson in the twentieth century. I sometimes wonder how it was determined that they were false.

In another museum in Tbilisi, I became captivated by a painting of a beech forest in the snow. I found the painting marvelous in every way, took a picture of it, and kept looking at it on my phone after we left. I was aware that part of what drew me to this image had nothing to do with the painting itself. It had to do with my great-grandparents' home province of Moldavia, which I had read was adjacent to a territory called Bucovina. Bucovina means "Land of the Beeches." According to what I had read, Bucovina was once a locus of high Jewish culture in the nineteenth century.

What is high Jewish culture?

It was because of the idea of a high Jewish culture that I was inclined to visit Bucovina. It was also because of this culture that I preferred to identify the region of my ancestry within Romania as Bucovina, not Moldavia, even if you elevated Moldavia by calling it High Moldavia, as Patrick Leigh Fermor had. It still sounded moldy. In my mind, I pictured Bucovina looking exactly like the painting: silvery beeches and gleaming snowmelt forming a path into the white woods. I could see myself walking down this path, although it would of course not be snow-covered in July. But it was where my great-grandparents walked. Perhaps it was in these beech woods that my Grape Zaidie had eluded the wolves on his way to visit my future Great Boiby. The very name of this homeland of mine, to say nothing of its high Judaic culture, sounded majestic to my ears, even aristocratic.

I wonder if I would have felt differently about Bucovina if I had known that the German word for "Beech Forest" is *Buchenwald*.

While we were in Georgia, my mother forwarded me some fresh information that my cousin, Uncle Larry's son, had just posted on social media. It was a picture of Grape Zaidie as an old man, probably taken not long before he died. The photograph seemed familiar to me. If it was true that my memory of having met Grape Zaidie as a small child was incorrect and that I only knew him through a photograph, it seemed likely that this was the photograph. Under it, my cousin had written that Grape Zaidie, Moshe Sigel, had emigrated in 1910 with his wife and daughters (the one who survived the sea voyage and the one who did not) from a town called Darabani. They went overland from Darabani to Bremen, Germany. My cousin expressed amazement at the difficulty implied in this journey of more than a thousand miles.

From Bremen, the Sigels sailed steerage to Ellis Island on a German-built steamship that had sunk in a New York Harbor dock fire a year earlier and was repaired and recommissioned. According to the ship's documents, the steamer was "suitable for the transport of large numbers of cattle."

Had I not gotten my cousin's coincidental message secondhand, I wouldn't have known about the existence of Darabani. This knowledge confused me. The information circulated in my family was that my great-grandparents were from Dorohoi. There was a marriage certificate confirming this—in fact, Heather had found it online before we left for our trip. I expressed no interest whatsoever in the marriage certificate.

Now that we had new information that located my great-grandparents in Darabani, I told Heather that it was possible my great-grandparents had been married in Dorohoi but were from Darabani. Then I questioned the very existence of Darabani. I said it seemed plausible that the toponyms *Darabani* and *Dorohoi* were similar enough on paper that they might have actually been one and the same place; perhaps there had been a scribal error at Ellis Island. But had I looked at a map I'd have seen both towns, about twenty miles apart. I did not look at a map.

It might have cheered me to see that Darabani's position on the map made it likelier to be considered part of Bucovina, Land of the Beeches, rather than Moldavia. That alone would be a good reason to go there and stand where my ancestors stood.

Heather decided she wanted to take a brief trip from Tbilisi down to Armenia, Georgia's neighbor to the south. We had discussed going there while we were planning our trip but had left open whether we would actually do it. Now she decided it would be missing out not to go.

I declined to join her. I was happy in Tbilisi and wanted to do some writing there. But at the very last minute I changed my mind. We took a long minibus ride to the Armenian capital, Yerevan, whose modern look and feel surprised us. The Soviets, we learned, had destroyed most of the old architecture and infrastructure. We lamented the disappearance of history but conceded that modernity probably held some advantages.

We had decided to stay in Armenia for only two nights. In order to get the most out of our short visit, Heather hired our second and final private driver of the trip. We got into his car early the next morning and soon saw a strikingly high and beautiful mountain in the distance. This, our driver told us, was Mount Ararat, where legend holds that Noah's Ark made landfall. I had had no previous idea where Mount Ararat was, or that some of the very earliest Biblical history reached as far east as Armenia.

Ararat sits right on Armenia's border with Turkey, which claims the mountain. Armenia is the oldest Christian nation in the world, founded in the fourth century (Georgia appears to have been the second), and many Armenians believe Noah's Ark is still up near Ararat's summit. But there is no way to find out. Access to Ararat is barred, our driver told us. We could see a road going along its lower slope, however, with many vehicles on it. When we asked our driver about this road, he said it was a UN military route, absolutely off-limits to the public.

The next day we went to the Armenian Genocide Memorial Complex.

"At the hands of the Turks," the museum's literature says, the Armenians suffered "the first genocide of the twentieth century." I did not know much about Armenia or the genocide, or that the very word *genocide* did not even exist when the Armenian Genocide took place, in the years before and during World War I. The term was coined in 1944, but it had still not yet been officially defined a year later, when the Nuremberg Trials began. The Nazis were accused of crimes against humanity, not genocide. Two years after the trial ended, and one year after Israel was granted nationhood, the UN Genocide Convention was established to formally define genocide: any of five acts, enumerated and elaborated by the Convention, "committed with intent to destroy, in whole or in part, a national, ethnical, racial or religious group."

There are many parallels between the Armenians and the Jews. Among the most striking is one of the last things you see in the Armenian Genocide Museum, just before you exit. Emblazoned in very large lettering on a wall is this text:

"Who, after all, speaks today of the annihilation of the Armenians?" – Adolf Hitler

Hitler was reported to have concluded a 1939 speech with that rhetorical question, by way of giving orders "to send to death mercilessly and without compassion, men, women, and children of Polish derivation and language." Poland had by far Europe's largest Jewish population in the years before World War II.

The country with the second-largest Jewish population in Europe in the years before World War II was Romania.

There is some uncertainty over whether Hitler actually said, *"Who, after all, speaks today of the annihilation of the Armenians?"* His speech wasn't recorded. There is less doubt, however, that the Nazis got the idea to eradicate the Jews from observing the Turks' efforts to destroy the Armenians earlier in the twentieth century. During World War I, Germany's alliance with the collapsing Ottoman Empire, and then with the Young Turks after the Empire dissolved, included support of the Turks' scheme for Armenian "deportation"—a euphemism for annihilation. At least one historian, an Armenian, suggests that the Germans may have encouraged and even helped orchestrate genocidal operations.

In 1933, the German-Jewish writer Franz Werfel published a historical novel as an early warning of the potential for a coming slaughter of the Jews. The novel, *The Forty Days of Musa Dagh*, is about the Armenian genocide.

xl.

When we got to Kazbegi, Heather was unable to hike up to the glacier. Not because of the weather but because she was ill.

With what? Mild food poisoning? A little bug? Possibly she had mild altitude sickness, or even homesickness caused by turning fifty in a place so distant and unfamiliar. Fortunately, the hotel, a chicly restored Communist-era tourist resort, was a pleasant place to rest. Our room had an awe-inspiring view of the 17,000-foot Mt. Kazbegi.

She did feel well enough to manage a hike up to the monastery on our first full day. Although it was not a great distance, the climb was steep, strenuous, and crammed with tourists. So was the monastery itself. We intended to ascend higher the next day, as far up the glacier as we could go, but Heather went to bed feeling worse, and there was a chance of early afternoon rain.

I went to bed that night with a beating pulse, slept fitfully, and woke up before 5:00 in the morning. I threw a few things in my daypack and set out in total darkness. I reached the monastery shortly after sunrise. I barely stopped. Above the monastery, the trail was nearly empty. I saw virtually no other hikers. For quite a while I was accompanied by a very amiable dog. I could not tell if the dog meant to serve and protect me or if it was merely happy for some human company in this habitat, where it was obviously quite comfortable. The dog declined my offers of water and food and would frequently run up ahead of me, or go off the trail to one side or the other to investigate something. But it kept rejoining me for well over an hour. Eventually, it simply didn't return from one of these detours. I wished my fellow pilgrim well.

The trail grew so steep that at one point the rise directly in front of me obscured Kazbegi itself. I added great effort to my step and pushed myself hard up this section of the trail for half an hour or so. When I reached the top of the ridge, I was greeted by an even more astonishing view of Kazbegi—closer, higher, enormous, like a god. It was a hundred times as magnificent as the view from the ridge in the Albanian Alps, and it goaded my spirit. The sky, in defiance of the forecast for rain, was powerfully and deeply blue, causing Kazbegi's snowcap to gleam. It was difficult for my eyes to behold and for my spirit to contain itself.

My heart was pounding as hard and fast as it ever had—from the difficulty of the climb, I knew; but the sight of the peak from the ridgetop seemed to make the sound echo more loudly in my chest.

I continued upward until I came upon a pack of cigarettes lying right on the trail. In it there was a single cigarette. I don't smoke anymore but it seemed I should take it.

Eventually I reached glacier altitude. The black volcanic terrain was increasingly treacherous under a layer of ice, and rivulets of snowmelt widened and deepened until they were roaring violent cascades. Crossing them meant taking wide detours off what little trail remained visible.

Mostly I just clambered up the icy volcanic slab as best as I could. I orienteered by keeping my sights on what appeared to be a building in the high distance. The trail guide signs and blogs had not mentioned the existence of a building that high. I was already very high up, perhaps higher than I had ever climbed.

I hoped to make the building my turnaround point, but it was obviously at least another two hours' climb, and the glacier had become so slippery that I found myself taking one step up, then sliding two steps down in my running shoes, which had barely gotten me over the Theth-to-Valbona trail and were certainly no good for ice.

I took a few steps higher up to a rock outcrop, sat down, lit the cigarette with the lighter I had picked up on the street in Tbilisi, and smoked it. Then I got up and went back down the mountain. At the monastery I found Heather waiting for me. We walked down the mountain together.

Then we flew to Romania.

3.

Impairing

i.

One of our outings in Bucharest was to a bookstore to buy a Romanian guidebook. It is well known that the worst place to buy a guidebook is the place covered by the guidebook, because that is where you will pay the most money for it. But Heather and I agreed that we really did need one, and in addition to feeling ill I also felt remorse for not having packed the copy we had at home. This now seemed an unforgivable error, if not an act of near sabotage. At the very least, it seemed as neglectful as coming all the way to Romania with no greater sense of purpose than merely to stand in the place where my ancestors stood. And how could I think of getting there without a guidebook?

The bookstore included a substantial section of English-language translations of Romanian authors. I took one of them from the display, partly because of its title, *Existential Monday*, which appealed to me, but mainly because of its cover image: a beguiling photo of a man looking down at a second apparition of his own head, which levitated just above his palms, so that he looked like a fortune teller gazing down into the crystal ball of his own face—which, in turn, stared out in dead-eyed frankness, as though it had lived ten million of the title's existential Mondays and contained every fortune ever told.

I had never heard of the author of *Existential Monday*. His name was Benjamin Fondane. On the back of the book, I read that Fondane was a Romanian-born Jew who moved to Paris as a young man, spent time in Argentina, where he associated with Jorge Luis Borges and worked with Victoria Ocampo (it was Ocampo, I later learned, who invited him there), then returned to Paris, where he was "the most daring of the existentialists." And that he died at Auschwitz. Also on the back of the book was a credit of the photo to Man Ray, who took the famous photo of Proust on his deathbed three years before making this image of Fondane.

This was clearly a book I ought to read. I walked around the store with it, but at the last minute I put it back on the shelf. Instead of *Existential Monday*, I bought *In the Heart of the Heart of the Country* by William Gass. A curious choice. The only Gass I had previously read was his final novel, *Middle C*, which is about a family who escapes Austria in 1938 by pretending to be Jewish.

How do you pretend to be Jewish?

Was William Gass Jewish? If he was not, did I consider his authorship of *Middle C* problematic?

It is not entirely true to say that I read *Middle C*—or rather, it is not true to say that I read the entirety of *Middle C*. It's a little over 400 pages long. I read the first 380 or so and then stopped. I admired the writing but didn't care about the characters. It almost seemed that Gass didn't care about the characters.

"I write because I hate," Gass once said. "A lot. Hard."

I read most of *In the Heart of the Heart of the Country* while lying in bed all day in Zodiac House. This must have been what I did during the sick day in Bucharest of which I have no memory.

In addition to not buying *Existential Monday*, we also did not buy a guidebook to Romania. It was too expensive.

ii.

The next day—I suppose it was the next day—we went on the Jewish Bucharest tour. Its text began: "The story of the Jews in Romania is not a happy one."

The website went on to inform us that in the years before World War II, Romania's Jews numbered 800,000. Perhaps as many as 200,000 of Romania's 800,000 Jews lived in Bucharest, the capital.

In 2019, there were about 5,000 Jews in Bucharest.

Why did I want to take this tour? To stand where my ancestors stood?

My ancestors did not stand in Bucharest. They came from Bucovina, or High Moldavia, where Domnul David told Patrick Leigh Fermor he must go if he wanted to meet a lot of Jews. The Jewish part of Romania.

Romania has a lot of parts.

It is the tenth biggest of Europe's fifty countries (if you don't count Russia, whose boundaries extend well into Asia, of course). It is nearly the size of Wyoming and would be the twelfth largest of the fifty U.S. states, although Romania has not always been so large. In fact, it has not even been Romania for very long. The country was established in 1859, only about thirty years before my great-grandparents were born, when two principalities, Moldavia and Wallachia, united to form the country we have since called Romania. About sixty years later, after World War I, Romania was awarded additional territory on three sides, considerably widening its boundaries.

This was the country's recompense for having entered the war on the side of its eventual winners (and for the efforts of its queen all throughout the war to persuade the Powers to think well of her country when it was over). Most notably, Romania took possession of Transylvania, as well as part of Bucovina. Long before that, Bucovina had belonged briefly to Poland. Russia occupied it during a late-eighteenth-century war with the Ottomans, under whom Bucovina had been a vassal territory, as the pashalik of Ali of Tepelena had also been. After the Russians defeated the Ottomans, they gave Bucovina to the Austrian Habsburgs as a gratuity for having helped them prevail. Later, Bucovina's boundaries were redrawn again. Some of it became Romanian while the rest was made part of Ukraine.

It is interesting to me to think about a place—especially about having one's ancestry, and particularly one's Jewish ancestry, in a place—that has always known its identity, autonomy (or lack of it), and overall status in the world to be subject to the decisions of other, larger places. It is interesting to me that there are territories that seem to have the necessary size and hallmarks of sovereign nations—unique names, cultures, customs, landscapes—yet never have been. Bucovina never belonged to itself and only provisionally to other countries. If countries could be nomads, Bucovina, the place I considered my ancestors to have come from, would be one of them. It is a wandering Jew of a place.

As we walked down into the historic city center to take the tour of Jewish Bucharest, I was aware that although my stomach felt somewhat better I was still quite weak. I slouched after Heather as she navigated with her phone. She asked me more than once if I was feeling alright and suggested, gently, that we might go back to Zodiac House so I could get more rest. I objected and said I felt fine, or at least fine enough to continue. I had a water bottle and was trying to stay hydrated in the hot sun, but whenever I took another swig, I felt that same sloshing around in my guts, followed by bloating. Yet I remained terribly thirsty.

While we walked downtown from the affluent neighborhood where Zodiac House was, Bucharest changed before our eyes. By the time we were near the old Jewish Quarter, we had entered a zone of crumbling Soviet-era cement-block buildings. Everything was gray, lots of debris, many abandoned shopfronts. The Jewish Quarter itself seemed especially rundown.

We were looking for our first stop on the tour of Jewish Bucharest, which was called the "Lost Synagogue." It was not actually the first stop as the tour was plotted out online, but it was the one most proximate to our route from uptown, and it didn't matter to us which order we chose.

The actual name of the Lost Synagogue was Beth Hamidraş Temple. The Jewish Bucharest website informed us that Beth Hamidraş was built in the eighteenth century and had been "abandoned, it would appear, for decades." There is a difference between lost and abandoned, I thought, but to be fair, the online Jewish Bucharest tour called Beth Hamidraş "lost" in quotation marks. In any case, it did seem lost. We could not find it despite assiduously following the website's directions. We finally spotted it after circling the same block numerous times, obscured behind other buildings that appeared to have been constructed later. Perhaps not, though. Jewish houses of worship have always tended to be discreet, deliberately and protectively half-hidden behind the cover of other architecture. They were also generally smaller and lower-profile than churches—probably, in some places, by official decree—and sometimes sited in declivities so as to appear even shorter. These hiding practices did not stop a band of fascists from raiding and burning Beth Hamidraş in 1941. It was the Sabbath and a religious service was in progress at the time. Twenty-three Jews died in the fire.

Beth Hamidraş was surprisingly tall and ample, yet even after we spotted it, we were frustrated in our efforts to get near it. The surrounding buildings blocked the approach. We edged our way toward the synagogue as best as we could, but even then it seemed to possess mysteriously evasive capabilities, to be able to retreat or duck slightly when anyone got too close. Its evident dereliction also helped it resist detection, as though its tatters were a deliberate disguise, an aristocrat going around in rags.

There did not seem to be a way to get to the synagogue, not even by trespassing across private property.

We walked around the block yet again, where there was another, newer synagogue, but its handsome, well-kept exterior was surrounded by locked gates and it was clearly not open for visitors. So we went back to Beth Hamidraş, this time to try to gain access from the other side. We passed a row of small storefronts, most of which were, like the synagogue, abandoned and quite dilapidated. There was no one around except for a man sleeping in the entry alcove of one of the storefronts, covered with newspapers. I startled myself nearly stepping on him, although he did not wake up at the noise I made. He was reeking. There was a pile of human excrement near him.

We came to a long sliding gate through which we had a reasonably clear view of the synagogue, just slightly obstructed by the gate's bars. We stood there for a moment. This appeared to be as close as we were going to get, so I took a few pictures with my phone. While I did that, Heather tried the gate. It slid open. Behind it was a large parking lot, to the right of which loomed Beth Hamidraş. It seemed to have grown even taller, as if in anticipation of visitors. Its windows were broken. It looked less like it was in ruins than as if it had been sacked. We snapped a few pictures.

A dog came toward us.

Not from the synagogue but from another building across the parking lot. It was not charging or racing but pacing, a purposeful lope, as though so confident in its territory that swift attack was not necessary. As it grew closer, I could hear a low growl, almost a hum. The dog's cracked teeth were slightly bared.

I have heard many times that the worst response you can have to a hostile dog is to show fear. Be calm, firm. Especially do not turn and flee. And never look a dog in the eye.

I kept looking at the synagogue and ordered my eyes not to look at the dog. In my peripheral vision I measured its distance from us, which was closing.

The dog began to make more noise. I spoke to it firmly but coolly, with calm indifference. We're just taking a few pictures. We mean you no harm. Mostly I tried to keep ignoring the dog, as I tried to ignore the man in Istanbul who would not let me watch the card game on the bridge.

The dog continued to bark, growl, snarl, signaling that it was prepared to attack. A real Romanian dog, just like in the book I read. I had no stick to ward it off.

Instead of being frightened, I became angry.

I have an instinctive reaction to being denied access. It's a trait inherited not from my Romanian side but from my father, who inherited it from his father. Though of generally amiable and amenable disposition, I have seen them become enraged when entry was not granted them, when an authority halted them, when accommodation was not made. I have seen them do this even when clearly in the wrong. Because I have witnessed both my father and grandfather react in unacceptable ways in these circumstances, I have always made a conscious effort to try to maintain mildness of temper, respect for the rule of law, and social graciousness. Heather will tell you that I am not always, or entirely, successful.

I began screaming at the dog.

I don't remember what I screamed, only that my voice was as loud as it ever gets. The dog started to bark just as loudly. I wanted to attack it—more than it wanted to attack me, I sensed. I almost sensed that it knew what I knew: that I was in the right, that I was only trying to look at a synagogue, not doing anything wrong, hurting no one, I was Jewish, this building belongs to my people, who are you to try to stop me, leave me alone. I have forgotten about Heather although I hear her voice behind me, what is she saying, it doesn't matter, I'm the one saying, and that doesn't matter either, the dog is not attacking but it will not let us pass. Still we are in danger, even in my rage I can perceive this. Let's go, come on, I say to Heather, let's go, let's go. But she doesn't follow me. Why won't she follow me? I cross back over the threshold and the gate slides violently shut right in front of my nose. The dog is on its hind legs and its snout is pushing through the gate, inches from mine, barking and snapping at me while I scream back at it. Then it drops down to all fours and moves off. So do I, down the street, away from Beth Hamidraş.

After a few moments, Heather appears.

She tells me we could have been mauled or killed. That she could have been. I antagonized the dog and left her there.

I shout at her: *You're the one who opened the gate!*

You were in the wrong, Heather says.

All I can hear is the word *wrong*. Wrong, wrong. You were wrong.

iv.

Everything I've recounted about the Romanian dog at Beth Hamidraş is wrong.

There was no dog. That was a man.

I put a dog in his place because what I remember of him is wrong. The problem is this: I remember the man very clearly, his crooked teeth and gait. I remember steadfastly ignoring him when he approached us and then arguing with him when he made it clear that he would not be ignored. I remember the sound of his voice and some of the things he said, word for word. This clarity is the problem, because I also know that my memory, the way I remember the memory, is wrong. I remember what happened, but not what I did. I screamed at a man on his own property, ignored my wife, turned on my heel, and left her there with him as he slammed the gate shut behind me.

To rectify my mistaken memory, I have changed the man into a Romanian dog.

On the street in the Jewish Quarter, Heather said to me, I don't know what is wrong with you, but you can't get through it unless you get yourself well.

I don't remember what I said back. I was drenched in sweat, dazed, hearing her from far away.

We agreed to split up for the rest of the day. I don't remember whose idea it was to split up. I told her I'd see her later and started walking away, as I had walked away from the man.

In a few minutes, we were walking together again.

We walked to the National Museum of Romania. On the way, we passed the balcony where Nicolae Ceauşescu stood and gave the speech I had studied in college when I learned to mimic him in my role as the lone Hungarian in *Mad Forest*. In the speech, Ceauşescu denounced a popular uprising that had recently occurred in the Transylvanian city of Timişoara, trying to reestablish the authority of his collapsing regime. Instead, another protest broke out among the large crowd on the square. Flustered, the dictator paused awkwardly. He resumed but eventually broke off again because of the unrest, and finally left the balcony and retreated inside the Central Committee headquarters. The next day, he and his wife fled Bucharest by helicopter, which the Romanian military forced to land. The Ceauşescus were detained and almost immediately brought before a tribunal. The charge was genocide, a charge that, in 1989, could be made with definition. After a one-hour trial, they were convicted, led outside, and shot to death.

In the National Museum of Romania, I resumed the Jewish Bucharest tour, but one of my own design. I found a painting called *The Jew with the Goose*, painted around 1880, a few years before my great-grandparents were born. The Jew in the painting was holding, in addition to the goose, a piece of paper. The descriptive plaque next to the painting identified the piece of paper as a petition and the goose "for bribery."

How were these identifications made, I wondered?

The last galleries we walked through held the modern

art collection, which contained a number of sculptures by the most famous Romanian artist, Constantin Brâncuşi. I spent quite a while standing before a small bust. The head and neck were in a contortion of agony, the eyes closed in silent suffering, the right arm sawed off just below the shoulder, well above the base. The sculpture was called *Torment.*

On our way back to Zodiac House, we stopped into the Athénée Palace Hilton, once "the most elegant grand hotel in the Balkans," Frances Stonor Saunders writes in "The Suitcase," an account of her family history that begins in Romania in the 1930s, when Bucharest was known as "the Paris of the East," as Salonika had been known as the Jerusalem of the Balkans. A dance competition was going on in one of the hotel's ballrooms, its doors open to public view. Heather and I watched stylish Latin-lover types tango and trip their way across the floor, occasionally spilling out into the lobby in a feverishly altered state of body and soul—much as I was, only theirs was the inverse of mine: full of brio, blood, strength, desire, life.

We went back to the bookstore where I had bought William Gass's *In the Heart of the Heart of the Country* but not Benjamin Fondane's *Existential Monday* and bought a Romanian guidebook for a lot of money. I collapsed into bed with it when we got back to Zodiac House and opened it to the section about Moldavia. Neither Dorohoi nor Darabani were mentioned. They didn't even appear on the map.

Our last day in Bucharest. I was feeling better again.

That's what I said to Heather during a morning of rest, then said again to Julie over breakfast. I was happy to be able to tell Julie that I was on the upswing. It was probably the carp, or the gizzards, or the run, or the Pilates—all easily brushed aside, in any case. These things happen when you're traveling.

After lunch, we bid Julie a warm goodbye and said we'd see her when we were all back in the States. I was already looking forward to this. Then Heather and I bought train tickets to Moldavia.

That night, we went out and heard some music. When we arrived in Bucharest nearly a week earlier, we had spotted an announcement for a couple of outdoor rock concerts. At the time, we expected to be gone before the concerts took place, but here we still were. So we walked down to the city center where an enormous bandshell had been set up just in front of the equally enormous Palace of the Parliament, as it is officially called. It is the world's heaviest building, according to the *Guinness Book of World Records*, thus in its own way the largest, and the second largest administrative building on earth (only the Pentagon is larger). It would be even heavier if it wasn't mostly now empty. According to Julie, the Palace of the Parliament is known colloquially in Bucharest as the Korean Wedding Cake. It was built by Ceaușescu, who is said to have gotten the idea from his 1971 visit to Pyongyang, hence Korean. "Wedding Cake" because it is layer upon layer of overdecoration that resembles white icing, a giant monument to overbaked bad taste. An entire neighborhood was razed to make room for it, and it is surrounded by landscaped grounds that spread out over many blocks. We didn't even try to walk around them. It would have taken an hour.

It was drizzling, which made an outdoor concert a dubious proposition. Nonetheless, I was determined to go. That was because, amazingly, I was familiar with the group playing that night and had known their music since high school. But I had never seen them play live. It was the Cure. Had we come to this outdoor stage the night before, we would have heard Bon Jovi.

It was hard to imagine the Cure, the English goth-pop band, playing in Bucharest, Romania. In fact, it was hard to imagine the Cure at all. But they still existed and had been inducted into the Rock and Roll Hall of Fame only five months earlier. Their bandleader, Robert Smith—the only remaining original member—had just turned sixty.

Tickets were quite expensive and we had no thought of buying them. While Heather sat on a covered café patio and had a beer, I meandered over to the bandshell, looking for a way to slip inside the barricades. I thought it would be easy enough to do. Like much of the territory we'd been over by then, from Albania to Baku, Bucharest seemed full of cracks and rather penetrable. But the perimeter was tightly secured. (Traces of the old communist regime, I thought.) There was no getting in there. This time, I didn't have the affronted response to being denied entry that I'd had at Beth Hamidraş. I was content to stand at a great distance. Heather found me after she finished her beer, and we stood in the intermittent drizzle, listening to the Cure playing all those songs from the heyday of our alternative-radio youth—"Just Like Heaven," "Boys Don't Cry," "Why Can't I Be You." It was suddenly so obvious that the Cure had actually been a dance band all along. I found myself bopping my head and tapping my toes. I felt better. And better still because we were leaving Bucharest the next morning.

Gass. *Torment*. The Cure.

4.

Despairing

i.

The next morning I felt less well.

Not so much physically ill again as out of it. Feckless, foggy, sullen, unwilling.

We arrived at the Bucharest train station rather early, largely because there was a longish gap between checkout time at Zodiac House and the departure of our train to Iaşi, in High Moldavia. Heather and I got into another tiff when she walked us into a pharmacy to get me some remedies—hard to do when you don't know exactly what is ailing you—but I insisted that I was fine, or on my way to fine, and no longer needed them. After that, we decided to separate while we waited for the train.

In 1936, when Bucharest was the Paris of the East, the train station was "rowdy with commerce," Frances Stonor Saunders writes. "Vendors with trays hanging from their necks piled high with Turkish delight, to be chased down with cold spring water carried in wooden jugs and served from a metal cup on a chain clipped to the vendor's waist. Fifty bani for half a Turkish delight, one leu for a whole one. Others yell 'Braga racit!', cool millet beer, poured into glasses from a pump on the seller's back."

In Pittsburgh, during the Great Depression, my great-grandparents owned a neighborhood grocery store. "We were poor," my Boiby told me, "but we were never hungry." You never see begging Jews, homeless Jews—I have sometimes heard Jews say this. I wonder how Jews know this.

Grape Zaidie found a way to gain a little extra income from the store's merchandise by opening packs of cigarettes and selling them individually for a penny each, which served both the customer and the Sigels. One penny per cigarette represented a significantly higher profit margin. The store also sold individual eggs. My Boiby was fond of telling a story about a thief who slipped an egg into each front pocket of his pants. He went to the register, proffered a penny, and asked for a single cigarette. Grape Zaidie gave him the cigarette and rang up the sale.

"One cigarette," he said, "and two eggs."

"No, just a cigarette," the thief said.

"And two eggs," Grape Zaidie repeated, genially.

The thief grew defensive, even offended, and protested vigorously.

"That's one cigarette—" Grape Zaidie said again, and clapped the thief on both pockets, which went sticky-wet with the evidence—"*and two eggs.*"

I'd have been happy among the vendors of 1936, downing a millet beer or chewing on half a Turkish delight for fifty bani, half a leu, or if I was flush, a whole one for a whole leu. The leu is still the currency of Romania. One of the most pleasing things about our trip was the array of moneys we got to use, especially to the child numismatist in me. What I liked best was how similar the names were, even anagrammatic: lira and lari; lei, luma, leke. *Pennies, nickels, dimes, and quarters.*

Long gone were the hawkers with tin cups clipped to their waists and beer pumps strapped to their backs, but the station was lively with vendors of many types. For a few lei I bought a bag of *covrigi*, Romanian for pretzels, the national snack. There are *covrigi* stalls everywhere in Romania, and for whatever reason the very word *covrigi* seemed to be much oftener heard on our trip than anyone would have reason to be talking about pretzels, as though the ubiquity of a foodstuff can permeate a country's very consciousness and become what preoccupies it. There are flavored *covrigi*, stuffed *covrigi*, and just plain *covrigi*. I had tried them once or twice in Bucharest but was generally not in the mood to eat.

Nonetheless I bought a number of them, loaded up on a few other goodies as well—my own little pharmacopeia—and sat in a small café over a coffee. Mainly it was to kill time and make a few notes in my notebook, but I also hoped for a laxative effect to get me to the toilet before we boarded the train for the long ride to Moldavia. My gut was uncooperative, though; but at least I no longer felt bloated, gassy, balled up. I thought I probably hadn't had food poisoning after all; but then, what did I have? I was achy, weak, and still clammy despite the July heat, but now I was feeling sniffly and slightly congested. Something respiratory seemed to be coming on. My original illness, whatever it was, was turning into another one.

Except I denied to myself that I had any illness. I was getting better.

ii.

It was very late afternoon when we detrained in Iaşi. It would be useful to know how to say this word. Iaşi is pronounced like "Josh," but with a Y: "Yosh." Most of the i's at the end of Romanian words are silent. The sculptor Brâncuşi is Brancoosh. The Romanian gymnast is Nadia Comaneech. Romanian Jews, apparently, did not observe these rules of pronunciation. When saying "Iaşi," they pronounced it Jassy, to rhyme with gassy and starting with the same *J* sound as in *Jews*.

It would also be useful to define names and borders. Moldavia's northern border is with Ukraine. To the east is a country called Moldova which has, confusingly, also been known as Moldavia; part of it is sometimes referred to as Bessarabia, sometimes spelled Basarabia. The etymology sounds like it must have an Arab connection (something like "lower Arabia"), but it is geographically nowhere near Arabia and doesn't seem to have anything to do with it. Historians can't agree on what Bessarabia/Basarabia does mean. It may have been a name applied by Western cartographers, but why would they have chosen it? In Bucharest, Heather and I had gone into a food market called Bessarabia that sold mostly Russian goods.

Julie told us that she once took the train from Romania to Moldova. This was less to visit Moldova itself than to experience the border crossing. Russia and many of its former satellites, including Moldova, use a wider gauge track than the rest of Europe to make it harder for potential enemy invaders to penetrate the country by rail. At the border where one gauge standard gives way to another, the wheels have to be converted. Julie's excitement about witnessing this conversion evaporated during the many hours of dead time it took.

Another thing that would be useful to know is how my ancestors came to be in Moldavia before they left and came to America.

They, of course, refused to speak about Romania, leaving a blank where my family's history might have been. But Patrick Leigh Fermor provides an account.

"In flight from the appalling conditions in Poland and the Russian Pale," Leigh Fermor writes in his memoirs, Jews established themselves in what he calls "the remote principality" of Moldavia. In Leigh Fermor's account, Jews migrated south, where they had been invited to settle and establish a middle class between the region's feudal landowners and "a vast and callously exploited peasantry." Owing to "Jewish acumen or a general Romanian inaptness for commerce, and probably both," Leigh Fermor writes, managing to repeat two stereotypes in a single clause, the Jewish population grew into "a semi-alien bourgeoisie of middlemen and retailers." They flourished in their new land and "increased from two thousand families to close on a million in a hundred and thirty years." When Leigh Fermor arrived in 1934, there were many towns and cities where Jews "now outnumbered the Romanian inhabitants and monopolized the commerce of the province."

No other livelihood was available. Jews weren't eligible for citizenship, property ownership, or public service, barred from "nearly every route to advancement and honour." They were forced to "expand and excel in the only field that was not barred by prejudice." The peasantry now felt itself doubly exploited: first by their landowning overlords, and then by the Jewish merchant class. Both peasant and prince, for their different reasons, converged on an anti-Semitism that eventually reached what Leigh Fermor calls "a nearly mystical intensity."

I read this account before I left the States and made no note of any of it.

I did write down a line from another book I read before our trip, an account of modern Romanian history and politics. In it, the author cited the exhortation of a Romanian politician to his people not long before the outbreak of World War II: "Work, civilize yourselves, and you will rid yourselves of the Jews."

During World War II, Romania ridded itself of many Jews. One way this was done was by crowding them onto trains and deporting them. Some of the trains rolled around Moldavia for many days. It is unclear whether this was a deliberate way of killing the passengers or the result of disorganization or indecision on the part of the authorities. In any case, by the time these trains finally came to rest, most of the Jews inside them were dead. Some of the Jews who survived were shot or killed in some other way. But most were simply unloaded at the Dniester River, which was then under Romanian control and is now in Moldova—or rather, half of it is, depending on one's geopolitical alliances. On the other side of the Dniester from Moldova is a breakaway republic called Transnistria, "Across the Dniester." Had I not been ill, or with my sights set on the land where my ancestors stood, I might have liked to visit Transnistria, mainly to acquire some of its coins.

Many Jews deported from Moldavia to what is now the border between Moldova and Transnistria drowned in the Dniester. There were no camps set up there, not even extermination sites, nothing at all. The Jews who didn't drown themselves starved, froze to death, or, if they lived long enough, died of disease.

iii.

The population of Iași was 40 percent Jewish around the time my great-grandparents were born—Patrick Leigh Fermor puts it at 50 percent—and Heather and I found many traces of Jewish life as it once was. On the way to our apartment in the city center, we walked past one of them: a plaque that marked the spot where (so far as anyone can confirm) the world's very first professional Yiddish theater performances occurred. The plaque, we soon discovered, was among the stops on one of Iași's themed walking tours. (These were the work of tourist-board officialdom, unlike the blogger's "Jewish Bucharest.") The Yiddish Theater plaque was part of the *Traseul Evreiesc*: the Jewish Tour. At every stop on the tour, which we took on foot the next day, we found an identifying marker bearing a dubious cartoonlike picture, not to say caricature, of an Orthodox Jew in full *payot* (the famous traditional hair curls). One of the stops was a small Holocaust memorial obelisk whose inscription promised, "We will not forget."

We will not forget. It's a phrase that seems so clear but when I think about it, it isn't. Who are "we"? Are "we" the grandchildren of the perpetrators? The tourism board who created the *Traseul Evreiesc*? The people, whoever they were, who carved the words *We will not forget* into the obelisk? Or the people, like Heather and me, taking the tour, now enjoined henceforth not to forget? Or perhaps the few hundred aging Jews left in a city that was once as much as half Jewish but was now, by the most generous estimation, 0.02 percent Jewish?

The Holocaust obelisk was on the grounds of the *Sinagoga Mare* (Great Synagogue), another low-slung example, unassuming and modestly sunken on a slope. It was closed. To gain admission, a sign posted on the door instructed us to go and make the necessary arrangements at the Jewish Community Center, which was not far away. The old woman staffing the place called up the man who had the key. We passed the time waiting for him in the Jewish Community Center's one-room museum, much of it devoted to the infamous "death trains" that carried thousands of Jews out of Iași to their gruesome end at the Dniester, in June 1941.

When the man with the keys arrived, we handed him a few lei and he walked us back to the synagogue, let us in, and stood around somewhat impatiently while we gave ourselves a quick tour. I have virtually no memory of its interior. Nor do I remember any of the other sites on the *Traseul Evreiesc*. Either they were of little note or I was still too befogged to absorb them. The site we had happened upon while walking into town from the train station, though it was nothing but a plaque, was the only one I ended up remembering. The history of Yiddish theater in Iași owed to the passion of a single person, a writer and impresario named Avram Goldfaden who was originally from Ukraine. The first part of Goldfaden's adult life was something like a Jewish peddler's, but what he peddled was his poetry and plays. He came to Iași, which he would have called Jassy, in 1876, having already tried and failed to gain literary traction in numerous places from Odessa to Munich. In Jassy he finally caught what every artist needs: a break. A theater production he presented outdoors in a public garden—presumably on the spot where the *Traseul Evreiesc* plaque stands—happened to catch the approving eye of Romania's most famous poet, Mihai Eminescu.

Goldfaden's act was "total theater," according to the account of one of his contemporaries and collaborators: "In many of his plays he alternates prose and verse, pantomime and dance, moments of acrobatics and some of *jonglerie*, and even of spiritualism." It was apparently something like avant-garde performance art before there was avant-garde performance art, forty years before the Jewish Romanian Tristan Tzara founded Dada, and more than a century before I worked for the avant-garde theater company whose artistic director claimed she must be an Ashkenazi Jew. How I would have loved to be a Jewish performance artist in Jassy when my great-grandparents were alive in Moldavia. I would have written plays, just as I do in this life, and belted out songs, just as I did as Hyman Kaplan and Seymour Krelborn. I'd have nailed the sets together myself and stood in the park ringing a bell, calling, "Theater in the park tonight! Theater in the park tonight!" I'd have sold the concessions myself. If of my radical new "total theater" someone were to ask me, "Do you think of yourself primarily as a singer or a poet?," I'd have answered as another Jewish performer did, many decades later: "Oh, I think of myself more as a song and dance man, y'know." Bob Dylan. Robert Zimmerman, y'know.

Eminescu's praise put Goldfaden on the map and allowed him to traipse all over it. Goldfaden eventually founded a theater company in Bucharest. It's still active, the oldest continuously operational Jewish theater on earth. We didn't know about this, but we would have if our Jewish Bucharest tour had not abruptly ended after Beth Hamidraş: the theater was part of the tour. Later, Goldfaden immigrated to New York City and established himself there. By the time of his death in 1908, he was hailed as the father of the modern Jewish theater. And now we were standing on the spot where it started.

Where my ancestor stood. I consider myself a song and dance man.

A bust of Goldfaden stands in Iași outside the historic National Theatre, which is Romania's oldest. It is just a few hundred meters from the plaque in the park. We did not happen to see the bust, but we did tour the theater itself. It's a stately neoclassical building, one of the loveliest in Iași, built not long after Goldfaden's time in the city. It was just a few minutes' walk from the place where Heather and I stayed, and we passed it nearly every time we went out. In the tradition of theaters in summertime, it was closed for the season, but on the door was a sign with a phone number on it. Heather called it, made no headway with the party on the other end (who didn't understand English), and we stood pondering what to do. There were four other people standing nearby, looking like they wanted to see the theater, too. One of them, a man about my age with similar features and complexion, offered to try the phone number himself. "I speak Romanian," he said with an offhand shrug, in English so perfectly American that it was almost too perfect, and no wonder— he turned out to be Canadian.

He dialed the number and we were amazed when he not only started speaking Romanian but spoke it as perfectly as he spoke English. After he got off the phone and told us that the theater guide would be right down to give us a tour, he explained how he knew the language. His mother—he pointed her out to us, standing nearby, along with his brother and his stepfather—was born outside

Iași. When he was growing up in Canada, they always used her first language around the house, Romanian, rather than English.

"It's kind of amazing to be able to speak it here," the man said. This was his first trip to Romania, accompanying his mother on a long-awaited return visit; and suddenly this obscure language—which in his youth he had always considered a sort of secret code, a private family argot—was understood everywhere he went. This delighted him, but it also put him slightly on his guard. In Canada, he could communicate freely in Romanian, share confidential and even negative thoughts with his family. In Romania, he had to stop and think before speaking his mind. It struck me that this might be just slightly like living in Ceaușescu's Romania or Hoxha's Albania, where anyone on the street could be an informer, any room could be bugged, any wrong word punished. Still, I envied him the way I envy people who can sight-read music and run their hands effortlessly all over the keyboard, when all I can do is pick out chords by ear. I envied him the way I occasionally envy observant Jews, raised in the faith, who know all the prayers and rituals without any conscious awareness that they ever learned them at all. I even feel this envy, at a remove, toward hymning Christians. But it's only when Jews rock back and forth and incant the Torah aloud that I feel that ache in my muscles, the faint inner breathwork of longing and despair.

It turned out that the Canadians we met in front of the theater were Jewish. Of course they were.

It also turned out that when the mother was a girl, she had performed in this very theater.

A man came with keys and let us in. It was hard for me to take in the theater itself. Mostly, I marveled at the old woman. It must have been an astounding experience for her, after many decades away, to walk again in this place.

We learned that she had emigrated from Iași to Israel in the late 1960s. Not by choice. After World War II, her parents had an opportunity to leave Romania but miraculously much of her family had survived the Holocaust and maintained their homes and livelihood, so they chose to stay. Life under the oppressive Communist regime that followed, however, grew increasingly precarious, and by the 1960s, the young mother worried for the safety of her new family and knew they had to find a way to leave.

In 1944, Romania changed sides in the war. This was not only because it had become clear by then that the Axis had been the losing choice. It was also because Russia might now come sweeping into Romania and annex it, or worse. In the event, Romania wound up going communist itself, although it never became an SSR; but it did join the Warsaw Pact and was firmly under the Soviet Union's influence if not its outright dominion.

Despite its ban on religious practice and a particular hostility toward Zionism, Romania established diplomatic relations with the newly formed state of Israel, the only communist country to do so. An annual quota of Romanian Jews was permitted to emigrate. This permission was not granted out of largesse: Romania demanded payment for these souls, whom the fledgling Israeli state badly needed in order to populate itself. A similar arrangement took hold in surrounding countries, most of which got better rates: Hungary earned a thousand dollars per Jew sold; Romania only managed a hundred. Supply and demand—even after the genocide of World War II, there were still a lot of Jews in Romania compared to almost everywhere else. They were less collectible.

The Jews-for-cash practice lasted a few years until, in 1952, the further Stalinization of Romanian communism clamped down on emigration. But when Ceauşescu took control in the mid-1960s and sought to unyoke Romania from Moscow's control, he strengthened political ties with Israel. (Romania was the only Warsaw Pact country to preserve diplomacy with Israel after the Six Days War in 1967.) He resumed the sale of Jews to Israel, much of it via a single Mossad agent who made his career brokering these deals. The arrangement was accompanied by other forms of political and economic diplomacy. The Romanian army's Russian-made tanks were serviced by Israeli technicians, and Israel imported far more Romanian goods than the country really needed.

But they were choosy about one commodity. Israel wouldn't take just any Romanian Jew. It wanted Jews it could use. And that's how the old woman on the theater tour with us left Iaşi.

Her first marriage was to an engineer who helped construct some buildings on Iaşi University's campus. Doctors and engineers were the Jews whom Israel most eagerly wanted to import. Actresses were of no interest or value, and Israel offered no family exemption to include her as a spouse. Not only did Romania profit from the sale of her husband, she had to pay Israel for the privilege of emigrating with him. Had she not had a college degree, she would not have been allowed in at all. The couple would have been separated, leaving her a single mother of a toddler—the older of her two sons now touring the theater with us. Her family scraped together the money and paid her way.

Not surprisingly, she had a low opinion of Israel. Eventually, she divorced her husband. By then, they had a second son, the one who had made the phone call that got us into the theater.

After the divorce, she met another man at a social gathering of expat Romanians in Israel. She married him. There he was, going around the auditorium now with his two stepsons. As soon as their period of residential obligation to Israel was complete—not more than a few years—they moved to Canada.

Why was I so deeply envious of this family?

Why did hearing this story make me long for the very city in which I was now standing? And what was this longing? To see Iași as they saw it, buildings my father built, the theater where my mother performed? A longing to be born in Israel but to belong to Canada, yet to speak native Romanian? A longing to speak it here and be—suddenly, finally, in middle age—understood? To have anyone understand me here, especially myself?

Although his mother expressed gladness at being in the theater again, and the son gladness to have brought her to her birthplace and to speak her native language in situ, he was as resentful of Romania as his mother was of Israel. Although his father's buildings still stood on the university campus, instead of delighting at their enduring confirmation of his father's work and skill, he deplored it. "Romania did everything they could to kill all their Jews, but they made sure to keep my father's buildings," he said. He wanted them torn down.

I could have urged him to cherish the buildings, including the National Theatre in which we now stood, simply because his mother had once performed in it. I wanted him to delight in his ability to speak the national language, whereas I descended from peasant stock whose towns were not even on the map and who had erased every trace of themselves in Romania. How easy it was for him to disparage what I longed to possess.

But what I really wanted to say to him was nothing so rational. What I wanted to say was, *Don't leave me here all alone!*

I showed him the picture of my Grape Zaidie that my cousin had posted. Do you know this man? This is what I wanted to ask him, what I felt I was asking him.

Instead I said I didn't know why my family had left Dorohoi in 1910.

His mother, standing nearby, said that many Jews left during the years before the Great War to avoid conscription.

After a few minutes, we began to bid the Canadians goodbye. They told us they were headed to the village outside Iași where she had grown up. Her eyes were twinkling in anticipation. "Good luck with your search," her son told us, warmly.

The search for what? For whom? Do you know this man? I. I. I. I am.

It suddenly occurred to me that Heather and I had not paid the few lei our guide had quoted for our tour. He seemed to have left while we were talking. I expressed dismay, remorse.

"It's taken care of," the son said, with a genial offhand wave. He had paid our way. I almost began to cry.

A car and its hired driver were waiting for them on the street. After they drove off, I realized I hadn't even gotten his name.

Heather and I went to lunch. She related something to me that the Canadians' mother had said while I was out of earshot: that bringing her sons to Iași completed her life's circle. At this I cried almost as hard as I had cried on the sofa at Zodiac House. I had to hide my face, lowering my gaze to my plate. Then I got annoyed that it took fully half an hour to get our bill at the end of lunch. But it was probably for the better. I had time to collect myself.

We got back to our rental apartment in the very late afternoon. Heather took some time to rest. I must have been exhausting her. I knew how badly she wanted me to get well, and how badly she wished to take up the reins of my search, if a search was even what it was. It seemed

I had come to Romania not to undertake a search but to undergo a trial.

She told me much later that she had her own suffering in Romania: the pain of the descendant of the guilty, the oppressor, the non-Jew. We were having separate experiences of the same circumstances. I am no closer to anyone on this earth than I am to Heather, yet I felt as alone and anguished and irretrievable as I had felt ten years before, writhing on the breathwork table and a strange woman called to me, *Adam, do you have any Jewish heritage?*

While Heather rested, I went out on my own for an early evening stroll. I was the one who should have been resting, of course, but I craved some time to reconvene with myself. I walked up Iași's handsome pedestrian promenade in the cooling hours, bought a string of *covrigi* from a street vendor and even felt well enough for a plastic cup of cheap Romanian wine. I texted Heather and invited her to meet me at the promenade's end by an imposing statue of a national hero on horseback, Stephen the Great, a revered fifteenth-century prince who stabilized Moldavia for half a century. The statue was on the grounds of the massive Palace of Culture, which loomed beautifully at nightfall, floodlit, eternal. But a plaque said construction on it began just a few years before my great-grandparents emigrated. When they were born, it wasn't there.

The next day, I felt well enough.

No fever, minimal aches, untroubled digestion, cooperative respiration. We did some lighter sightseeing. I continued to insist on doing a lot of walking. Iași, Romania's second largest city, revealed itself to be very pleasant, well-proportioned, lively and habitable, as Thessaloniki had been in Greece and Tbilisi in Georgia. Iași is known as the cultural capital of Romania. We visited the university, toured one of its handsome historic buildings—surely not one that had been built by the Canadian's father—and laid eyes on the library named for Mihai Eminescu, the famous poet who discovered Avram Goldfaden.

Later, we returned to the Palace of Culture and visited a few of the small galleries and museums it houses. One of these contained a painting that depicted four men gathered in a tight secretive cluster, like the men conducting the Three-Card Monty game on the Galata Bridge in Istanbul. The secrecy was intensified by the heavy garb traditionally worn by Orthodox Jews and by their enclosure in dark, menacing shadows.

The painting was called *A Good Deal*.

Much later, I looked up this painting online. But the *Good Deal* I found, dated 1899, depicted an entirely different scene of Jews: two men, not four, one of them whispering a secret into the other's ear.

Afterwards, we continued beyond and below the palace to the outdoor grounds of an enormous, gleaming new mall on the edge of town. A folk performance festival was going on. I had seen events like this in Albania and Macedonia: troupes from all over the Balkans and even farther, performing traditional dances to traditional music in traditional costumes. But this was the first time I thought: There are no Jews in this festival. Jews are not folk.

vi.

In the morning I felt unprepared.

Unprepared for what? How can you be either prepared or unprepared when you don't know what you have
been preparing for? Or when all you have prepared to do
is stand where your ancestors stood?

When we went to the Jewish Community Center in
Iași for access to the *Sinagoga Mare*, we took the opportunity to ask the woman there if she had any insight into
the Jewish community in Dorohoi. She wasn't optimistic
about our finding much up there, nor especially interested in us or our purpose in the region, but she did call the
Dorohoi Jewish Community Center on our behalf and relayed that we could stop in when we got to Dorohoi.

My great-grandparents had never spoken about Dorohoi, not to anyone. And now I, their great-grandson, was
going.

Except I remembered that one of us had already been
there.

A second cousin, a Sigel I vaguely remembered from
childhood trips to Pittsburgh but no longer knew, had
visited Dorohoi some years earlier. I had heard a little
about his trip but wasn't much interested, partly because
he himself didn't seem much interested in what he found.
I recalled only one detail, a fragment, perhaps even a mis-
remembered one, which I had heard second- or thirdhand
from my mother after it passed through the family net-
work. The second cousin reported that Moldavian farm-

ers were still using horse-drawn carts. Some amount of disdain accompanied this observation.

As though cramming for a test, I emailed my mother to ask for contact information for whichever cousin had passed on the information about the horse-drawn carts. I sent him an email briefly explaining my whereabouts and purposes, which I described as "a sort of speculative ancestry tour."

What was a speculative ancestry tour?

To get to Dorohoi we had decided to rent a car. At the rental agency I had the opportunity to present my international driver's license for the first and only time on the trip. There was the photo of my face, bright and youthful and healthful. There was the beam and charge in my eyes, all full of readiness. What a difference from that face to this one, which appeared when I adjusted the rearview mirror.

Our rental car was small and blue, just like the Peugeot we had rented in France in 2017. I got behind the wheel. That's how we travel. I drive, Heather navigates.

We pulled out of Iaşi. The drive was fine. The roads were fine. There weren't many cars. When we reached the Moldavian farmlands, we passed farmers driving their horse-carts full of hay down the road, as my second cousin had seen. The carts had license plates on them.

The landscape was bucolic and pastoral: rolling hills, grazing livestock, fields of grain. The heart of the heart of the country. It reminded me just slightly of Burgundy. Or did it remind me of Burgundy because it was with insubstantial purpose that I had gone there, too, in a rented car that was also small and blue?

I could not stop feeling thirsty no matter how much I drank, yet I did not want to drink no matter how thirsty I felt. I barely sipped from my bottle of water. But I had to pee so badly that I was forced to pull the car off the road and go behind some shrubs. I checked for dogs first. For wolves.

vii.

Dorohoi was a small town. The only interesting building looked like an old schoolhouse, but it was under
major renovations that had evidently stalled. Heavy ma-
chinery sat parked on its lot and the walls were ripped
away to reveal some of the building's interior, stripped to
its shell. Even some of the shell was stripped. You could
see all the way through it.

We proceeded directly to the Jewish Community
Center, which the woman at its counterpart in Iaşi had
phoned the day before on our behalf. It was closed. There
was a sign on the door in Romanian. We drove back into
town and found the tourist office. It was also closed.

We were hungry, or in any case Heather was. I had
had no appetite for days, which is to say that I had no
interest in eating even though I knew I was hungry. But
every time I ate, I felt terrible afterward: bloated, roiling,
cramped, stupefied, odorous, disgusting. Nonetheless it
was lunchtime and we had not eaten anything other than
a morning pastry before we left Iaşi. We left the rental car
by the closed tourist office and walked down a steep hill
toward town. It was midafternoon and nothing seemed
open. After trying a convenience store where there was
only more water and a pizzeria that looked open but
was taking its afternoon break, we went to a place called
Splendid. It was an old hotel, the only building other than
the stripped-down schoolhouse that looked historic. The
Hotel Splendid's restaurant was open. We took a table on

its spacious, attractive patio and ordered food. Soup for me. It came with a basket of warm, herb- and seed-topped pita bread called *lipje*, which was so delicious we ordered another basket as soon as we tasted it. Much later, back in the States, we discovered that this particular type of *lipje* was not Romanian at all but rather a traditional bread of Israel.

We had no plan for the night because I had no plan for the day. The wellness I had reported to Heather that morning in Iaşi had almost totally evaporated. I was hot, dazed, aching. My breath was shallow and slightly wheezy, and I had trouble seeing anything clearly, like the menu. I was immensely tired and could have slept sitting upright at the table in the hot sun. My skin felt like the driest, thinnest, flimsiest cover. I would bleed through it uncontrollably, like my Uncle Larry, the hemophiliac.

I was prepared to give up on everything.

Heather went into the lobby of the Hotel Splendid and booked a room. The Hotel Splendid appeared to be Dorohoi's only place to stay. It did not appear in any of our phones' lodging apps, which like the guidebook contained no tourist information about the entire town of Dorohoi. I could not remember the last time I had been to a place so totally unrecognized by the world.

After lunch we walked back up the hill. The tourist office was now open. The two women staffing it were friendly and wanted to be helpful, but they spoke little English. Our trip had taken us to remote places in the Balkans and the Caucasus, and there was always someone who spoke

English. But not in Dorohoi. Only our waiter at the Hotel Splendid spoke a little.

We explained our purpose as best as we could. As we tried to do this, my feelings of physical unwellness and mental fog were saturated with a peculiar sensation that has occasionally visited me since early childhood. I described this sensation to my mother as "the missy feeling" but could not say much more about it. It doesn't entail missing anyone or anything, and although it causes a profound displacement, it isn't homesickness either. When I was a child, the missy feeling could arise right in our house, even around my mother. It is a hollow, gnawing feeling, a sense of non-belonging, not only here but anywhere at all. There is no home to be sick for. The missy feeling is a perception that the world is going on all around me yet entirely without me, but I am not inside myself either, I am a ghost, everything is unimaginably far away, and I will never return to life. The missy feeling eludes description partly because it is itself an elusive condition, organized around both an inner vacancy and an outer dislocation. It is, paradoxically, a feeling as familiar to me as any I've ever felt, and it would be a sort of comfort were it not so constitutionally estranging.

We said to the women in the tourist office that it seemed evident to us there were few Jews left in Dorohoi, were we mistaken about that? One of the women gave a sympathetic, almost mournful half-smile. No, there weren't many Jews in Dorohoi, she agreed. She brought forth a book which appeared to have been published by a local historical society. It was an annal of students at Dorohoi's former Jewish school, a list of names for each schoolyear dating back decades, although not as far back as when my great-grandparents lived here. We paged through it briefly. The name *Sigel* appeared a few times.

The book didn't appear to be for sale, but the woman in the tourist office invited us to keep the copy we were holding, as a sort of consolatory text, it seemed, like a fragment of scripture.

viii.

We drove farther north to Darabani. There were no beech trees. We must not have been in Bucovina. We passed settlements of small farmhouses in short rows. The frontage of every property was laid out with the harvest of midsummer produce. Wreaths of plump garlic bulbs were stacked on the tables. I suddenly, powerfully wanted a wreath of garlic—needed one, I felt. I made a note to buy one on the way back down to Dorohoi.

Darabani was a tiny town, and it was almost completely closed at this hour of the very late afternoon. A line came into my head from a book I'd read in preparation for our trip, a Balkan travelogue by a Polish writer named Andrzej Stasiuk. Of a small town in Romania he wrote: "Time burns slowly here, like the edge of a fabric." When I read that sentence, I had a powerful desire to go to a place where time burned slowly like the edge of a fabric. Darabani was such a place.

The only open business was a pharmacy. Heather insisted we go in and get me some medicine.

Pharmacists overseas do more than fill prescriptions. They are like doctors themselves. To walk into a pharmacy feels much more like entering a clinic where an expert in a white coat will lavish attention and expertise on even a slight headache, a bitten cuticle, and prescribe a means of relief.

But what was my ailment? I now felt simultaneously congested and leaking, both feverish and cold, bloated yet undernourished, at once full of nerves and utterly drained of all energy, of all blood like Uncle Larry. I did not know if I needed painkillers, expectorants, a febrifuge, a stimulant, a coagulant, a laxative, an anti-nauseant, an anti-anxiety, an antibiotic, or nothing at all.

Heather is a gifted interpreter of health and provider of remedy. She may have saved my life when she took me to the hospital on the night I had appendicitis. But she now stood in deference to the pharmacist—and, as I now understood, to me, in both body and soul. She companioned me uncomfortably but deftly: booking a room at the Hotel Splendid, then suggesting we drive from there right up to Darabani but refraining from telling me what to look for once we got there. Walking me into the pharmacy and then standing aside. There was only so much she could do.

The pharmacist, a solicitous and matronly type, took each of the symptoms I described very seriously and demonstrated sincere concern. At no point did she suggest that these symptoms did not seem to add up to any identifiable illness. What do you give someone who isn't sure what is wrong with him but, when questioned, agrees to every suggestion of what it might be? Did I feel this complaint? Yes. What about that one? Yes. And also this one, and this one, and that one. Yes, yes, yes. For every symptom I named or assented to, the pharmacist selected a medication. I left with a bulging bagful. In return, we gave her Romanian lei amounting to about twenty-five dollars, just slightly less than what we were paying to stay at the Hotel Splendid that night.

While I had been sick in bed in Bucharest, or possibly Iaşi, I had at least gone as far as to search the keywords *Jews* and *Darabani* on my phone. I found a study which gave historical population trends in Moldavia's settlements. Iaşi was down from tens of thousands of Jews to about six hundred. Dorohoi had a hundred or so left. Darabani, which was more than a third Jewish in 1910, the year my great-grandparents emigrated, with about 2,500 Jews, now had zero. It seemed to me now that this was why the town square where we stood was utterly empty, betraying not a single sign of life.

Another report I found online noted the locations of Jewish cemeteries in the region. The report had been conducted via very thorough fieldwork. It gave the location of a Jewish cemetery in Darabani. Under the "Restoration" column appeared the code for *Not Maintained.* Under "Threats": *Uncontrolled Access, Weather Erosion, Vegetation.*

Here is a sentence that appears in my notebook under a date that corresponds with that of our drive up to Darabani: "Europe is, has always been, a charnel house of Jews." The sentence appears in quotation marks in my notebook. I am diligent about citing quotes when I write them down, which is often, but I did not cite this one, and after reconsulting all the books I read before going on our trip, then searching the sentence online, I can't find it anywhere. Did I make it up myself and surround it with quotation marks, as though someone else, an invented author, had written it, or as though I was planning to write it at some point, perhaps this one? Europe is, has always been, a charnel house of Jews.

The field study located the cemetery just outside the center of town. We could walk to it easily—easily, that is, if I had felt well. Instead we went at a trudge, my legs and breath heavy but hollow. We went along the main road until we came to the turnoff indicated by our phone maps. The road we turned onto was gravel. It went into a residential area where there were both established houses and new ones under construction. We took the gravel road to the next turn, a small lane. It seemed doubtful that a derelict cemetery was right in the middle of this neighborhood, a sort of subdivision. But the map was insistent.

We were just a few dozen yards from the exact dot on the map when we came to a barrier across the lane.

I almost laughed. Another one? Here?

I was not going to cross it. Not after Beth Hamidraş.

We turned around and went back down the lane to the wider gravel road. Although we had been walking for only about half an hour, I was exhausted, overheated, depleted, airless, my muscles and bones groaning.

Heather and I stood where the gravel road met the narrow lane, the barrier a short way away. I put my water bottle down on the side of the road and sat on the ground next to it. I sat with my knees up and wrapped my arms around them for support. I put my head between my knees and closed my eyes.

I don't know how long I sat that way. Heather used her

phone's map to find another road that might lead to the cemetery from the opposite direction. If we went back up to the main road, we could get there. She asked me, gently, if I wanted to try that. Or perhaps we could try to go back down the lane that was roadblocked and see if we might find someone to ask for permission to pass.

No, I said. Let's go.

I think I may have said that a few times.

Let's go. There's nothing here. This is not where I come from. I'm not Romanian. I'm Jewish. Let's go.

I did not get up.

I stared down at the ground. Gravel, grass, the shadow I cast.

When the mind swings by a grass-blade/an ant's forefoot shall save you.

Of the thousands of lines in Pound's *Cantos*, my favorite.

I lifted my head at a noise. There was a mule drawing a cart, a man following. They took no notice of us as they passed by, very slowly. I watched them until they were out of sight. It took a very long time.

After the man and mule and cart were gone, Heather said, gently, We can go. But it does look, she said, it does seem, only if you want, if you have the strength for it, like there is another way around to the cemetery. We don't have to, but if you would like to see, to try, before we go.

I looked up at her. My companion, my wife.

I said, Alright, let's look.

She helped me up. We walked back up to the main

road and then along that road to another gravel road. We turned there, and then we turned again, past more houses each with an acre or so of cultivated land behind it: produce, chickens, goats, sheds, plows. Behind one of them there was a cow, standing heavy in the backyard in the afternoon, right behind the house, like a pet.

When I was a young boy, perhaps four or five years old, we lived in a house with a small plot of land where my parents kept a garden. Tomatoes, a few rows of corn. Behind our property, which was probably half an acre, was a stand of woods that marked the end of the world as I knew it. Although we were not far from town, our neighborhood bordered farmland and probably had been farmland itself not many years before. One day I was looking through the sliding glass doors onto our garden. My mother was in the kitchen nearby.

"There's cows in the yard," I told her.

She laughed. Of course, sweetie. Cows in the yard.

"There's cows in the yard," I said again.

I think she admired my invention. The mind of a child makes a great advance when it begins to comprehend that anything is possible.

"Look," I said.

There were cows in the yard. Three or four of them. They were eating everything in our garden.

The farmers whose cows they were eventually showed up. They were very apologetic, abashed, friendly. They led the cows away and came back later with a gift of corn and tomatoes.

A stout older woman came out from the back door of her house and overturned a basin of water near the cow. She took no notice of her cow, nor of us.

Next to her house was the cemetery.

There it was, as though it was simply the next house over. The adjacent properties came right up to each side of the graveyard and then stopped short at the fence.

There was a gate. It had a chain around it but it wasn't locked. *Uncontrolled Access.*

The woman went back inside her house. We walked into the cemetery.

Many headstones. Most were fallen or half-fallen, in some cases in small domino topples, one upon the other upon the other, as though seeking support or commiseration. They were quite old. Had I been able to read Hebrew I could have known exactly how old. The engravings were worn. *Weather erosion.*

We walked around, carefully. *Vegetation. Not maintained.* The cemetery was overgrown and there might be snakes. We were trespassers. But on whose property were we trespassing? The graveyard was much larger than it looked from the lane. It seemed to expand before our eyes and feet, as Beth Hamidraş had in Bucharest. The cemetery spread itself out over a hillside that marked the edge of town. There was a sweeping view of the valley and the ridge beyond, beautiful in the late afternoon sunlight. An image of the snow-covered, wind-whipped cemetery in Pittsburgh rushed through my mind.

There were apple trees, bearing fruit. Fallen apples

were on the ground. There seemed to be apples everywhere, just as there were headstones everywhere. The more headstones we found, the more of them there seemed to be just beyond them, thousands it seemed, like a crop in its most abundant season.

I put my hand on one of the stones. It was very warm. I left my hand there, waiting, like a mother taking a child's temperature. You are not forgotten, I heard myself whisper.

We will not forget?

Who are we? Who were we? Who buried these people? They may have been my people, the buried and the buriers? It didn't matter. What mattered was that Jews buried Jews here. No one slaughtered them in pogroms, packed them onto trains, left them by the river to starve or freeze. Jews lived here until they died here, and then other Jews buried them here.

It was Heather who said that, not me. She said it that night, after I lamented that the cemetery had suffered such neglect. Heather saw this neglect as something else, as uncontrolled access into the past. Yes, she was right.

If this was not my story, it could end here, with an epiphany atop a great prospect, in the place where my great-grandparents stood and where some of their kin, my kin, were surely buried, the bodies of the dead. But it is my story, and the epiphany is someone else's. I found it that night in the Hotel Splendid.

ix.

On the way back down to Dorohoi from Darabani, all the wreaths of garlic had been taken in for the night. I took this as a bad sign. I made a note to try to find garlic somewhere, anywhere.

I lay on the lumpy mattress in our room in the Hotel Splendid and looked for information about Jews in Dorohoi. Enormous mosquitoes hung heavy from the window air conditioning unit, which did not keep the room comfortably cool. The mosquitoes looked as swollen and exhausted as I felt. It seemed as if they had been there for decades, waiting for blood, and were now too old and immobile to fly over to us and draw ours. When I got up to take a shower, the cheap laminate floor felt like sand underfoot. The shower stream was weak and lukewarm. The stall leaked water onto the bathroom floor.

I found an article written five years earlier by Andrew Solomon. I had read and admired Solomon's work. The article, a personal essay, recounted his 2013 trip to Romania. His official purpose was to publicize a book of his that had recently been translated into Romanian. The reason he chose Romanian, which is not a widely spoken language, was that his ancestors were Dorohoian Jews, like mine were, who had immigrated, like mine had, via a German ship to the United States, and refused, as mine had, ever to talk about Romania. He wanted to see their hometown, as I did and had now done, as he had done in 2013.

First Solomon flew to Bucharest and publicized his book. Then he went to Dorohoi hoping to "have a surprising sense of identification with the place." He described seeing "farmers in oxcarts" on the ride through Moldavia, in a car with a hired driver, over the gently rolling hills where "life seemed to have changed little in the last century." He went to a Dorohoi cemetery that was in "a state of profound neglect."

I read all of this with great interest, of course, and I remembered something my first cousin, Uncle Larry's son, had written to me not long before I came to Dorohoi. We were exchanging texts about our family after I let him know I had seen the picture he posted of Grape Zaidie and the details of our family's emigration from Bremen. My cousin told me he'd easily found the details of the Sigels' immigration online via a quick, virtually spontaneous search of a free Ellis Island database that contained many records like our family's. He texted me: "Our family story is so common it almost feels universal."

It was in personal retracings of the story that it became somewhat less universal. Like me, Solomon communed with the gravestones in the cemetery, and a few bore his family name, as the stones in the Darabani cemetery surely bore mine. But Solomon was able to identify these names because, unlike us, he had hired a translator who could read Hebrew: "one of the last Jews in the county, who runs a sideline in genealogy."

Solomon also found fruit trees in the Dorohoi cemetery, as we had in Darabani's, but his were wild cherries, not apples. He went so far as to pick and eat the fruit, which tasted "so sharp and so sweet"—like his feelings, he did not need to add. As he devoured the cherries, "the red juice stained my hands"—blood, he did not need to add—and he had what he called "a revelation": he suddenly pictured his Romanian immigrant grandparents as children, climbing these same cherry trees, picking the fruit and eating it just as he did more than a century later, just as I might have done if the apples had been ripe and I had been well enough to climb the trees.

I could not imagine my ancestors climbing trees and picking fruit. My hemophiliacs, their mutterances. That's it—you're a Sigel.

On his way out of Dorohoi, Solomon took stock of the farmers in their oxcarts and the other Moldavian "peasants," as he called them, whose forebears had driven his, and mine, out of Moldavia and to America. "Instead of feeling outraged at their history of aggression I felt privileged by it," Solomon writes. Their aggression forced Jews to "expend their vigor on solutions—some of which can be exquisite. I looked at what had happened to us in two generations, and looked at what hadn't happened to them in two or three. Oppression sometimes benefits its victims more than its perpetrators."

Despite sensing from Solomon the same faint superiority and disdain my second cousin had expressed toward the peasants and their carts, I ought to have taken comfort from his magazine story. Here was my tribesman, journeying back to our mutual origins and giving voice to our story so common it's almost universal, to the "semblance of common identity" shared by semi-alien but essential outsiders who are also, paradoxically, middlemen. Solomon's ancestors and mine may very well have known each other in Romania. Perhaps they had been in school together, or business, or even marriages. We might share not only history but blood, so sharp and so sweet.

Why, instead of taking comfort from his story, did I feel outraged by it?

Why did I feel like something had been taken from me? Why, instead of my family story feeling almost universal, did it feel like it was no longer even my family's?

Heather suggested I think about getting in touch with my mother.

She had in fact already been in touch with my mother. It was the only thing she had done without my knowledge or consent. The reason she did it, in her own words, which mine could never replace:

> I knew that if you were truly struggling in a way that was related to your Jewish identity in a place where white Christians had persecuted you then perhaps my face was not the one you needed to see. I thought your mom would have been what you needed in that moment. So I actually texted her and said I thought being here was hitting you kind of hard and maybe a talk with her would be nice. I told you that your mom and I texted and she was hoping to talk to you. And you absolutely

refused, several times. Then I had to tell her that you weren't up for it but thanks anyway.

I called my mother. I told her I wasn't feeling quite 100 percent. Probably nothing major, a little bug. I told her about the historical society book I had been given in the Dorohoi tourist office, and that there were some Sigels in it. I did not tell her about the Romanian dog in Bucharest, sobbing on the sofa in Zodiac House, or dropping to the ground outside the cemetery in Darabani and refusing to get up. I did not tell her I had come all this way on behalf of our family with no greater purpose than to stand where my ancestors stood and had not even managed to remain standing.

Hearing about the historical society book from the tourist office, my mother suddenly remembered that her grandmother's maiden name was Leibowitz. For both my mother and me, her recall of the name Leibowitz came as a sudden revelation. I immediately opened the book, found the name Lipovici, the Romanian rendering of Leibowitz, and confirmed its existence, our existence, in Dorohoi.

The discovery ended our conversation on an upbeat, hopeful note. After the call ended, I took some of the many medicines I had bought at the Darabani pharmacy, a virtually random combination, as though to chase and reinforce the effect of the name Leibowitz on my spirits.

X.

Despite what the actress in the National Theater told us, it seems unlikely that the Sigels left Romania so that my great-grandfather could avoid military conscription.

Pogroms were common in and around Dorohoi when my great-grandparents lived there, decades before Moldavian Jews were put into trains and rolled around the countryside until they were dead or deposited at the Dniester to die there. The word *pogrom* is of Russian origin, meaning "total destruction." Every man, woman, child, and beast. The term seems to have been applied specifically to the violent destruction of Jews, who eventually adopted the word to describe what was done to them—what Patrick Leigh Fermor meant by "the appalling conditions in Poland and the Russian Pale." Any violent destruction the Russians visited on other people, or on their own, would have had to be called something else. What some Armenian communities suffered at the hands of the Turks could not have been properly called pogroms, either. Perhaps there is an equivalent Turkish word, also used by Armenians. *Genocide*, coined later, provided a universal term for the violent destruction of one group by another.

One series of pogroms in 1907, three years before my great-grandparents emigrated from Dorohoi, is known as the Romanian Peasants' Revolt. The "vast and callously exploited peasantry" Patrick Leigh Fermor identified in his discussion of Moldavia were furious at the deepening

inequality and neglect they suffered, despite supposed re-
forms, under wealthy landowners, most of whom lived nowhere near the land they owned and seldom even visited.
The peasants' only available recourse was to take action
against the landowners' local property administrators—
that is, against the "semi-alien bourgeoisie of middlemen"
who suffered the violent destruction. The Romanian government had to step in and quash the Romanian Peasants'
Revolt, one of the few times a European government came
to Jews' defense, although it was not the Jews' interests
or security that Romania had in mind. Nor was it those
of the gentry. It was Romania's. The state was the largest
landowner in Moldavia.

xi.

The next morning, we went to the Dorohoi synagogue, which was right in the middle of town. There had once been two dozen of them—surprisingly, not during the flourishing of Moldavian Jewry in the early twentieth century but after World War II. The Jewish population steadily dwindled following the 1907 Romanian Peasants' Revolt, then plunged on a single day in 1941 when 3,000 Jews were rounded up in Dorohoi and deported to the Dniester. After the war, the new Romanian government programmatically resettled Dorohoi with Jews, who built more synagogues. The Romanian civil authorities liked to hold up Dorohoi as a successful example of the recovery of the Moldavian Jewish population, a sort of postwar Potemkin village. One rabbi who had not perished was forced by the authorities to remain in town and minister to the resurgent Jews and their congregations. A plaque commemorating this rabbi was near the synagogue, which was the only synagogue left in Dorohoi for a plaque to be near. When Romania started selling Jews to the newly formed state of Israel after 1947, Jews left Dorohoi again, and the synagogues gradually closed and were eventually razed.

Except this one. Closed. Padlocked. Sign on the door, phone number. We were used to that by now.

Heather called the number. No answer. She left a message. While we waited to see if anyone would call us back, we wandered around and looked at the plaque commemorating the rabbi.

We were surprised to get a call back just minutes later. Come to the Jewish Community Center.

When we got there, we were greeted by an elderly woman named Viorica. Soon she was joined by an elderly man called… what was the name? Did he say *Yooj*? Ah, Euge—Eugene. Euge looked a little like my Zaidie. Not my Grape Zaidie, but Herbert Belans, Abraham Belansky, my mother's father. A different branch, a different *şöbəsī*, not Moldavians. Euge and Viorica did not speak any English at all, and there was no one else around. Who, I wondered, had called Heather back and instructed us to come here? We used our phone's translation app to explain our purpose, my family's connection to Dorohoi. They asked about names.

I said Sigel, and I showed them the picture of Grape Zaidie my cousin had posted a month earlier. Euge became somewhat animated. He spoke lengthily and with ardor, more to Viorica than to us, it seemed, almost as though she could translate for us. She couldn't, of course, and he was going too fast for our translation app to help us, but we were able to piece together that there had once been multiple branches of Sigels in Dorohoi: the doctor Sigels, the teacher Sigels, and so on. The Jews in Dorohoi had a lot of education, Euge said. We said we'd seen what we thought was an old schoolhouse under renovation. Yes, he said, that was the Jewish school. My great-grandparents had almost certainly attended it. Perhaps they even taught there. Of course, Jews would not return to it after the renovation was complete. There were fewer than a hundred left in Dorohoi. It seemed probable that most of them were Euge's age, too old to attend school or teach.

Heather and I both sensed that Euge had a deeper recognition that seemed to spark from the sight of Grape Zaidie in the photograph. I wondered if perhaps he knew my family personally. This was a preposterous notion: Euge had told us he was eighty-three—old as far as it went, but my great-grandparents had emigrated a quarter century before he was born. But why was he so animated? He even seemed just the slightest bit angry, as though he might have been able to help us if only we had supplied more information than a name and a photo of an old man in Pittsburgh. Yes, Sigel, but which branch of Sigels? Did I not realize that it was not possible to walk into the Dorohoi Jewish Community Center unannounced from the United States, disclose a name and photo, and expect to be recognized, received, rooted?

After a while Euge took us to the synagogue, which had no rabbi, he told us on the way over. As we entered, I walked right past the communal box of yarmulkes and he reminded me to put one on. It was an older temple, probably built before World War II. The interior was in somewhat rough shape, not especially clean and very cluttered, although not by overuse but its opposite: the disarray that comes from long neglect. There were many old prayer books that would have made fine specimens for, say, the Jewish Heritage Museum, had they not been so badly moldered. One of them began to crumble in my hands when I picked it up to look at the publication date, which was around the time my great-grandparents left Romania. On the walls were a few plaques, wooden boards hand painted with lists of names—memorials to the dead, I would later learn—bearing dates from the middle of the twentieth century. Among the names were Lipovici and Sigel. We remarked on this to Euge. Yes, he nodded, somewhat dismissively.

The synagogue contained a small museum. It was mostly dedicated to the Holocaust, particularly photos of the Dorohoi deportation of 1941. Euge went out of his way to emphasize that some Jews fought back, that they shot a few fascists. This seemed somehow pitiable to me. He also said that there were other Jews who shot themselves rather than submit to deportation. I mentioned that we'd been to the cemetery in Darabani, and that there were fruiting apple trees in it. Did you eat the apples? he asked, laughing. No, I wanted to say, that was Andrew Solomon.

I wondered for a moment if it had been Euge who took Solomon to the cemetery in Dorohoi, but then remembered that it was the hired translator who was Jewish, and of course Euge spoke no English. The caretaker who let Solomon and the translator into the cemetery was a non-Jew who said to them, enthusiastically, "I am not Jewish, but I like Jews." I wondered exactly what it was about Jews he liked, and whether he liked all of them.

Throughout our morning with Euge, communication was mediated, poorly, by our phone, which could "listen" to our voices and supply mangled translations that required further guesswork. The only word of Euge's I recognized was *covrigi*. I had no idea why his discourse had come to involve pretzels. It seemed that, eventually, every conversation in Romania did.

We drove Euge back to the Jewish Community Center in the blue rental car and spent a while in warm thank-yous and farewells. It seemed we had made some sort of progress, had gotten some kind of validation. Euge had spent nearly two hours with us (we had paid the fee to tour the synagogue, of course). Viorica was so sweet it was almost painful. She seemed to take a particular shine to Heather. The two elders were like a kindly great aunt and uncle. We snapped pictures, signed a guestbook, and left feeling that we might somehow see them again.

Which we very nearly did, almost at once.

xii.

We decided to go and see the Voroneț monastery, the most famous of the renowned "painted churches" of Bucovina, which meant that in addition to going to the monastery we were also going to Bucovina, finally.

We got back in our rental car and began the drive. En route, we agreed that Euge seemed to be indicating that he had more familiarity with the Sigels than we had been able to understand. Heather thought we should go back, perhaps right now, instead of going to Voroneț. We could find someone to translate.

I disagreed. Of course Euge couldn't have known my family. At best, he might have known some distant cousins a generation younger—and what would they have known of my great-grandparents, who cut Romania out of their lives as soon as they arrived in Pittsburgh? Still, Heather implored me, although gently: we might as well be sure. We could even go to Dorohoi's town hall and look up records. (We later learned that all requests for information have to be submitted in writing in advance.) But I was not swayed. I kept driving so resolutely and so straight-on that when we reached a turnoff we should have made, Heather did not have time to alert me, and we missed it. But that was alright—it looked like there was another road to Voroneț, and a more scenic one at that.

I have driven some very bad roads, all over the world. I have navigated dirt tracks studded with rocks the size of basketballs and craters large and deep enough that small bombs could have left them. Thousand-foot drops from the shoulder of the road don't trouble me. I've driven roads so treacherous that I've passed overturned trucks with their wheels still spinning, and barely gave them a glance.

But I had never driven a road like this one.

There were no cliff faces, no craters, and not much dirt. The lack of dirt was actually the problem. The road was almost nothing but rocks, huge ones, bigger and heavier than gravel. The Peugeot's tires sank into them and I had to fishtail the car deliberately in order to make any kind of progress at all. Getting up hills was so difficult that I worried I was going to overdrive the engine. The only breaks for several miles were the occasional stretch of bumpy creek bed that had been dried to a gulch, and the appearance of the odd sheep or goat. We had to wait for the animal to move, prolonging the trial. I gripped the wheel, hunched over it like a fighter pilot under attack, and hoped we wouldn't blow a tire or puncture something in the undercarriage. Like many rental cars in Europe, this one had a manual transmission, so I was constantly having to shift with a hand I needed to help me steer.

I stopped the car for a breather and to take in the surroundings as best as I could. I wiped sweat off my forehead, walked a few paces away from the car, which was still idling, picked up a rock, and threw it as hard and far as I could. I threw another one, and another one, and another one, until my arm was too tired to do it anymore and I was sweating profusely again. I turned around, and Heather was watching me with that half-mournful, half-frustrated look I had gotten used to seeing. We got back in the car and fishtailed forth.

What makes Bucovina's painted churches special is that it's their exteriors that are painted, and that this paint has lasted for many centuries. Voroneţ is a particularly marvelous example. Its painted façade is so distinctive that the monastery has donated its name to the color: Voroneţ Blue. We walked around it, taking in its vivid New Testament imagery and iconography. One entire façade depicted an extravagant, phantasmagoric Last Judgment, a Bosch-like spectacle both violent and visionary. I had seen quite a lot of Christian religious art and architecture on our trip, much of it extraordinary, some of it remarkably enduring: thousand-year-old Macedonian icon paintings; the unforgettable, almost impossible pinnacle-top monasteries of Meteora; remote complexes deep in Armenia and the lambent Orthodox churches of Tbilisi. I especially admired the quiet tenacity of these Christian Caucasian nations, which for centuries had withstood assaults by Russians and Turks and Arabs, survived genocide and oppression and depression. Clearly their faith had sustained them, and our entire trip had been buoyed by the presence of their ancient, abiding Christianity, which seemed more deeply rooted than any other form I'd ever seen.

Walking around beautiful, historic, remarkable Voroneţ, all I could think was, *These fucking Christians!*

I said this to Heather. She replied that she was feeling the same way.

On the way out of the monastery, we stopped at a workshop where artisans were decorating the famous painted eggs that went with the famous painted monasteries (the traditions are not actually connected). They would make good Christmas gifts. Some of the eggs seemed suspiciously machine-painted, but what did that matter? It was a historic regional practice among the Christian faithful here in the region of my Jewish people. We bought a number of the eggs. They're colorful, decorative. Two of them sit on a ledge above the desk where I'm writing this.

We stayed that night in Suceava, a mid-sized city of about a hundred thousand people that had once been the stronghold of Stephen the Great, the hero whose statue had been my rendezvous point with Heather in front of the Iași Palace of Culture. On the outskirts of town we found a comfortable, modern hotel of the sort that cluster around American airports. It had plenty of amenities, including a decent restaurant and, in our air-conditioned room, a blasting hot shower and a king-sized bed. We went to the restaurant and had more chicken soup, a particularly good regional variation called *Ciorba Radauteana* (named for the nearby town of Rădăuți), which we had also enjoyed elsewhere in Romania. Now we were having it where it came from. I wondered if *crap țărănească* was available in Suceava.

Back in the room, I showered the grime off of me, wrapped myself in the heavy robe hanging in the bathroom, and got into the bed. It was barely nightfall, but I fell almost immediately into heavy sleep and didn't wake up until the next morning.

xiii.

The next morning, we left Romania. At least for the moment. We were going to Ukraine.

Driving over the border seemed risky, so we returned the car to a Suceava branch, şöbəsi, of the rental agency. We wandered around town while we waited for a bus. There was a synagogue. It appeared to be a century old or more, and in good repair. It had the usual padlock and sign with phone number, but this one also had posted visiting hours. We made a note to try to visit it when we returned.

On the bus, I was sitting near a young woman in full Eastern Orthodox Christian clothing from headscarf on down, though most of it had a tattered look, as though it was the only clothing she owned and couldn't afford to replace it. Her head was half buried in a pocket prayer book, her eyes practically burning holes in it. Every several seconds, she would cross herself. *These fucking Christians!* I thought again. *These superstitious peasants!* I was beginning to understand how my second cousin and Andrew Solomon felt. I was beginning to feel it. I looked out the window. No beeches.

For the first time in a couple of weeks, I was not thinking about whether I felt well or ill.

We arrived in Chernivtsi, Ukraine. We went to the place we had booked, which was called The Yard. It was a hostel. I had never stayed at a hostel, not even when I was young enough to stay comfortably in hostels. The reason we chose The Yard was not strictly that it was cheap and Chernivtsi's hotels and short-term rental apartments were surprisingly expensive. We chose it because it was so incredibly cheap that we didn't quite believe how cheap it claimed to be—or if it really was that cheap, whether the laudatory reviews and encouraging photos, many of them posted just in the last few weeks, were hoaxes. It seemed like we had to stay there simply to find out for ourselves. When we clicked "confirm," I felt myself start back in my seat, as though I had just pressed a button whose consequence might turn out to be dire.

But The Yard hostel really was that cheap. It was five dollars a night each. And it really was that clean and modern. It was also located right in the center of Chernivtsi, yet peaceably nestled in a quiet courtyard. The reception desk doubled as an espresso bar. The manager we'd communicated with online after we booked, called Max, was there to check us in—except there were actually two managers named Max, it turned out, and this was the other one. But both Maxes were friendly and welcoming. We explained to this Max our business in Chernivtsi (Jews, roots, etc.) and he responded brightly that he was Jewish, too.

He took us upstairs and into the dormitory. It had eight "boxes": bed-sized berths, half-enclosed, each equipped with a phone charging station, a reading light, and a small shelf that could accommodate a book or two, a bottle of water, and a snack. (What more does a human being really need, I thought?) A couple of the boxes were occupied, one of them by a person sound asleep. It was lunchtime. We put our bags in lockers and chose adjacent boxes on the upper bunk level, on the side of the room that had windows. The mattresses were very comfortable and felt fresh. The design of the boxes afforded surprisingly ample privacy without any sense of claustrophobia, and the windows let in cheerful sunlight. A sign enumerated rules against making noise, which we were only too happy to observe. An air conditioner was going, although the dorm was a little on the warm side, but at least the air was dry and breathable.

We needed food, insofar as I could stand to put anything into my stomach since I got sick. Max recommended a well-established place—a Chernivtsi institution, we gathered, just near the hostel. It had a large menu with both "Ukrainian" and "Jewish" sections. I chose the Jewish section and ordered what turned out to be a beet salad. Was this Jewish food? What was Jewish food? A carp in the bathtub? *Mit tzibeleh?*

We walked around Chernivtsi, a small city of about a quarter-million people, although it felt quite bustling after Dorohoi and Darabani. If Bucovina was the heart of high Jewish culture, then Chernivtsi was the heart of the heart, although Jews would not have called it Chernivtsi. The city has long been a "chafing point between East and West," Frances Stonor Saunders writes in "The Suitcase"—another place where east meets west. It was always "a complicated place to account for because it kept migrating between the Kingdom of Romania, the

Habsburg Empire, Ukraine, and Russia." Even its name was complicated: "You say Cernăuți, I say Czernowitz, you say Chernivtsi, I say Czernopol."

Jews say Czernowitz. In the center of Czernowitz proudly stood a large movie theater which we wanted to see because it had once been a synagogue. It was known, naturally, as the Cinégogue. There were many traces of Jewish culture around the town, where a larger and comparatively prominent Jewish population remains despite the ravages of the twentieth century. The 1930 census counted 43,000 Jews, and as late as 1960 the postwar population, rebounding as it did in Dorohoi, was 37,000. Now it was down to two thousand. Still, we saw many buildings marked with Jewish Stars and visited Czernowitz's only active *shul*. In the early twenty-first century, it had been handsomely restored—controversially, we learned, owing to its modern look. In 2016, it had been outfitted with a kosher restaurant—my father's tongue sandwich at Hillel House went across my mind's table—and doubled as the city's Jewish Community Center, although it contained no museum. The fellow who took our money and handed me the obligatory yarmulke waited impatiently for us to zip through the place and let him get back to whatever he had been doing.

All day, walking in the summer heat, I felt spacey and tired, but I perceived that this was the fatigue of convalescence, not illness. I had crossed the border into the country of recovery. If I kept to our slow walking pace, if I merely took in sights and did not try to take anything from them, if instead of a *Traseul Evreiesc* I simply toured Czernowitz, then my recovery would surely continue at the same gradual and ungreedy pace.

Walking back to The Yard, we passed a tattoo parlor and I announced to Heather that I wanted a new tattoo. She quite rightly responded that getting a tattoo was a terrible idea, given my illness.

Illness?

I did not tell her that in my opinion I was in recovery. I seemed to want to protect this recovery, this opinion, by withholding it.

Another thought I withheld was the image I pictured on my skin. Would it have advanced my case for getting a tattoo if I had told her what I wanted? I wanted a Star of David. A Jewish Star. I could also have told Heather where I wanted this tattoo, this sign, signet, Sigel: on my hipbone, a part of my body virtually no one sees but me. I already had a red star there, symbolizing Mars, my birth sign's ruling planet. The Jewish Star would accompany the red star.

I thought I might get it the next day, in secret, in the city of high Jewish culture.

I slept poorly. I woke in the middle of the night in my box in The Yard feeling feverish and headachy. I took some ibuprofen, which put me back to sleep, but it wasn't a restful sleep. In the morning, I blamed it on the air conditioner. The thermostat hadn't been turned down any further since we checked in and I had noticed the dormitory was somewhat warm—too warm for comfortable sleep, I told Heather.

She had slept fine.

I perceived that I was dehydrated—always dehydrated, the one constant symptom throughout my kaleidoscopic illness. Constant insatiable thirst seemed to start at my very skin. But by now I had lost my vigilance and was only lugging water around, letting it get too warm to drink in the July heat, pouring it out and stopping to buy another bottle every few hours. Occasionally I forced myself to swig, feeling bloated and sloshing even though my organs were screaming for water, yet having to find places to pee all the time. It had all gotten to be intolerable. The more central water became in my mind, in my body, the more exhausting the effort to drink it.

The reason Czernowitz's *shul* had no museum was that Czernowitz had a formal Jewish Museum, located in a very beautiful building that had originally been constructed in 1908 as the Jewish National House. As with most Jewish houses, it did not stay Jewish. The building passed through Soviet and Romanian hands before a lower portion of the building was returned, years later, to Czernowitz's remaining Jews, who converted one of its rooms into the Jewish Museum only a decade before we visited.

"Here, in multinational Bucovina, there was no Pale of Settlement," the museum informed us. "Here the Jews managed to gain equality with other peoples. Here prevailed an atmosphere of tolerance, mutual respect, and cooperation among people of different nationalities and religious beliefs that was exceptional for those years. Here

Jewish culture flourished, influencing other cultures and being influenced by them."

One of the flourishings was literary. Czernowitz was the birthplace of numerous eminent writers, most notably the poet Paul Celan. It was also the formal birthplace of a Jewish language. In 1908, the city hosted the first World Conference on Yiddish. Much of the Jewish Museum's exhibition was devoted to this conference, whose purpose was to validate and elevate Yiddish from its status as the impoverished patois of the shtetls and street theaters (and Pittsburgh). It could be the speech of poets, too, and it was. Itzik Manger, born in Czernowitz in 1901, wrote in Yiddish and became its most celebrated exponent. He was known for recasting old stories, including the Book of Esther, into modern settings. He also adapted some of Avram Goldfaden's performance-based lyrics into formal verse. Manger raised Yiddish's esteem so effectively that he helped legitimize it in Israel, where it had previously struggled to gain acceptance. Israel had only recently rescued Hebrew from its long demise as a spoken language—a cultural and societal achievement nearly as extraordinary as restoring the Jews to their homeland—and the country was not eager to support the revival of a German dialect. Zionist activists and others were known to vandalize signage in Yiddish, even as the twentieth-century influx of European Jews to Israel continued to propagate it. Those European Jews eventually included Manger himself, who relocated to Israel in 1958, the same year Ezra Pound returned to Italy after thirteen years of institutionalization in America. As soon as his ship docked, Pound raised his arm in the fascist salute.

Although the museum occupied just a single room, its memorabilia collection was far better than what we had seen in Iași, to say nothing of Dorohoi, and better care had been taken over the curation, design, and aesthetics of the gallery itself. Still, the collection was nothing compared to the treasures exhibited in extravagant, sumptuous, almost careless abundance at the Ioannina Ethnographic Museum in Greece, which I suddenly found myself wishing I'd spent more time in and better appreciated. None of the Czernowitz objects really interested me: IDs and passports, bank ledgers and mercantile transaction logs—wherever Jews, there business—household items. Where was Abraham's saucepan?

I was most interested in the room's upper ring of images of the twelve signs of the zodiac. They were reproductions of the originals on the ceiling of the Cinégogue. We weren't sure if the frescoes were extant on the Cinégogue's ceiling—or, if they were, whether we could have seen them there—but there might be another synagogue where we could. The museum's display included a photograph of the ceiling of the *shul* in Suceava, which also depicted the twelve signs of the zodiac. It seemed imperative now that we visit it when we returned to Suceava the next day.

After its triumphant account of flourishing Jewish culture, the museum's proclamation concluded:

"Then everything disappeared in the flames of the Holocaust."

I emerged from the Jewish Museum sick again. I sat down immediately outside, right on the curb, as I had sat on the ground outside the cemetery in Darabani. A Jewish museum is a Jewish cemetery. I stared at the cement. I heard people passing by. I heard Heather say, in a voice that seemed summoned from far away, that it was time we had some lunch. The most dreaded moment of my day.

I agreed to this on the condition that I could have something brothy and mild. There was a Japanese restaurant a few doors down from the museum. I ate noodle soup. I felt sufficiently revived to continue walking about, but limply, distractedly, in near silence, reduced to mutterances.

At the northwestern end of town was the celebrated campus of Chernivtsi National University, a Viennese-built architectural confection that mixes Moorish and Byzantine elements with traditional classical forms. You had to pay to enter the campus, and then were allowed inside only one building. Access denied. Again, everywhere.

After the university tour, I went for a long late-afternoon walk by myself.

I had no destination in mind. I simply felt I must keep walking. I soon passed a scattering of vendors on a curb, selling their backyard produce off dirty blankets. One of them had garlic, and I bought two bulbs. I put them in my backpack that night and carried them with me for the rest of the trip, never taking them out of my backpack until we were back in the States.

I continued across town, at a pace barely faster than a shuffle, until I found myself looking at a sign that read *Synagoga Str*. I followed this street down through what was clearly the old Jewish Quarter, sliding down toward the low end of town, southeast of the city center. There was the derelict Jewish hospital and another large, looming, forgotten building that looked a little like Beth Hamidraş in Bucharest and was probably once a temple. I passed an old shopfront still signed:

J*sak* *Eisikowicz, Pictor de Firme, Fondat 1910.*

A painted sign, in Romanian, for a Jewish sign painter who founded his business the year my great-grandparents sailed away. Sign, signet, Sigel.

I was filled with a longing to have been in Czernowitz then. What a place it must have been, where Jewish culture flourished. I wanted not to find my roots here— where they were not, after all—but to have grown out of them here. I wanted to go back to 1900 and escape from Dorohoi, from Darabani, and plant myself here among the Jews, go to lectures at the wondrous university, admitted to its every room, attend the World Conference on Yiddish. I would have lived among my Jews on Synagoga Street and argued with them in Viennese German, over tea sipped through a sugar cube, about whether Jews should speak Yiddish or Hebrew. Here I would have been at home. Life isn't about finding yourself. Life is about *creating* yourself. In Czernowitz I would have created myself. Then, like, Avram Goldfaden, like Itzik Manger, Paul Celan, Benjamin Fondane, Pinchos Jassinowsky, I would have expended my vigor in the cities of the world: Odessa, Munich, Paris, Jerusalem, Saint Petersburg, New York.

In the novel set in the Burgundian town by the Jewish writer who changed his name for "the usual reasons," the narrator writes of Dean, the main character:

> He has already set out on a dazzling voyage which is more like an illness, becoming ever more distant, more legendary. His life will be filled with daring impulses which cause him to disappear and next be heard of in Dublin, in Veracruz... I am not telling the truth about Dean, I am inventing him. I am creating him out of my own inadequacies.

I am on a dazzling voyage which is more like an illness. No, I am suffering an illness which is more like a dazzling voyage. I am filled with daring impulses which cause me to disappear and next be heard of in Istanbul, in Bucharest. I am not telling the truth about myself, I am not finding myself, I am creating myself out of my own inadequacies. This novel set in Burgundy is not a sex book. This novel is a Jew book. The sex is Dean's substitute for faith, it *is* his faith, he practices it devoutly. Every act of this worship fulfills him completely and at once drives his desire for fulfillment deeper. It can only end in his death, and it does.

As I walked back toward The Yard, instead of a tattoo I got a haircut.

Heather met me at the barbershop. She had expected the worst and was relieved to find me shorn instead of inked. On the way back to the hostel, we stopped at a store and bought some bread, salami, cheese, and beer. We took these provisions back to the Yard, where we discovered a problem: eating was prohibited in the dorm, alcohol wasn't permitted anywhere in the building, and there was no common space other than the espresso bar, which Max, one of the Maxes, was closing up. Before we said goodnight to him, I asked him if he might turn the temperature down, just a few degrees, in the dorm—I discovered, in fact, as I heard myself making this request, that I had been trying all day to work up the nerve to do so. My language was tentative, conditional. I was all but asking him to say no.

Sure, he said, no problem. Had it not been cool enough the previous night? He was sorry about that. He would turn it right down.

We decided to try eating on the fire escape. Other hostelers had already had this idea. We found two other dorm-mates who hadn't been in the hostel the previous night. We wedged ourselves beside them and laid out our evening picnic. They were a French couple, probably in their early sixties (was it a relief or a disappointment to discover that we were not the oldest hostelers?). It transpired that they were traveling by bicycle. They had been cycling all over the world for years now, returning to France only occasionally to regroup or recover from the maladies that invariably befall those who take the rough road. It turned out that they had been to some of the same remote Albanian towns where I had stayed, although this did not seem to interest them at all when I said I had been to these unlikely places, too. Nor did they respond to Heather's addressing them in French, which she speaks fluently. Instead they responded in English and named off more of the places they'd been. They had little to say about any of them except that they had been to them.

I thought of Lee and his pilgrimage from Korea to Santiago de Compostela, but this couple were not pilgrims. They were not trying to get anywhere. They were trying to get away from somewhere. I wanted to tell them how lucky they were. You have been pedaling all over the world without having to wish to belong to any part of it. I wanted to tell them that no Jew can ever feel this way.

The dormitory room was cool, almost bracingly so after a hot shower. I climbed up into my box and got under the comforter. I texted my sister, with whom I hadn't communicated since Heather and I were in the Caucasus. I told her where I was and how sick I had been. It did not take me long to feel overwhelmingly tired. But it was a different fatigue from what I had felt in Romania: not the fatigue of illness or despair but the sensual sleepiness of a creature who feels, finally, protected and safe, the whole body going inward into a depth of restoration and recovery. My little box was completely and purely white inside. I turned out my reading light and slept heavily.

xiv.

The next morning we arose before five in the morning, took a taxi to the bus station, and crossed the border back into Romania. By breakfast time, we were standing in front of the synagogue in Suceava and Heather was dialing the number on the sign on the door. Soon after, a young man arrived. He was perhaps thirty. His name was Daniel, and he was friendly, cheerful, and seemed genuinely glad to have visitors. He spoke English. It was clear that he took pride in Suceava's temple, which was doubly delightful to us when he told us he was only half Jewish. (I thought of the man at the cemetery in Dorohoi who told Andrew Solomon: "I am not Jewish, but I like Jews.")

Strictly speaking, Daniel was the wrong half: his father was Jewish. Daniel himself was a Pentecostalist. He acted as the temple's caretaker and also helped look after Suceava's last few Holocaust survivors, elderly folk supported, he told us, by funds from Israel.

There on the ceiling were the zodiac frescoes. The last time I'd seen these images displayed in a house of worship was in 2017, in Burgundy, where they were carved into the tympanum of the cathedral in the town where the Jewish writer's novel was set. Astrology, the great superstition, engraved into all the others, over every system of belief, overlaid on every representation of the divine. All the tattoos I already had were astrological symbols, engraved in my body.

Daniel took us upstairs and showed us a small but impressive collection of memorabilia, most of it shoved into a provisional clump for future sorting and display. There were steamer trunks, religious artifacts, and much more. It would have made for an illuminating exhibition, and there was room on the upper level, but Daniel lamented gently that there weren't funds for that project. All the money that came from Israel was allocated to Suceava's Holocaust survivors.

There was a moment of slightly awkward silence. Then Daniel cleared his throat and said, in a formal tone: "I would like to say something."

What he said was this. There was no question that Holocaust survivors must be the first funding priority. This was beyond discussion. Yet there was no money for other elderly Jewish Suceavans in need of care because they were not Holocaust survivors. Daniel said he was on his own to tend to these others, and he spent a lot of time calling on shut-ins and the infirm.

He also lamented that there was no money for necessary renovation work on the synagogue or preservation of its contents. He gestured at the collection of relics piled in the corner and said that his dream of turning them into a display was completely out of the question. Nor was there money for a rabbi in Suceava. The only money, and the only attention, that could be paid was to the Holocaust, whose artifacts, narratives, and suffering dominate our museums, our literature, our very existence. The Holocaust is the barrier that separates us from our possessions and our history, the incinerator of Jewish time.

On the way out of the synagogue, we took down Daniel's email address. This was not only for the general purpose of staying in touch with him, but also because we hoped that he might be of some help in clarifying whether Euge had known more about the Sigels than we could understand when we were in Dorohoi.

We spent another night in the same generic but comfortable executive-style hotel with the powerful shower and the king-sized bed. They had been kind enough to stow our larger bags while we zipped up and down to Czernowitz with only our day packs. We ate another bowl of Moldavia's beguiling *Ciorba Radauteana*.

And the next morning, we left the land where my ancestors stood.

5.

Repairing

i.

I woke up feeling as healthy as I had been since Tbilisi. But sad.

We had discussed staying in northeastern Romania longer. Heather was willing, even advocating, to go back to Dorohoi and press Euge on the matter of my great-grand-parents. We could try to hire Daniel and bring him with us from Suceava as a translator. Or we could spend long enough in Dorohoi to file requests in writing at town hall and gain further information about the Sigels and the Lipovicis. Or simply stand a while longer in this place where my ancestors stood. As we pulled out of Suceava I felt a terrible longing, almost a desperation not to leave.

So why were we leaving?

Because I needed to get well. I knew that as long as we were here, I would not.

And I knew I was getting well because we had a terrible time getting to Transylvania. First we had a smelly train ride to a city called Bacău, a long and hot walk across Bacău to the place where we would get a bus, then a long and hot and anxious wait for the bus, which was so late in coming that we thought we must be in the wrong place and had missed it. When it finally arrived, we sat behind a family whose small children were very ill and kept throwing up. Their parents seemed only barely interested in this and occasionally supplied plastic bags into which the children, aged roughly two and four, unsuccessfully tried to aim their projectile vomit. The parents reclined their seats

251

so far back into our laps that we had to complain. The bus was hot, stuffy, reeking, and ran into a forty-five-minute delay in a town where a road was closed. When we finally arrived in Braşov, it was late, dark, raining, and we were soaked by the time we reached the apartment we had rented, which was cavelike and dank and mildewy. And I felt completely fine. Not as if I had recovered, but as if I had been traveling for two and a half months and was a little out of shape and weary. Which I was.

We toured Peleş Castle, not far from Braşov. It is properly a palace, not a castle, dazzling inside and out, a masterpiece. Peleş was built by King Carol I, who assumed power in 1866 after Romania's previous ruler—the newly formed republic's first—had been expelled from the country by other noblemen. Lacking an evident successor, Romania looked outside its borders for a monarch. Carol was a German-born prince with ties to royalty around Europe. His installation legitimized Romania's sovereignty. Under him a new constitution was promulgated, built on liberal ideologies: freedom of speech, the press, the right to own property. But non-Christians were barred from citizenship. I was in the home of the man who had warranted my great-grandparents' exodus from Romania.

We visited Braşov's synagogue, a temple in good repair and regular use. The interior was bright and cheerful, as was the docent, who was even less Jewish than Daniel in Suceava: not Jewish at all. He told us he had taken his position at the synagogue because he liked Jewish music. Sometimes he sang with the congregation.

Later that day, I went for yet another long walk alone. A Jewish cemetery popped up on the map my phone showed me—the phone seemed, by now, to have learned to identify this landmark for me everywhere we went—and I walked well out of my way to see it. It turned out to be deceptively hard to get to. And like Beth Hamidraş in Bucharest, it also appeared to retreat as I neared it, taking evasive measures. When I finally found it, after a strenuous uphill climb to the top of a steep grade, the only entrance took me into the adjacent Catholic cemetery. There was an iron fence between the Jews and Catholics. I walked right up to the fence and was just a few feet from the Jewish headstones, but there was no gate. Access denied again. I was accustomed to this by now. I continued up to the top of the cemetery and found a gate. The graves rose in rows up the Pittsburgh-steep hill. There was a sweeping view of the valley below Braşov. The grounds were in good stead and in active use, with freshly dug and filled graves in abundant evidence. It seemed clear that Europe's charnel house of Jews had not quite swallowed Transylvania.

A young man approached and asked me my business in the cemetery. He was perfectly friendly and wanted to tell me that I had to pay the entrance fee. Down at the foot of the hill there was a proper entrance and administrative building, occupied by a caretaker, which I somehow had not managed to find. The young man escorted me to the very old caretaker to whom I gladly handed a few dollars' worth of lei. Instead of going back into the cemetery, as soon as I paid, I left.

Before I had left the United States, a Jewish friend of mine told me that pastrami, which I always ordered at Hillel House on Friday evenings when my father took us so he could have his tongue, had its origins in Romania. Throughout our time in the country, I had dutifully scoured the markets for pastrami, even though I had not been in the mood to eat, but the vendors in every town seemed to sell almost every kind of preserved meat except pastrami, save for a few examples made of lamb, which fills Heather with revulsion, just as gefilte fish fills me with revulsion. On our last day in Braşov, I went into a locally famous delicatessen and found some beef pastrami. But when I took my first bite, I discovered that *pastramă*, as the Romanians call it, was nothing like the pastrami I knew from Jewish delis in the States. It was plainer and softer and without pepper, closer to what we call "baloney." Through a language confusion with the woman behind the counter, I ended up with more than a pound of *pastramă* instead of the few slices I had tried to order. I spent nearly a week forcing myself to nibble my way through it before finally throwing away the remaining portion, which was roughly equal to what I had wanted in the first place. I consoled myself for having satisfactorily revised the old joke told by a Jew, as delivered by Woody Allen in *Annie Hall*: "Boy, the food at this place is terrible."

"Yeah, and such small portions."

It turns out pastrami is probably not Romanian at all, but derived from Turkish *pastirma*.

ii.

Three days later, we went for a twenty-mile hike in the Carpathians.

We had to get to the trailhead by very early-morning bus and then by ski lift. In between, we had a long trudge up a mountain road when I mistakenly disembarked us a stop too early. Although I was now sounder of body, I was still foggy of mind, and I got very upset with myself over this mistake. I refused Heather's initial efforts to soothe me, scolding myself as we huffed uphill, and she eventually grew frustrated and cross until we finally got into a spat of the sort that married couples have all the time. In a way, it was reassuring: we had room for this now.

The hike was quite long but, owing to our starting point, almost entirely downhill. Our day rambling in the beautiful Carpathians ended in a pleasant and reasonably affluent village called Rășinari. Something about this name twinkled in my memory, but nothing was illuminated until we reached the heart of the village and came to the Emil Cioran Museum.

Although I had not read any Emil Cioran, I might have wanted to visit the museum had it been open. I had learned of its existence, and a bit about Cioran, in the Andrzej Stasiuk book in which village-time burns slowly like the edge of a fabric. Perhaps this was the very village. One of Stasiuk's destinations was this museum, which was also Cioran's childhood home. I had to remind myself that in 1911, when Cioran was born, this town wasn't in Romania but still part of Hungary. He wrote in Romanian, however, and extensively about Romania, and is today considered one of the country's greatest writers and philosophers. In his twenties, he immigrated to Paris, where he got to know both Benjamin Fondane and Paul Celan. Cioran was a frequent visitor to Fondane's apartment, where Fondane would hold forth, spellbinding the younger Cioran with his garrulous intellectual discourse and making him wish afterwards that he had been writing down everything Fondane had said.

Cioran was not Jewish. He was the son of a priest and an early enthusiast of the Nazis who described himself as a "Hitlerist." He also wrote in praise of Romania's fascist Iron Guard, the paramilitary force that had set Beth Hamidraş on fire and was responsible for the Iaşi pogrom Heather and I had seen memorialized in front of the *Sinagoga Mare* and in the associated museum. There was a bigger pogrom in Bucharest in 1941 whose details are too gruesome to recount.

Cioran later recanted his support of the Iron Guard and was at pains to disown most of his early works. He even redacted the unseemlier politics from one of his first books. He died in 1995 with the highest literary honors.

One prominent American scholar called Cioran's oeuvre "a philosophical romance on the modern themes of alienation, absurdity, boredom, futility, decay, the tyranny of history, the vulgarities of change, awareness as agony, reason as disease."

The scholar was William Gass.

The Emil Cioran Museum was closed. It had the air of a place that opened perhaps only a few times a year. There was no number to call on the door.

The next day we left Romania.

iii.

From a town so small it seemed it could not possibly have an international airport, we flew directly to London. We stayed with one of Heather's friends who'd met up with us in Istanbul. She was keen to see a play that was popular at the time. *The Lehman Trilogy* chronicled the rise-and-fall story of the powerful Lehman Brothers investment bank, from its nineteenth-century origins to its 2008 collapse. Lehman was founded by three brothers, Jewish immigrants from Bavaria who made their first fortune as middlemen in the cotton industry in Alabama. Their business flourished so greatly that it outgrew cotton, and in fact outgrew commodities altogether. In the pivotal moment of the play's first act, the eldest brother pulls rank on the two younger ones, radically changing the nature of the business and setting the Lehmans on their historic course with a single, five-word sentence: "We are merchants of money."

The Lehmans' Jewishness was only a minor theme of the play, but explicit acknowledgments of their heritage stood out, especially the reciting of the mourner's kaddish that occurred three times, once per act. After each death, the period of mourning was shortened, first from the traditional weeklong period to three days and then, in modern times, to a mere three minutes. The audience was given to understand that this was an act of sacrilege. They were asking for it, and they got it, the ruin they deserved.

Throughout the play, small details mounted up, little

more than brief asides, to keep reminding us that we were watching Jews. (So did, during the early section chronicling the original immigrant brothers and their establishment in America, the actors' delivery of their lines in a generic transcontinental, not to say rootless cosmopolitan, accent.) But in their very smallness and infrequency, each detail functioned as a little snag that allowed it to go almost without saying that of course Jews were money merchants and money merchants were Jews: practitioners of all those dark arts Ezra Pound had ranted about on Rome Radio. The play subtly, almost slyly, led the viewer to the unmistakable conclusion that what doomed the Lehmans was the family's descent from the rectitude and honorability of their religion into the shamefulness of their bloodline, which carried Jewish greed, Jewish money-grubbing, Jewish immorality. Days of mourning reduced to three minutes. The tribe that had come up from Pharaoh in Egypt making its early profits from enslaved Black cotton pickers in Alabama. Two of the immigrant Lehmans were slaveowners themselves. The play ended with the three brothers saying their third and final kaddish of the night. It landed false and hollow, on an unearned elegiac note, because by then they had sold away their Jewishness, financial bankruptcy begotten from religious bankruptcy. The play seemed to be saying that if only they'd been more Jewish, they might have ended less Jewish.

The playwright was an Italian Jew.

"Historians be warned," a historian writes, "it's not easy to write well about rich Jews."

We went to the Tate Britain to see the Vorticists. A number of works in the museum's collection were the same ones that had been shipped to North Carolina to appear in the small-town exhibition for which I had constructed the play about Pound and the Vorticists almost a decade earlier. The most remarkable of these—a piece so far ahead of its time and so unnerving that it still looks futuristic—is a sculpture called *Torso in Metal from Rock Drill*. (Pound named a section of his *Cantos* after this sculpture.) The sculptor was Jacob Epstein, a U.S.-born Jew who expatriated at age twenty-one, became a British subject like his modernist contemporary, T. S. Eliot, and produced his entire oeuvre as an Englishman.

Walking out of Hyde Park the next day, I came upon an arresting sculpture wedged uncomfortably in front of a modern building. Moving closer, I discovered the sculpture to be an Epstein, *The Rush of Green*, an exhilarating depiction of a family, led by their dog, leaping toward the park at the piped instigation of Pan behind them.

I spent the next day or two, sometimes alone, sometimes with Heather, walking around London on my own *Traseul Evreiesc* by plotting a course from one Epstein to the next. His *Rima* in Hyde Park proper, commissioned to honor the naturalist writer William Henry Hudson, was defaced with swastikas in 1935. His somewhat ghoulish *Ages of Man* series caused a scandal and now survives in mutilated form on the façade of Zimbabwe House, under which we saw people queuing up for free food from a charitable organization. His haunting, half-mummified

Madonna and Child looms weirdly over Cavendish Square. I much preferred this tour to visiting cemeteries or *shuls*.

Although we did go to one. Bevis Marks is the oldest continuously operating synagogue in Europe. In the traditional way of synagogues, Bevis Marks had been built well off the street, deliberately half-hidden and even harder to spot now that it was further hemmed in by new construction and obscured by the business-hours bustle of the City of London. Its entrance door was discreetly located in a side wall rather than at the front. Inside, Bevis Marks was typically unostentatious. Jewish religious structures are pleasingly modest. It would be almost impossible to imagine an exterior painted like the blue monastery at Voroneţ, or ornately decorated inside with stained glass, flying buttresses, and so on. Still, it was a beautiful old house of worship, easily the loveliest synagogue we had seen, no doubt because it was also the wealthiest. Among its most powerful benefactors was Moses Montefiore, an unimaginably rich nineteenth-century financier who married into the Rothschild family and used his considerable influence and wealth to drive philanthropic works, from building flour mills in Palestine to helping abolish slavery in the British empire.

Near the synagogue was a street called Jewry Street on which was an establishment also called "Jewry." It was hard to tell exactly what its business was, and impossible to find out by going in: it was closed in the early afternoon. It turned out to be a swanky cocktail bar.

We went to London's Jewish Museum, too. It was in

Camden Town, which I knew only as the domain of Amy Winehouse, the preternaturally gifted but drug-doomed chanteuse who, I had recently discovered, was Jewish. There was her statue: another, accidental, destination on my tour of Jewish sculptures in London.

The Jewish Museum had a good deal of ethnographic content in its permanent collection, but the highlight was a temporary exhibit called "Jews, Money, Myth." Seeing it right after *The Lehman Trilogy* deepened the exhibit's impact. It offered a thorough, highly evidentiary critical examination of the associations between Jews and money. Its topmost floor included a substantial video about antisemitism. It suddenly dawned on me how strange it is to be of a people the hatred of whom is baked into any display of our own history and culture. This is what you encounter as a Jew in any Jewish Museum: the evidence and images of how much you have always been despised, for whatever combination of reasons. The usual reasons.

iv.

On returning to the United States, we spent a week or so housesitting for an old friend of mine from college who lives in New Jersey, a short commute from Manhattan. We do this most summers, mainly so we can revisit New York.

I moved to New York two weeks after graduating from college and felt almost immediately suited to the city. I was happier and more comfortable in my five years there than I have ever felt anywhere else I have lived, including my hometown, which is where I live today and which has never felt like anything to me but a place like any other. Were I to be compelled to flee it, I would not have much to say about it afterwards. Perhaps my great-grandparents refused to talk about Romania not because what happened to them there was unspeakable, but simply because there was nothing to say.

I had known for many years that both sets of my paternal great-grandparents were buried in New York: the Jassinowskys in Queens and the Sobseys just east of Queens on western Long Island. I had never visited their graves. Now it seemed essential.

Heather and I took a commuter bus from New Jersey into Manhattan, then the Long Island Railroad to a stop near Bethpage. From there, we walked nearly two miles along a highway to New Montefiore Cemetery. The Sobseys are buried in a section of New Montefiore called the Workmen's Circle, which was founded in 1900 to provide resources for Jewish immigrants, including burial services. It was not easy to find the Workmen's Circle, and harder still to spot the graves—but then, all at once, there they were: Benjamin and Rose Sobsey. My middle name is Benjamin, and there lay the man who gave it to me, whom I never met, under a stone bearing two-thirds of my name.

We gazed at the stones for long, silent moments. Then Heather got stung by bees. She spent the rest of our time in the Workmen's Circle with a swollen eye.

We backtracked by taxi, commuter train, and subway to Queens, where we went to Mount Carmel Cemetery and found the Jassinowsky plot. *Poet, Composer and Beloved Cantor of the Jewish Center,* read the headstone, which occupied the prime spot at the top of the sloped section maintained by the Jewish Center, the Upper West Side *shul* where my great-grandfather spent most of his career.

It's generally agreed that the name Jassinowsky probably originated in Poland, but as I stood in front of my great-grandfather's grave I decided the Jassinowskys weren't from Poland at all. As their name plainly announces, they were *from Jassy*: the Jews' name for Iaşi. This meant I was not a quarter Moldavian but half, and that twice as many of my ancestors had stood where I had just gone to stand.

There was no trace of the footstone of Pinchos Jassinowsky's wife, my great-grandmother Lillian. We knew she was buried here, and it seemed important to confirm this. I suddenly dropped down to my knees and began to dig with my bare hands.

While I dug, Heather called the cemetery. Yes, Lillian was buried there. The footstone had probably sunk under the earth. The Jewish Center must not have paid its maintenance dues. Eventually I uncovered a corner of her stone.

When we got home, I sent the funds to have the footstone raised.

We had a thirty-minute walk to the subway. It started to rain, and then very suddenly to pour, an afternoon midsummer storm. We were in a residential neighborhood way out in Queens and there was nothing much in the way of shelter. We stopped into the first available place, an Irish pub. The barmaid's name was Colleen. She had an Irish accent. A few men sat in various states of slump in the middle of the day, well into their drinking shifts. We ordered shots of Irish whiskey. On the television above the bar, the Yankees were putting the finishing touches on an easy Wednesday afternoon win over a second-division team up in the Bronx, a few miles north of us, where it wasn't raining. Some things were the way they should be and always were. The Irish pub was full of the Irish, my great-grandmother's footstone would soon be raised, the Yankees win again.

My grandfather, my father's father, used to tell me about going to see the Yankees. Babe Ruth was on the team then. My grandfather grew up in Brooklyn and was a Dodgers fan, but he was often in Manhattan on weekends, and it was easier to get from there to Yankee Stadium. He was in Manhattan because his father, Benjamin Sobsey, whose grave Heather and I had just seen, owned a greasy spoon in Hell's Kitchen, and my grandfather was made to work in it on the weekends. It was called the Copper Pot. This was during the Great Depression. For a nickel, you got a bowl of soup and all the bread you could eat. Maybe there were individual cigarettes on the counter for a penny each. Hell's Kitchen was dangerous then, and the Copper Pot's clientele was largely rogues and ruffians. But everyone respected the place, my grandfather told me. No one ever caused trouble. You were safe there.

In high school in Brooklyn, my grandfather was on the football team. His position was tight end, and he was a favorite passing target of the team's quarterback, who also happened to be Jewish. When it came time to go to college, the quarterback urged my grandfather to follow him to Columbia University, which was then a college football power, where they could go on being a dynamic Jewish duo—and then, who knew, maybe the pros? My grandfather had to decline. He couldn't afford Columbia and had a scholarship offer from Michigan. But at Michigan he was kept mostly on the bench because the coach didn't want Jews as starters, and his lack of playing time drove him off the team. The quarterback who went to Columbia was named Sid Luckman. He went on to become a star with the Chicago Bears, and he's in the NFL Hall of Fame.

Our housesitting stint came to an end and it was time to go home. But I felt we already were.

6.

Postparing

I went home and got on a scale for the first time in three months. I was almost afraid to look down.

I weighed exactly what I had weighed before we left. To the pound.

Nothing else seemed to have changed either. I worked, I wrote, I ran.

Was something supposed to have changed? Why had I gone to Romania?

I kept telling Heather, lamenting to Heather, kvetching to Heather, that if only my purpose in going to Romania had been more substantial than merely to stand where my ancestors stood, then I would not have gotten sick. If I had not gotten sick, then I would not have been too incapacitated to undertake a search. If I had been able to search, then I would have found.

But what would I have found? If you do not know what you are looking for, how can you expect to recognize it should you find it?

I tried to identify or even invent a purpose for having gone to Romania, after the fact. I imagined returning with this purpose in mind to Romania, where I would find connection, belonging, and revelation, as Andrew Solomon had, so sharp, so sweet. But instead of establishing a purpose that would have changed everything about my trip, I merely felt a longing to repeat it almost exactly as it was. I was longing to eat *crap țărănească* again in Bucharest. Longing to take another Pilates class with Cécile. Longing to take the tour of Jewish Bucharest—the whole tour, without screaming at the man outside Beth

Hamidraş. Longing to find Benjamin Fondane's book again, only this time to buy it. Longing to take the tour of the theater in Iaşi, only this time to get the name and address of the Canadians who spoke Romanian. Longing to drive up into Moldavia and this time buy its garlic. Longing for another basket of *lipje* at the Hotel Splendid in Dorohoi and another bowl of *ciorba Radauteana* in Suceava. Longing to lay my eyes again on the zodiac ceiling of the synagogue, to sleep in a box in the Yard Hostel, and to get a tattoo. Longing to park the car in the middle of Darabani in the late afternoon, to go into its pharmacy for a bounty of medicines, and then to go in search of the Jewish cemetery only to fall upon the ground, surrounded by fallen apples. Longing to go right back to all the places I had gone, and to be sick in Romania again!

Instead I felt bored. Terribly, hopelessly, lifelessly bored.

I went back to work. In fact I went back to work before I started working. The very evening I arrived home, I delivered to my Albanian colleague the plastic bottle of his father's homemade raki. It had survived our long trip without the lid popping off in the back of a minibus, or the bottle exploding in a jet's cargo hold, or confiscation at a border checkpoint, or simply being drained of its contents somewhere between Albania and Azerbaijan. My colleague was quite overjoyed to lay his hands on the bottle. It was like a sacred relic to him, but a living one, an ardent spirit of family and country. Thus I was quite surprised, and dismayed, when he almost immediately opened the bottle right there in the restaurant and in the dull lull of five o'clock between afternoon setup and the first trickle of customers, poured copious shots for anyone who happened to be working that evening's shift. Within half an hour, the bottle was nearly empty.

Andrzej Stasiuk, whose footsteps I followed to Emil Cioran's house in Rășinari, where time burns like the edge of a fabric, writes: "I love traveling to little-known countries. Then I return, consult books, ask people, and gather a mountain of facts to determine where I actually was."

I needed to determine where I actually was. I coined a word for this form of retrospective travel: *postparing*.

Ask people. Consult books. Gather a mountain of facts.

I emailed Daniel, who had led us through the synagogue in Suceava. Would he mind calling Euge and Viorica in Dorohoi and clarifying with them whether they had known my family? He replied that he would be happy to do that for us.

I reread *The Carp in the Bathtub*. How do the children save the fish, and what are the consequences of their subterfuge?

Ah. The children do not save the fish.

They are caught and scolded; the carp is caught and scalded. Their mother turns it into gefilte fish. As a consolation, their father buys them a pet housecat.

It turns out that the tradition of keeping a carp in the bathtub before a major holiday feast is not exclusive to the Jews and the Seder. Christians all over Eastern Europe have long done the same in advance of Christmas. The practice is regional, it seems, not specifically Jewish, although the Christians may have adopted it from the Jews. In Poland, gefilte fish is known as "carp Jewish style."

Carp is not the only species used to make gefilte fish, although the others are also freshwater fish, such as pike. Walleye, the fish recommended by the maître d' to Uncle Larry and his table of guests from the Midwest, is similar to pike, inhabits the same waters, and is sometimes called "yellow pike," but is not in the same family as pike.

("First of all, walleye isn't *sea* food.")

I consulted *The Diary of Anne Frank* to see if I had correctly remembered my character Otto Frank's line, *"Was ist los? Was its passiert?"* I had. I then read through to the end of the script. After the war is over, Mr. Frank returns to the hiding place where he peruses his daughter's journal, in which he comes upon the sentence for which Anne Frank is best remembered: "In spite of everything, I still believe that people are really good at heart." Anne's voice is heard saying this line. Surprisingly, it is not the last line of the play but the second to last. The final line is delivered by Mr. Frank, my character. I had no memory of this line whatsoever, and it did not summon any recognition in me when I re-read it, postparing. Mr. Frank says: "She puts me to shame." It's strange to me that the last line of *The Diary of Anne Frank*, spoken by a concentration camp survivor, is "shame," and that he is the one who is shamed.

I also read the original diary, a biography of Anne

Frank, and a speculative biography of Anne Frank that took the form of her imagined obituary had she lived into her old age. In Anne Frank's diary, I was most affected by her very strong, articulate, and nuanced feminism, and by the entry that recounts a fearful night the hiders must spend in a room that has no toilet: "The wastebasket stank, everything went on in a whisper, and we were exhausted. It was midnight. I made my bed between the table legs. The smell wasn't quite so bad when you were lying on the floor, but Mrs. van Daan quietly went and got some powdered bleach and draped a dish towel over the potty as a further precaution."

While reading these writings, I came across a Google Doodle devoted to Anne Frank, which excerpted eleven lines from the diary and designed images around them. One of the lines was her expression of the sentiment that she felt like "a caged bird." In another, she said goodbye to her cat before the Nazis took her away. It was interesting to me that two of the eleven lines involved housepets. The eleven-line scroll concluded not with the line about the reeking wastebasket but, naturally, with: "In spite of everything, I still believe that people are really good at heart."

I also came across a magazine cover in the supermarket bearing Anne Frank's face and the headline: "Anne Frank: Her Inspiring Life." This was as strange sounding to me as "Now we can live in hope."

Gather a mountain of facts. I went to get my coin collection. Pennies, nickels, dimes, and quarters. I knew exactly where it was. The binders of coin flips were in a box that had sat on a table in my mother's basement for years. It was one of the few remnants of my youth she had made a point of safeguarding. My mother lives three miles away from me and I could have claimed the collection at any time, as I could have visited my New York ancestors' graves at any time but only just had. By the same impulsion, I now wanted my coin collection. I had not yet come across a famous Jewish writer's characterization of "a 'collection' as a manifestation of a philosophical project or even as an idea of personal identity."

The coin collection was not in my mother's basement.

I looked all around her house, in closets and chests. It was not there. She lives alone and no one ever goes down into her basement. She is sure that she never moved the coin collection, and I believe her. But it's gone.

I didn't hear back from Daniel in Suceava for a couple of weeks. I emailed him again and got no reply. I assumed either that he'd learned nothing, that he hadn't been able to reach Euge and Viorica at all, or that he'd simply forgotten.

I had a deeper question. It had started nagging at me. A Jewish Question.

What have people got against the Jews?

What have they *always* had against us?

The Crucifixion. Yes. But Christians aren't the only ones who hate Jews. Everyone hates Jews, including people who were hating Jews long before there were Christians. There had to be a more persuasive answer to the question of what everyone had always had against the Jews.

I had a related question: What are Jews, exactly?

(*What IS he?*)

It seemed to me that the best place to begin looking for answers was in the book the Jews wrote about themselves.

Like almost any westerner I had read bits and pieces of the Bible, and of course I was familiar with the most famous episodes, like David and Goliath, but nothing more. I was one of the People of the Book my own people had written and I had never read.

I bought a recent translation by an eminent scholar of both the Bible and comparative literature. His translation included copious annotations, glosses, and lexical exegeses. I read the translation slowly, often aloud, sometimes alongside the King James Version, usually with my computer awake in front of me so I could search further. This was what I spent my time doing when I wasn't working or running. For six months I didn't write.

In the translator's annotations, I discovered something fundamental to the Hebrew language. If you revocalize the same cluster of consonants with different vowels, the meaning changes. I first learned this from the translator's gloss on the root HRM. Vocalized *herem*, it is often translated as "to put under the ban," but this phrase was opaque to me and required some translation itself. *Herem* essentially means "total destruction," that is, "pogrom." I was surprised to find this concept in the Hebrew Bible.

It happens that my hometown's consonants are DRHM,

HRM plus D, and Dorohoi's are DRH. As I had decided in Mount Carmel Cemetery that Jassinowsky means *from Jassy*, I decided that my hometown is a revocalized Dorohoi, confirming it as a place that shares the same root as the place from which my great-grandparents emigrated, a place where there is total destruction, therefore unspeakable and unspoken.

What are Jews? Abraham is obedient to God: surely his sacrifice of Isaac is the greatest act of faith in all of literature, and he enacts our covenant; but later he bargains over figures with God. Isaac is weak; Isaac's son Jacob, patriarch and namesake of the Israelites, is devious and self-dealing. Among his sons, Joseph dissembles, Judah strays, Reuben defiles. Aaron fabricates the golden calf. Moses complains, Moses *kvetches* about the burden God sets on him. He says he is not up to the task of leading the Israelites through the wilderness to the promised land. He complains about this stiff-necked people, the chosen people, and they complain to him, about him, the one who has been chosen to lead them. The Book of Judges is full of violence, apostasy, and brutality. It ends with civil war that nearly destroys the tribes, caused by one of the most gruesome atrocities I've ever read.

I began to have something against the Jews myself. I could identify with none of them. Then I identified with one. I found him at the moment in the Bible when the Jews set down roots as a nation and demand a king.

I was surprised to discover that the first king of Israel was not David, who slew Goliath and gave the Jews the star my sister and I learned to draw by setting one triangle upside-down over the other. The first king of Israel was Saul. I don't think I had ever heard of Saul before I encountered him in the Book of Samuel, as I had never heard of Thessaloniki before I went there.

My question, What has everyone got against the Jews, became a more specific question: What has everyone got against this Jew?

The Israelites demand a king, "like all other nations have, to fight our battles for us." Saul is the one the Lord chooses. He is not chosen for any particular reason. He has not appeared in the Bible until the moment of his choosing. The choice dismays the prophet Samuel. Samuel is not dismayed by the specific choice of Saul. Samuel does not think Israel should have a king at all. There is only one authority, and that is the Lord, Who nonetheless heeds the Israelites and commands Samuel to anoint and crown Saul, which Samuel does grudgingly, sourly, enviously. It seems clear to me that the prophet wishes to be king himself, if Israel must have a king. Not Saul, a farm boy who belongs to a lowly clan from Gibeah, the town where the horrific act that caused the civil war among the tribes occurred.

As soon as Saul takes the throne created for him, he makes a harmless mistake: an understandable one, even a defensible one. For this, Samuel excoriates him and tells him he has squandered the kingship. Nonetheless, Samuel sends Saul out on another errand, that is, to fight another of Israel's battles. Saul triumphs, but he makes another mistake: he does not *herem*, HRM, the enemy. He spares their counterpart king, perhaps as collateral, and the fattest livestock, perhaps as sacrifice to the Lord. Samuel denounces him again. Saul has not only squandered his crown, but his seed will also be cut off from the kingship forever.

I identified with Saul because he wants, wants so badly, to fulfill what is expected of him, what he expects of himself, what Samuel has commanded, and goes to such lengths to do it, and the longer the lengths the less he knows what to do and the deeper his failure. He is a simple man. His only quality is that he is tall. Is this why he was chosen king? Because of his height? I only went to Romania because of my face.

The Lord repents the choice of Saul. It is the first time the Lord has repented since the creation of the human race, who were all consequently destroyed in the Flood save Noah, whose ark made landfall on Ararat. Instead of destroying Saul, the Lord floods him with troubles until Saul destroys himself.

The greatest of these troubles is David, whom the Lord anoints to replace Saul. Saul, disposed to fight through troubles, as I am, as Aries is, tries to maintain his kingship and continue to fight Israel's battles. But it is an unwinnable fight. Saul pursues David, expending his vigor on the wrong solution, against the wrong enemy. In scene after scene, he suffers denial, disdain, deception, humiliation, possession, dispossession, madness, illness.

Saul is lost from the very start.

He first appears when his father sends him in search of some mules that have gone missing from the family's farm. Saul, going out after the lost mules, gets lost himself. His accompanying servant, not Saul, recognizes where they are: near the town where Samuel lives. That is how Saul's fate is set. He goes to find his mules and instead he founds a kingdom.

I identified with Saul because he undertakes a family errand involving land, only to fail on the errand and grow helpless and bewildered, relying on the strength and intelligence of a companion. I identified with Saul because his purpose is simple but in pursuing it, he happens upon the unimaginable complexity of the heritage he carries inside him, and finds himself onerously crowned with this heritage.

Just after Samuel anoints Saul, the prophet sends him home, telling him the mules have been found. We never see these mules found. On the way home, Saul encounters a band of prophets, as Samuel has told him he would. These are not prophets like Samuel, not wise men or tribal leaders but roving mystics who play a trance-inducing music—holy rollers. Samuel tells Saul that he, Saul, will prophesy, roll holy, with them: "You shall become another man." The prophets play Saul into a fugue state. He prophesies, he rolls holy, he becomes another man. When this session of spiritual transport is over, he collapses and lies spent in the road.

I identified with Saul because he is sometimes visited by a mysterious evil spirit, sent by the Lord, which torments him with melancholy and rage. Sometimes this rage leads him to rash violence, as the rage caused by an evil spirit led me to the brink of rash violence against the Romanian dog, the human being, outside Beth Hamidraş.

Saul pursues David. Samuel again sends the prophets out to intercept Saul and derange him once more. This time, Saul strips off all his clothes and goes into an even higher delirium, and when it is over he collapses at the side of the road, as I collapsed at the side of the road in Darabani and withdrew into a trance from which I did not emerge until I heard a passing sound, which was the sound of a mule.

I identified with Saul because his way is blocked. The road, his kingship, his spirit. Mostly what is blocked is knowledge. Samuel gives him a book, the *Mishpat Hammelek*, the Duties of the King. It is a book Samuel wrote. Saul is unable to understand it. Instead he consults oracles, but the oracles are silent. Finally he consults a necromancer. He has forbidden this practice in his own kingdom.

The spirit he commands the necromancer to summon is that of Samuel, who has died of old age. Samuel's ghost, irate that Saul has disturbed his eternal rest, excoriates him one final time. Tomorrow, he tells him, you shall be with me. You shall die.

The next day, Saul does as Samuel the prophet has commanded. He dies. He commits suicide. He is the first true suicide in the Bible.

And that is how the nation of Israel, how the Jewish people, sets down roots.

Saul is not a villain. Saul is a victim.

(Adam, do you have any *Jewish* heritage?)

For months, all I read about was Saul. More translations, more annotations, more essays, more lexical exegeses. The more I read about Saul, the less sense he made. The less sense he made, the more I identified with him. I ran out of books to consult. There are many biographies of David, but there is no biography of Saul, the first king of Israel.

I decided to write one. I decided to write it in the same form as I wrote my biography of Ezra Pound—as a play. But it would not resemble my Ezra Pound play at all. It would not be an unstageable four-hour verse drama. It would be more like the performance piece I created for the Vorticist exhibition, which I did not write but assembled from other books. I would assemble my King Saul play from the chapters of the Book of Samuel that involved Saul. I would not have to go all the way to Jakarta to write the play, because I could write it in my house, and I would never have to withdraw it from production because I would never submit it for production. If the play were ever staged, I would have to play Saul myself. I would have to become another man, Saul.

But not only Saul.

I bought *Existential Monday*, the essay collection by Benjamin Fondane, which I had picked up and put down in the Bucharest bookshop. It took me a long time to open the book. For months I kept putting it in prominent places around the house, but not as a reminder to read it. It was so I could gaze at Fondane's two faces, the one on his neck and the one levitating in his hands, which gazed back at me: "A face marked by rage, by pity, and by joy," Fondane called it in one of his poems.

I showed the book to a friend of mine, another writer, summarizing Fondane's biography and work, attempting to interest her in him.

All she said was, "What a face!"

Was that not why I had chosen to go to Romania? Because of a face? The sign, signet, Sigel that was the map I was using when I arrived in Dorohoi and showed the picture of Grape Zaidie to Euge so he could tell me where I was, and who?

Fondane was born Benjamin Wechsler near Iaşi in 1898, a dozen years before my great-grandparents left Dorohoi. By age fourteen he had already published his first poem, under a pseudonym, and after trying on a few other pen names he settled on Fundoianu, which was the name of the Moldavian estate his family had come from. On reaching adulthood he moved to Bucharest, where he published widely—poetry and essays—and staged épater le bourgeois plays, a song and dance man. Then he went to Paris and Gallicized his name, as Cecilia Dumitrescu would do.

Fondane soon came under the influence of the proto-Existentialist philosopher Lev Shestov, another Jew with a changed name: Shestov was born Yehuda Shvartsman in 1866, in Kiev. He is not widely read today, but Shestov was much admired in his time (Camus discusses his work in *The Myth of Sisyphus*), a highly trained philosopher of great rhetorical discipline and scholarly mastery. His primary acolyte was Fondane, the Thoreau to Shestov's Emerson. At the very end of one of the essays in *Existential Monday*, Fondane pays tribute to Shestov, putting himself in the third person to avow that "the author [Fondane] did not set off on this path on his own, but was led onto it by a teacher whom he loves and reveres above all."

It understates Fondane's debt to Shestov to say that he modeled his philosophical thought on the teacher he revered and loved. Fondane's work is often an obvious paraphrase, at times to a nearly plagiarized degree. But Shestov, who wrote in Russian, was apprised by his own translator that "your philosophy has a better chance of making its mark on the world through Fondane than through you."

Reading Fondane and Shestov was uneasy going for me. I'm not a philosopher, unless Shestov is correct that a philosopher is not "a thinker with a stern face, a profound look which penetrates into the unseen, and a noble bearing—an eagle preparing for flight," as he says in his early book, *All Things Are Possible.* "A thinking man is the one who has lost his balance, in the vulgar not tragic sense. Hands raking the air, feet flying, face scared and bewildered, he is a caricature of helplessness and pitiable perplexity. The business of philosophy is not to reassure people, but to upset them."

All Things Are Possible contains the kernels of Shestov's philosophy, a business elaborated throughout his oeuvre and passed down through Fondane. His thesis is that only Faith can overcome Necessity—that mountain of facts we climb in vain on the mule of our Reason, which is "the one substance which can never be destroyed," Fondane says. With faith all things are possible.

Had I not known since childhood that all things are possible, through another Jewish text that I memorized and sung aloud as H*Y*M*A*N K*A*P*L*A*N? *"Anything is possible / When a man is free."* Had I not known even before that, when I was a small child and there were cows in the yard and the children rescued the carp from the bathtub? Had I not known all things are possible when I called Moishe Sigel Grape Zaidie and spelled his daughter's title B*O*I*B*Y? Jassinowsky means *From Jassy.* My hometown is Dorohoi, revocalized. Cécile Dumetrier from France, not Cecilia Dumitrescu from Romania. Not Robert Zimmerman from Minnesota but Bob Dylan from New Mexico. Not Benjamin Wechsler from Moldavia but Benjamin Fondane from Paris. Adam Sobsey, Sabzi, Şöbəsī, from Moldavia, Pittsburgh, Persia, Turkey, Sheki, New York. Life isn't about finding yourself. Life is about creating yourself.

What if you were created Jewish?

This cannot be uncreated. You may pass for Melanesian, Polynesian, Indonesian, Nepalese, Surinamese, Dutch-Chinese, change your name, passport, and language. But even a stranger in the mall will still know you are Jewish.

In Paris, Fondane established himself as a writer of

philosophy, criticism, and poetry. Some of his verses took the form of a sort of Dada film script. He called them Cinépoems. The Cinépoems prefigured Fondane's foray into filmmaking. To make this film, he sailed to Argentina on the invitation of the writer Victoria Ocampo. The film he made was never shown and is almost certainly lost. He returned to Paris and became a fixture among the existentialist literati who included some of his fellow Romanian émigrés, such as the founder of Dada, Tristan Tzara—another Moldavian Jew, born Samuel Rosenstock in Bacău two years before Fondane was born in Iaşi. Just after World War II, still another Moldavian Jew, Isidore Isou—born Isidore Goldstein in Botoşani—who was then founding what would soon evolve into the most important artist-intellectual school of postwar France, the Situationist International, interrupted the Paris premiere of Tzara's latest play and shouted: "Dada is dead!"

By then, Benjamin Fondane had been dead for two years.

Fondane saw the Shoah coming. He was made a French citizen in 1938 and soon enlisted in the military. That same month, he gave Victoria Ocampo a sealed envelope containing all the correspondence between himself and Lev Shestov, along with the manuscript of a book he was working on based on that correspondence. With it were detailed instructions for the elaboration of this material should anything happen to him. Fondane was mobilized in 1940 and stationed not far from Paris. Twice he was captured by the Germans. The first time, he escaped; the second time, he was released because he had to have an emergency operation. The reason for the operation was acute appendicitis.

After he was released from the hospital, in February 1941, Fondane went back to Nazi-occupied Paris, where he refused to wear the yellow star. He continued to go out and about as he pleased, attending university lectures, frequenting bookstores, and associating with fellow intellectuals and artists like Emil Cioran. "If there were ever an authentic Jew whom Hitler should have arrested," he wrote in a letter to his Gentile wife, "it's me."

The reason he had to write his wife a letter was that they had been separated. Fondane was imprisoned at Drancy, the French internment camp outside Paris. He was sent there in 1944 after he was apprehended by the authorities, apparently betrayed by his building's concierge following a quarrel. His sister was arrested along with him. Twice while he was at Drancy, Fondane's wife and friends, especially Emil Cioran, arranged provisionally for his release. But he agreed to accept it only on the condition that his sister also be freed. The condition was not met, and he remained at Drancy. A few months later, they were both sent to Auschwitz on the last train that ever went there from Paris. Neither survived.

"One might be *compelled* to die, no doubt," he had written, "but nothing in the world can compel you to *accept* this death."

A word Fondane coined describes the condition of being compelled without accepting what is compelled.

Irresignation. Fondane never offered a definition of this word. "The deep structure of reality will never change," he says. "As long as reality continues to be what it is, we will testify to our irresignation in one way or another—by poetry, by cries, by faith, or by suicide—even should this irresignation be, or appear to be, absurdity and madness. Indeed, nowhere is it written that, in the end, madness cannot have reason over reason."

Irresignation is to refuse to stop fighting your people's battles for them even after they have taken your crown from you. It is to summon the dead via dark arts that you yourself have forbidden, and then, condemned by the dead to die, to kill yourself. Irresignation is to refuse to leave your sister at Drancy and seal your own death along with hers. Irresignation is to go all the way to Romania to stand where one's ancestors stood but then, denied access to where they lie, to sit on the ground and refuse either to go any further or to get up and leave until Saul's lost mule passes. It is to refuse to leave Beth Hamidraş synagogue and to scream at its vicious guard dog. Irresignation is Lee cycling from Korea to Spain, it is Patrick Leigh Fermor walking from Holland to Istanbul, it is Benjamin Fondane sailing from Paris to Argentina to make a movie that will never be shown and will not survive, it is Adam Sobsey flying all the way to Indonesia to write a play that will never be performed. It is to lie on a breathworker's table and writhe on it week after week, to lie on the theater floor night after night in the darkness and twist one's limbs and testify. *I, I, I, I am.* By poetry, by cries, by faith, by suicide.

Ask people. While I was deep in my reading of Fondane's poetry and philosophy—including some that has not been translated from the original French, of which I have a shaky grasp and found very difficult and slow going—I corresponded with an American poet and Fondane scholar who teaches at a university. When I brought up Fondane's refusal to accept his release from Drancy without his sister, the scholar vehemently objected: "We're talking about relatively obscure Jewish intellectuals (poets! and more or less 'degenerate' ones to boot) in the great machine of the Holocaust. To believe they were 'special' to the Germans enough to be liberated is just so much nonsense." It followed that the story about standing by his sister was also "pure fiction," the scholar wrote to me, "mythobiography." In any case, he concluded, "No one has any evidence!"

I could have countered that Fondane's provisional release wasn't granted by the Germans. Drancy was a French prison. The appeal was to the French authorities and wasn't founded on Fondane's literary importance but rather on his military service. Yet to draw a rebuttal from the mountain of facts, from Reason, seemed entirely beside the point. I might have done better to say that anything is possible when a man is free, and Fondane was surely free, an authentic Jew whom Hitler should have arrested and who gave his life for the sake of his roots. One might be compelled to die, but nothing in the world can compel you to *accept* this death. Death is about *creating* yourself.

I read a book about Jewish genetics. I did not intend to read this book. Heather happened upon it among the effects of her uncle who had recently passed away. He was an avid reader with an enormous collection of books. One was an edition of *The Protocols of the Elders of Zion*: the notorious, and notoriously spurious, antisemitic tract first disseminated around the time my great-grandparents left Romania. When young Patrick Leigh Fermor walked from Holland to Turkey in the year Hitler seized power, he had letters of introduction to members of the central European aristocracy, some of whom attempted to bestow on him their copies of *The Protocols of the Elders of Zion* with assurances that it would make a believer out of him, too.

I would have to read it to know what *The Protocols of the Elders of Zion* actually said about Jews. I was quite keen to read it, in fact, because I remembered that my question "What are Jews?" had been preceded by the question "What have people got against the Jews?" Even if what people had against us was demonstrably false, I wanted to know what it was. *The Protocols of the Elders of Zion* must have been quite compelling for it to convince so many people that Jews were evil. I was quite disappointed when it turned out to contain only vague, warmed-over drivel, and after a few chapters I stopped reading it, not out of offense but out of boredom.

The thesis question posed by the book about Jewish genetics asks whether there is identifiable Jewish DNA. Is our heroic tradition of learning embedded not only in our culture but in our chromosomes? Does Krelboyne run in our blood? Instead of an answer, the author, whose name suggests that he is Jewish, poses another question: "Intelligence, like behavior, remains a highly complex trait and there are plenty of data demonstrating that environmental factors play an essential role in determining it. Jews have a tradition of scholarship that is as old as the Torah. Education has always been a hallmark of Jewish culture. Are we prepared to attribute much or most of that culture to genes?"

Well, are we? And was this question any different from what I had read in *Essential Outsiders*? "For whatever combination of reasons, Europe's Jews have produced an astounding number of success stories in business."

I continued to consult books: books about Jewish souls, Jewish bodies, Jewish science, Jewish history, Jewish law, Jewish customs, Jewish searches, emigrant Jews, excluded Jews, Jews who were killed, Jews who killed themselves, Jews who survived, Jews in love, Jews in school, Jews in America, Jews in Auschwitz. I read thousands of pages about Jews, yet I know how few pages this amounts to in our heroic tradition of learning, the vast appendix to our Book.

Sometimes I pick up *Existential Monday*. Not to read it again but to gaze into the levitating crystal ball of Fondane's face and receive his gaze back.

I also read non-Jewish books that, on rereading, revealed themselves to be Jewish books. Rereading Patrick Leigh Fermor's memoirs, I came across an episode of which I had taken no note when I read it in advance of our trip. In the far northwestern highlands of Transylvania, young Paddy needs a place to take shelter for the night and comes across some Jewish lumberjacks. Mountain Jews. They offer him lodging in their cabin. It transpires that they are also hosting a rabbi and his sons, who are from the foreman's hometown. This cabin of Jews regard Leigh Fermor and his wanderjahr with perplexity. They can't understand what his purpose in walking all the way from Holland to Turkey could possibly be, unless it were in some way related to their own heroic tradition of learning. They ask him if his goal is "to see the world, to study, to learn languages?"

> I wasn't quite clear myself. Yes, some of these things, but mostly—I couldn't think of the word at first—and when I found it—'for fun'—it didn't sound right and their brows were still puckered [...] The foreman shrugged and said something in Yiddish to the others; they all laughed and I asked what it was. 'Est is a goyim naches!' they said. 'A goyim naches', they explained, is something that the goyim like but which leaves Jews unmoved; any irrational or outlandish craze, a goy's delight or a gentile's relish.

The Jews' hilarity over Leigh Fermor's explanation warms them to him. There follows a long night spent in communion over scripture, which culminates in Leigh Fermor and the rabbi reciting Bible verses in alternation,

Paddy in English, the rabbi in Hebrew. "By this time the otherworldly Rabbi and his sons and I were excited," Leigh Fermor writes. "Enthusiasm ran high. These passages, so famous in England, were doubly charged with meaning for them, and their emotion was infectious. Their poetry, their philosophy, their history and their laws were the lodestar of their passion."

The last of these verses is supplied from memory by the young Leigh Fermor. It begins, *Tell it not in Gath*. I leaped to attention: David's elegy for King Saul. This passage was the lodestar of my passion. I put Leigh Fermor down, pulse racing, reached again for my Bible and reread David's elegy for Saul, for me.

Their bonding over Bible verses leads the Mountain Jews to wish that it was the Sabbath so they could designate Paddy their *Shabbos goy*: the non-Jew who performs tasks of work and effort that are strictly forbidden to Orthodox Jews on the day of rest. Leigh Fermor is almost wistful that it is not to be so.

Postparing further, I discovered not just who I was but where I was. The deeper geography. By way of reading a history of the Armenian genocide, I realized that our three-month itinerary, from the Adriatic to the Caspian, had covered the precise and complete west-to-east span of what had once been the Ottoman Empire, and included a stay in its capital.

I had no inkling of this while planning the trip. I went to Albania only because I had an Albanian coworker, of course. Kazbegi, in Georgia, appealed to Heather because it called to her as a place to turn fifty. We extended our route from there to Azerbaijan because Baku was the most accessible touchpoint of the Caspian Sea. We chose Istanbul because it was on the way between Albania and Baku and the most convenient place to meet up with Heather's friends, not because we were interested in the city for its historical importance—or for any other reason at all. Our route was planned not on lines of Reason but leaps of Faith.

In the Around the World class, one of the places we had to bag on the map was Ankara. I learned it was the capital of Turkey and that Turkey had something to do with the Ottoman Empire. But what was "Ottoman," other than a footstool? Had there been a place called Otto, or Ottoma? In Around the World we also had to touch down in Ottawa, a word confusingly similar to Ottoma. But Ottawa had nothing to do with the Ottomans—or did it? What were countries, actually? When I was nine or ten years old, hopping Around the World from one spot to the next, assembling a mountain of facts about each one, nations could just be a matter of names like those engraved on the foreign coins I bought in the mall. German East Africa? British Guiana? The Dutch queen on the Surinamese coin? Where was Surinam? *What* was Surinam?

When I got older, the Ottoman Empire was a vague historical reference to something I didn't know about and didn't need to. But as soon as I arrived in Albania, I discovered the recency of the Ottoman Empire. It was still intact, barely, in 1910, the year my great-grandparents left

Moldavia. Was I, then, perhaps, part Turkish not just on the Sobsey/Sabzi side but also on the Sigel/Lipovici side, and did that account for Grape Zaidie's darkening of the blood and face? Were Turks dark?

Postparing further, I understood that our entire west-to-east course, from Albania to Azerbaijan, had followed the entire length of the route to the Holocaust.

The Balkan Wars, which immediately preceded—and largely triggered—World War I, cost the already fading Ottoman Empire its western territories, including Albania, which declared independence in November 1912. To try to shore up the empire's dwindling power, the Ottomans turned their attention toward Asia: an alternate name for "The Armenian Question" was "The Eastern Question." The genocidal answer began with the Sultan's initial decree that the Ottoman Armenians were to be relocated to Mesopotamia. In practice, and perhaps in unstated intent, this relocation plan was a cover for killing them.

The Armenian genocide intensified during the Great War, during which the Germans were allied with the Turks. A German vice consul to Turkey, who later entered the annals as Hitler's dedicatee of *Mein Kampf,* called the Armenians "the Jews of the Orient." (I thought of the Chinese: "the Jews of Asia.") Another German, a general stationed in Turkey during the war, justified the Turks' slaughter of the Armenians on the grounds that "the Armenian is just like the Jew, a parasite outside the confines of his homeland, sucking off the marrow of the people of the host country. Year after year they abandon their native land—just like the Polish Jews who migrate to Germany—to engage in usurious activities. Hence the hatred which, in medieval form, has unleashed itself against them as an unpleasant people, entailing their murder."

If it was true, and it almost surely was, that the Ottoman Empire's loss of its western territories, and the consequent existential threat to the empire those losses posed, had led to the genocide of the Armenians; and if it was true that the Germans first had the idea to exterminate the Jews by observing that genocide—a slaughter they endorsed, probably enabled, and possibly abetted—then our three-month itinerary had retraced the full overland route that led to the Shoah: from Albania, the western terminus of the Ottoman Empire, one of the lost Balkans that turned the empire's gaze eastward; across Epirus and through Salonika, the Jerusalem of the Balkans; by way of Istanbul, with its traitors' niche displaying the head of Ali Pasha Tepelena; then Armenia, from where the genocidal plague was carried as far east as Baku and back north and west by the Germans, who reopened and expanded Europe's charnel house of Jews.

The three weeks Heather and I spent in Romania were not a localized inquest into my ancestry. They were the confirmation of all I had seen and done along the way: everywhere I had gotten my passport stamped, walked over an old bridge or stood over old graves, visited a museum or walked any town's streets; from the Site of Witness and Memory and the Solomon Museum in Albania to Abraham's saucepan in Istanbul to the literal writing on the wall in Yerevan—*Who, after all, speaks today of the annihilation of the Armenians?*—and again on the wall in Sheki: ŞÖBƏSĪ. And I had traveled these spans of geography and history, Ottoman and Holocaust, in my own lifespan and on the territory of my own body: lying on the sofa filled with revulsion and a necrotic appendix after the Tree of Life slaughter; stretching myself to its furthest length on the floor of the theater in Alexander Technique and contorting myself on the breathworker's table; going Around the World in a childhood classroom to learn geography, and around the world in adulthood to write a play about Ezra Pound. Declining bar mitzvah, accepting a coin from Palestine in a shop in the mall, then standing in another store to be told, *He's Jewish.*

How am I Jewish?

I have not started to practice Judaism as a religion. I do not attend *shul.* I am not bar mitzvah. I have not written to town hall in Dorohoi to ask about my ancestors—although I did hear back from Daniel in Suceava. He spoke with Euge and Viorica. No, they didn't know my family. He was sorry he couldn't be of more help.

It occurred to me that I could possibly help him, by raising money to fund his exhibit of objects on the second floor of the synagogue, just beneath the signs of the zodiac frescoed on the ceiling. But I have not done that either. Each of these acts would only be acts of Reason.

I did make another discovery, however, right here in my hometown: it has a Jewish cemetery.

I had never known it was there, even though I lived for three years in the apartment building directly across the road from the entrance to the cemetery. I was living there when I practiced breathwork. But I never went into the cemetery.

The first time I went in was the day after my appendectomy in 2018. Under doctor's orders to take regular but short recuperative walks, Heather and I drove there and strolled along the cemetery's main drive. But we did not make it to the Jewish section, because we hadn't known it existed. It would not have mattered to me then anyway.

Nearly a year after we returned from Romania, the summer of 2020, we resumed walking in the cemetery because it was an uncrowded and relatively safe place to go during the Covid-19 pandemic. Exploring one day, we happened on its small section of Jewish graves. It was on a downslope at the cemetery's outer fringe, nothing like the lovely hilltop graveyards in Pittsburgh and Darabani.

The Jewish section was behind a gate that was padlocked—access to the Jewish dead, barred yet again—but we found a gate on the other side that was unsecured. Just inside the entrance was a Holocaust memorial: the site of witness and memory where one must stop and pay respects to gain access to the rest of the Jewish dead. Many of the graves predated the incorporation of the city itself. Familiar Jewish names. Silver, Goldstein. Pennies, nickels, dimes, and quarters.

I came up short at one of the headstones. I recognized the name on it.

It was the name of a girl with whom I had gone to junior high school. I did not know her well then, nor did I know what had become of her later. In 2011, I heard that she had killed herself.

I placed a stone on her headstone. There were many other stones on it. I was glad mine was not the only one, that she was well remembered and it was unnecessary to say *You are not forgotten*.

I placed my hand on her gravestone and left it there, as I had placed it on the stones in the graveyard in Darabani.

Here would be another place where this story could end, if it were not my story: another scene of communing with the dead of my tribe in a cemetery on a summer afternoon, in my hometown, as I had communed with the dead of my tribe in a cemetery a year earlier, in their homeland.

But it is my story, and as I stood with my hand on my former schoolmate's grave, a question occurred to me. A Jewish Question:

What happens to Jews after we die?

There is no Jewish Heaven or Hell. I did not know this until I came home from Romania and read the Hebrew Bible. It contains a few references to a realm called *sheol*, which is derived from the same Hebrew letters that give us *Sha'ul*, Saul. SHL, revocalized. This is mere coincidence, as the shared DRH between my hometown and Dorohoi is a coincidence, but it is a satisfying one. It is likewise a satisfying coincidence that *sheol* also sounds like *shul*, which is in fact a Yiddish term derived from the German *schule*, school. Nonetheless: *Sheol, Sha'ul, Şhul;* Death, King, Learning.

Scripture has little to say about *sheol*, and Ecclesiastes warns us against asking what we will find there, because we will find nothing: "no doing nor reckoning nor knowledge nor wisdom in *sheol*." Dig holes in the ground and bury the dead in them. That is as far toward *sheol* as we go. Jewish eschatology ends in the cemetery.

A few weeks after we discovered the Jewish cemetery in our town, Heather and I got together with Julie, our friend who lives a few blocks from where we live for most of the year and the rest of the year in Bucharest, where she took us for carp and Pilates on our first night and I began to get sick. Back home, Julie told us that Cécile, the Pilates instructor, had recently got sick herself. When it wouldn't go away, as a precaution she went to the hospital—and died there.

Of what, we asked?

Julie didn't know. No one who knew Cécile seemed to know. No one seemed to know anything at all about Cécile. When the coroner came, it was discovered that she didn't even have an identity card.

Shortly after Julie told us about Cécile, I began writing this book. Shortly after I began writing it, some people raided the U.S. Capitol. A few of them waved Confederate flags and swastikas. Some wore t-shirts bearing slogans such as *Camp Auschwitz* and *6MWE. 6 Million Wasn't Enough.*

(We will not forget?)

These images were duly alarming, but only to Reason, and Reason was not behind the vandals' actions. I knew this from Fondane: "It is boredom that is the source of sudden changes, of wars without reasons, of deadly revolutions. The historians will say *afterward* that political, economic, and social causes explain this outburst. But they will not have grasped the elementary fact that the people were bored."

The half-dazed grandmother holding a little American flag in the rotunda like it was a lollipop, as though she was on a group holiday tour. The four men sitting empty-eyed under a Revolutionary War painting not long after they had broken into the Capitol and dirtied it a little and were now waiting around for whatever was going to happen next. Bored.

As for the ones with the swastikas and t-shirts, I wished them all dead, just like I wished the man who walked into the Pittsburgh *shul* and killed eleven Jews. The difference was that I repented feeling that way about the man in Pittsburgh, but about the men in Washington I did not.

Two days after the attack on the Capitol, someone hung a Confederate flag outside the Museum of Jewish Heritage, in which my great-grandfather's sheet music hangs.

Benjamin Fondane took his essay title "Existential Monday and the Sunday of History" from another Jew, Kafka: "You are destined for a great Monday! But Sunday will never end."

It is always the Sunday of history. The deep structure of reality will never change. The world is always about to start hating Jews again, hating all of us, *herem*, and we must either live marked or maligned, or we must flee, or else die. This has been true for thousands of years, and it will be true for thousands more. I was fortunate to be born and to have lived, so far, within a brief era and geographical borders of relative safety. I hope I do not live long enough to know the next catastrophe.

A few weeks after the attack on the U.S. Capitol, and about the same time I was finishing my first draft of this book, I was visited by another physical ailment, my first since Romania. For as long as I could remember, a small nodule had resided inertly just inside my left shoulder blade, directly behind my heart. A calcium deposit, a lipoma, or perhaps an accrual of fatty tissue: a curious fact, a small, amusing anomaly. Doctors' diagnoses differed, but they agreed that as long as the nodule wasn't bothering me or getting larger, I could disregard it. It wasn't and I did, for many years.

Suddenly the nodule swelled, turned red, and began to hurt. I resisted treatment until I had no choice but to see a specialist. He recommended an injection of steroids. The injection was worse than ineffective. Almost overnight the nodule swelled again, turned redder, and became more painful. Over the next two weeks, it grew from the size of a marble to the size of a golf ball, became infected, unspeakable. I found it difficult to sit and write. Soon, I had to sleep on my right side only. Then I could not sleep much at all. The growth had to be removed, like my appendix. Postpared.

During the procedure, I lay awake and alert on the table, facedown, feeling only distant pressure where the surgeon cut into me. We talked while he worked. I felt that one of us was speaking from beyond the grave. The surgeon told me that the growth was lodged much deeper than he had expected, and it was surrounded by a great deal of scar tissue. The operation took three times as long as he had scheduled, partly because three layers of stitches were required to sew up the incision his work had required him to make.

At one point during the operation, a question occurred to me: why did he think this had suddenly happened after so many years? He said there were many possible reasons. Or there could be no reason at all.

I recovered quickly, as I did from my appendix. I am generally a very healthy person. Instead of a tattoo I have a scar.

7.

Preface for the Present Moment

i.

Four years passed.

I worked, I ran, I wrote. I wrote this book seven times until it seemed it could not be done again. Yet I felt undone with it even though I sensed that to continue to harbor it could become somehow dangerous, like the threat of infection. I sensed that to release the book I needed to release myself. I needed movement, travel. I thought of going back to Romania.

Instead, I went to Pittsburgh.

Where my ancestors lived.

I did not go there just to stand where they lived. I prepared. I made necessary arrangements. I asked my mother for her memories of locations and addresses. I booked a place to stay and contacted New Light synagogue, where the Sigels were members for three generations, from my great-grandparents to my mother. I explained my relationship to the Sigels and asked if I might visit New Light while I was in Pittsburgh. I was invited to do so. I was also offered a visit to the congregation's cemetery across the Allegheny River, where I would find not only the Sigels' graves but also, in the cemetery chapel, memorial plaques bearing their names.

I said I was interested in my family's history and asked whether New Light might have any archives. I was glad to hear that they did, gladder still that these materials were preserved at the Rauh Jewish Archives in Pittsburgh's Heinz History Center. I was given contact information for the archive's director, who was quick to supply me with the precise box and folder numbers that held New Light's materials. The director also asked me for my family's name and general history. He soon sent me some digital reproductions of newspaper clippings, images, and other evidence of my family's existence.

New Light did not appear on any map. Its website directed visitors to another synagogue, called Beth Shalom. When I asked where I would find the congregation, I learned something I had not known. New Light's membership had been in long and deep decline. Consequently, so had its treasury. In 2017, the congregation sold its building, which it had had built to great fanfare and cost in the 1950s, when my mother was in grade school. They moved into another synagogue about three-quarters of a mile away, conducting services in a small unused sanctuary within the larger. The larger synagogue was Tree of Life. The eleven dead on October 27, 2018, the day before I was hospitalized with appendicitis, included three members of the New Light congregation. I arrived in Pittsburgh one week after the fifth anniversary.

Following the attack, Tree of Life suspended all activities. New Light moved into Beth Shalom, which was also nearby in the Squirrel Hill neighborhood, a stronghold of Pittsburgh Jewry for many decades and to this day one of the most Jewish enclaves in America. En route from where I was staying to Beth Shalom, my eye was caught by an imposing but blank and blocky building looming above Shady Avenue. As I passed it, I saw the words on its façade: TREE OF LIFE.

My breath caught. My fingers tightened around the steering wheel and I felt myself leaning toward it, my limbs, eyes, and organs instinctively clenching and bracing, as if for impact.

Entering Squirrel Hill, I saw many Israeli flags flying on front porches. The flags cheered me until I remembered that hostilities had broken out in Gaza only six weeks earlier.

New Light's president and vice-president were waiting for me inside Beth Shalom. They showed me the congregation's sanctuary, a small room with a capacity of perhaps two hundred people, although only about fifteen or twenty generally attended services, the president told me. His name was Cohen. Postparing, I had learned from the book about Jewish genetics that the surname Cohen indicated a member of the priestly caste. Since then, I had the reflexive habit of regarding all Cohens I encountered in person or in books with some measure of deference.

We got into Cohen's car and made for the cemetery across the river. I asked him why the cemetery was so far away from Squirrel Hill. In the nineteenth and early twentieth centuries, Cohen explained, when many of Pittsburgh's synagogues were established, including New Light, landowners did not want to sell valuable land to Jews, Catholics, or Blacks, who had to settle for distant hillsides so steep they were neither arable nor habitable, good for nothing but graves.

We were among them now. Cohen pointed out that the arrangement represented a hierarchy of sorts: Jewish, then Catholic, then Black, in order of distance from Pittsburgh. Jewish cemeteries occupied both sides of the road around us. Many of their associated congregations no longer existed, Cohen said. That was why so many of the gravestones were nearly black with soot and grime, some of them toppled over.

Just like Darabani, I thought. Just like Romania.

I asked him to pull into one of these derelict cemeteries. I got out of the car and snapped a few pictures, out of some sense of duty.

We pulled up to New Light's cemetery. The steep grade grew even steeper. I remembered the hearse fishtailing in the snow on the final climb as we drove Uncle Larry's body to its grave thirteen years earlier, the last time I had been in Pittsburgh.

It was no trouble to find the family plot. It was so close to the parking lot that I could see "Sigel" on the headstones from the passenger seat. I got out and circulated. I had forgotten to bring any memorial stones. I would not have had enough in any case. It would not have occurred to me, although it should have, that I would find not just my family but the extended Sigel clan, all my great aunts and uncles and their spouses, along with my Romanian great-grandparents, my Boiby and Zaidie, and my Uncle Larry.

Except that my Uncle Larry was not buried here.

I was perplexed. I walked around the plot several times, but there was clearly no headstone for Larry M. Belans. Had the family never had a headstone made? This would have been in violation of the Jewish tradition of installing and unveiling a headstone within a year of the loved one's death, as it is also a violation to cremate a Jewish body or leave it anywhere on the surface of the earth, as the Zoroastrians do. Jewish bodies are quickly interred, ritually mourned, and punctually marked with headstones.

I mentioned Uncle Larry's confusing absence. Cohen had the cemetery directory with him. Uncle Larry's name was not in it. Still, I was sure he was buried here. I attended his funeral. I walked down the hillside to a lower plot that seemed to be unfinished. There was a newer-looking headstone sitting alone, surrounded by piles of gravel and lumps of earth that still looked raw. When I got close enough to read the inscription, I saw that it named a second cousin of mine who died suddenly and unexpectedly—early-onset heart failure, we learned—just days after Uncle Larry had died in 2010. On the stone were the dates, which spanned thirty-six years. At once I understood that the Sigel plot up the hill was full. My Uncle Larry must be buried near where I was now standing, and his absence from the directory a mere administrative oversight or lapse in maintenance, like the sinking of my great-grandmother Lillian's footstone below the ground in the cemetery in Queens when Heather and I had visited it five years earlier. But my second cousin's grave stood alone. The only other stone nearby, about a dozen paces away, was much newer. It was a memorial to the three members of the New Light congregation who had been killed in the shooting on October 27, 2018. Their names were Richard Gottfried, Daniel Stein, and Melvin Wax. The inscription read, "Holy Martyrs."

The absence of my uncle's headstone seemed suddenly of no importance.

This memorial to the martyrs was only a small piece of New Light's remembrance of the attack. At the bottom of the cemetery drive was a small carriage house. Cohen opened the door with his key. Much of the interior had been converted into a fuller memorial. The names of all eleven holy martyrs were on a plaque. There were two large works of stained glass which New Light had commissioned. An impressionistic iconography was worked into the design, which had been adjusted, Cohen explained, in consultation with the families of the dead.

Under a vitrine were preserved the shofar blown by Richard Gottfried for High Holy Day services at New Light; Daniel Stein's Torah study guide, showing his handwritten dates of portions read; and Melvin Wax's travel prayer book, "used throughout his life," according to the captioning text. I thought of the sacred relics in the Privy Room at Topkapı, those replicas of Abraham's saucepan, Moses's staff, David's sword. But I knew the objects before me now were authentic. The accompanying text indicated that they had been provided by two of the men's wives and the daughter of the third.

Also on the wall were memorial plaques from New Light's previous building, the one it had sold. The names of my relatives appeared on these plaques, as I had been told they would. As I had seen on the wall of the synagogue in Dorohoi.

On the opposite wall was a large diorama of New Light's history, which dated to 1899. The original congregation had been chartered as Ohel Jacob, Tent of Jacob. It was rechartered in 1909 as Oir Hudish, New Light, for reasons that remain unclear, although it may have had to do with Ohel Jacob's absorption around the same time of another Romanian congregation. Oir Hudish was consequently known as "the big Romanian shul." Scanning the diorama's text and its accompanying photographs, I recognized it as identical to the History page of New Light's website, with which I had familiarized myself before coming to Pittsburgh. The key to this recognition was the arresting Yiddish word *fussgeyers*, footgoers. The Romanian Jews who came to Pittsburgh were known by this epithet for their having crossed Europe overland in order to sail to America, like my great-grandparents trekking from Dorohoi to Bremen.

Another word I encountered for the first time on New Light's website was *haimish*: "People call us the 'most haimish shul in town,'" the website says. *Haimish* is a Yiddish word that means homey, cozy, familiar.

On the way back to Beth Shalom, Cohen invited me to attend a New Light Sabbath service during my stay in Pittsburgh. I told him I would be sure to do that, and immediately felt that same tightening and bracing in my body that I had felt when I drove past Tree of Life.

ii.

I went for long walks around Pittsburgh. *Fussgeyer.* The weather was surprisingly clement. Not long before the trip I had asked a friend who traveled extensively for work to recommend activities in the city. She told me to make sure to enjoy the nice weather, because I wouldn't get very much of it. Her discouraging response matched my gray memories of Pittsburgh. Yet Pittsburgh was sunny, warm, dry, lustrous, vivifying. The slanting November light burnished the city's handsome Gilded Age architecture and infused the yellow-gold leaves of its many large sidewalk ginkgoes with an auric radiance—intensified, it seemed to me, by the powerful accompanying stench of the trees' fallen fruits that had split or been crushed on Pittsburgh's old cobblestones, releasing one of nature's rankest smells.

It pleased me to take note of the smells, the weather, the architecture, Pittsburgh. One of my strongest regrets after returning home from Romania was that I had been so overcome by my illness that I had observed and absorbed almost nothing of the place itself. I had been to Romania but scarcely seen it, felt it, experienced it—only my own throes.

Walking down Baum Boulevard—it is named for the family from whom descended L. Frank Baum, the author of *The Wizard of Oz*—I came upon Ritter's Diner. I stopped short. I remembered Ritter's. Not from my childhood visits to Pittsburgh, but because I had eaten here once as an adult. My sister and I took our Zaidie there, perhaps twenty-five years earlier. He was quite elderly and had such difficulty chewing and swallowing that he choked violently on his food. For several moments he could not breathe until he ejected the food back up onto his plate. He was so shaken by the incident that we paid our bill immediately and left.

It surprised me that Ritter's was still in business—it looked already quite old when I had come here long ago—and that I had happened on it entirely by accident. This pleased me, but I was perplexed, as I had been perplexed not to find Uncle Larry's gravestone in the New Light cemetery. Under what circumstances had my sister and I brought my Zaidie here? Why had we been in Pittsburgh together at all? It was long before Uncle Larry died.

The neighborhood where I was staying was called Highland Park. I chose it because it was inexpensive and because of associations with my Zaidie and my sister. I remembered him taking us as children to the Highland Park reservoir and walking around it. I put on running clothes and ran up to the reservoir. I recognized it at once—or thought I did. Perhaps I only told myself I recognized it because I knew I had been to it before. Memory is a strong substance but a weak faculty. Even if I recognized the reservoir, did that matter? I ran four, five, six times around it to cover my accustomed distance. With each additional circuit I felt as though I had run off another accumulation of years and memories. How many times around the reservoir would it be necessary to run until I would never have been here in my life until now?

Walking around the Highland Park neighborhood after running, I came to a large and unusual circular structure made of stone that appeared to be of some age. As I got nearer, I saw a sign in front of it advertising apartments for rent, but the building did not look like it was suitable for apartments. It was as imposing and windowless as a fortress. My eyes traveled up the façade to the words *B'Nai Israel* and some Hebrew writing. Ivy grew well over thirty feet up the begrimed stone wall, browning and dying as it climbed. Damaged, dirty pediments and other architectural forms lay stacked and scattered about. Through two ground-floor windows I could see the evidence of extensive water damage, walls whose layers of paint had been peeling for years, and stray pieces of furniture in such disarray that the temple looked as though it had been sacked. I had some awareness that I might be trespassing, that a Romanian dog might appear at any moment. But there was no sign of life, not even around the apartments, which I now saw were in a modern building that jutted out directly, jarringly, from the synagogue's rear left flank. It seemed almost an insult to the original Jewish structure.

I stood in dismayed perplexity for quite a while. Then I texted a picture to my mother and asked if she recognized B'Nai Israel. After a few seconds, she replied, "It's where your Dad and I got married."

My parents' marriage ended when I was eight years old and they took me out of Sunday School. I was not standing where my ancestors stood. I was standing before the place of consecration without which I would not exist. B'Nai Israel was the fortress of my origins. And they were derelict. I began to fret. Beth Hamidraş lurched into my mind.

Why here, I asked my mother, and not at New Light? Because New Light was too small, she said. B'Nai Israel hosted its own congregation's weddings as well as those of other congregations. "All the Jewish girls got married there," my mother told me.

Among the important locations my mother had remembered of her Pittsburgh youth was a house owned and occupied by her grandparents, my Great Boiby and Grape Zaidie, in their late life. The house was large enough to accommodate boarders. Presumably this was their means of income in the late 1940s after closing their grocery (*That's one cigarette—and two eggs!*). For a brief time, the boarders included my mother, her brother, and their parents. The family needed a temporary place to live while they sought a permanent home.

My mother remembered that the house was white and green and that, immediately behind it, down an alley, was a mechanic's garage, also painted green. A few more paces down the alley past the garage was a synagogue, which her grandparents regularly attended—not New Light but another one called the Margaretta Street Shul. They had bought the house for its proximity to the shul, as Jews who observe a certain fidelity to Sabbath law are forbidden to drive or operate anything mechanical on that day, even light switches.

My mother could still recall the address of the house, and soon we had called up an online street view on her computer. The house was still white and green, the same shade. Behind it was the same garage, also green, and as soon as my mother saw its name, Bruno's, she lit up with recognition. Down the alley, just visible, was what appeared to be a rear corner of the shul. My mother said that corner was where the women's entrance was. They went directly upstairs into the gallery while the men lined up and went in through the front door on Margaretta Street.

After we looked at this together, I didn't write down the address and forgot all about the house, garage, and shul.

On the way back from B'Nai Israel to where I was staying, I crossed Mellon Street and remembered that this was the street the house was on. I even remembered the address. I was only two blocks away from it. Three minutes later, I was standing in front of it.

I was standing where my ancestors slept. I was sleeping in their neighborhood.

Just as, at Ali Pasha's monastery in Ioannina, I felt borders redrawing themselves around me, now I felt them reknitting within me, like roots spreading, strengthening, connecting.

I took a few pictures. The porch screens were drawn, and I could not see the young woman until she emerged from behind them and asked, warily, if she could help me. When I explained that my family had owned the house long ago, her demeanor changed. She encouraged me to stop in at the garage and speak with her uncle, who would likely have memories and "loves to talk," she said. Her family owned both the garage and the house. How long had they owned the house, I asked her? She didn't know. As long as she had been alive. I suggested that perhaps her family had bought it from my family. The young woman and I both laughed at that suggestion in our different registers, as the young Albanian translator in the Solomon Museum and I had laughed when he told me that Jews bought wheat from local Albanian farmers in the fall and sold it back to them at twice the price in the winter.

The mechanics were busy and I did not want to disturb them. I walked further along the alley. The Margaretta Street Shul appeared to be defunct, like B'Nai Israel, and headed for dereliction. On its rear façade was a mural captioned with a quotation from the Christian portion of the Bible. In the adjacent gravel lot, which was directly across the alley from the garage, about a dozen cars were parked. A mechanic was working on one of them, his upper body buried in its "distillery of ducts and hoses," as the innards of a car are described by the Jewish writer in his book set in the Burgundian town. When the mechanic emerged, I introduced and explained myself. This was the young woman's uncle. He told me his grandfather had bought the house long ago to live closer to his place of work, as my great-grandparents had bought it even longer ago to live closer to their place of worship. The mechanic had grown up working in the garage, from which the frequent sight of the Margaretta Street Shul's women lining up before services at the rear entrance had left a lasting impression on him. He also remembered a regular chore on late Friday afternoons, while he and his family were closing up the garage for the weekend, when the congregation's men would ask him to come over and turn on the lights for them. "I was their, ah…" he trailed off, unsure if he might be on the point of using a derogatory term. *"Shabbos goy,"* I supplied. "Yeah," he smiled back, relieved.

It was with some unhappiness and even bitterness that he told me how the congregation had come to leave the building decades earlier. It seemed that bad blood had developed with another synagogue in the neighborhood (B'Nai Israel, I thought to myself). The mechanic didn't know why this happened. One of the rival congregation's members had taken it upon himself to increase hostilities by habitually calling the authorities to complain that the synagogue's members had parked their cars illegally on the surrounding blocks. The Margaretta Street congregation had been parking in this way for years and no one minded. The cars weren't in anyone's way and posed no nuisance. Still, the traffic police dutifully came over and ticketed all of them. This went on for some time. The antagonism escalated until the Margaretta Street congregation abandoned its shul and decamped for the suburbs. Much later, the mechanic continued, a Christian organization moved into the building, which explained the quotation muralled onto the wall, but then they, too, had left. The shul was now owned by an anesthesiologist who had evidently intended to rehabilitate the property (although for what purpose the mechanic did not know), but it had sat neglected for years. The mechanic volunteered that he wished the building could be turned into a community arts space. I could imagine myself moving into my ancestral neighborhood and running the arts space, presenting theatrics, perhaps even in Yiddish like Avram Goldfaden in Iaşi. I consider myself a song and dance man.

The mechanic was called over to help with a sedan of a deep and vivid magenta color I had never seen on a car in my life. It was parked under the deep green façade of the garage. The shop had been very busy lately, the mechanic told me, almost in confidence, as we walked toward the car, betraying a little fatigue and stress from overwork. He jokingly asked me if I was looking for a job. (At least I think he was joking.) The colleague who had called him over was much younger, likely still in high school, probably his nephew or son. The older mechanic reached down into the distillery of ducts and hoses, his body straining with contortion and effort. He came up as though from a well, clutching a hard clear plastic reservoir or receptacle. "Yeah, it's cracked," he said, showing it to the boy.

I had a suddenly powerful urge to bring him my car. It was not in need of any repairs, but perhaps he could find a cracked part. I was eager to resume commerce between our families more than half a century after our first and only transaction, the sale of the green-and-white house from my ancestors to his. I murmured something to the effect of having Bruno's perform a pre-trip inspection, as I would have to drive four hundred miles home in just over a week's time. The mechanic's response was both wary and weary. I apologized for taking up his valuable time and excused myself, leaving the family to its generational business and ancestral home.

I texted some pictures of the alley and its landmarks to my mother, who responded with glee, and to my first cousin who had called our story so common it was almost universal. During my multiyear stint of postparing, he had become something of a family archivist and I thought the images might interest him. He replied: "I was bar mitzvah'd around the corner."

This confused me. Uncle Larry had moved their family to Indiana before my cousin was bar mitzvah age. Why had my cousin been bar mitzvah'd here? "The same rabbi that bar mitzvah'd my dad was still at Margaretta Street," my cousin explained, "and it was easier for us to come there than for all the extended family in Pittsburgh to schlep to Indiana." He did qualify, however, that it bothered him that women were restricted to the balcony, so the ceremony was held in a smaller chapel inside the shul where all genders were permitted.

I took the opportunity to ask him about the perplexing absence of his father's grave from the New Light cemetery. His answer was no less perplexing. "My dad asked (weirdly, on his birthday a couple weeks before he died) to be cremated, which was unexpected given tradition, so we talked about it quite a bit. That's what he wanted, that's what we did."

The necessary arrangements.

That was why I didn't remember a single moment of Uncle Larry's graveside service. There wasn't one.

But when had I been to New Light cemetery?

It hit me all at once. It was the same day I went to Ritter's.

My Zaidie didn't choke on his food because he was old. He choked because he was recovering from pneumonia. His lungs and esophagus were weak. The infection was so serious that he had to be admitted to the hospital, where the doctors feared he might die. A few days later, my Boiby had a sudden heart attack in the way of some spouses whose conjugal connection runs so long and deep that it becomes impossible to live without the other. She survived the attack, but her body was by then so fragile from years of osteoporosis and undernourishment that she died a few weeks later.

Meanwhile, my Zaidie, improbably, recovered, only to bury his wife.

My mother, my sister, and I flew to Pittsburgh for my Boiby's funeral. On the morning of the funeral, while my mother prepared herself for the day's events, my sister and I took our disconsolate, debilitated Zaidie to Ritter's. After the choking incident, he required extra time to recover in his room. My mother worried we would be late for the service in the funeral home. After that, the hearse skidded in the snow on the way up to the cemetery. It was January 1997, thirteen years before Uncle Larry died. And now it was thirteen years since.

The circumstances of my previous visit to New Light

cemetery were settled, then. But after the hearse skidding in the snow, I don't remember anything about burying my Boiby.

iii.

I passed Tree of Life again on my way to New Light Sabbath services at Beth Shalom. I kept myself from tensing or bracing by fixing my gaze on the road and willfully averting it from the building, as you might from an animal that may be dangerous.

I remembered to take a yarmulke from the box in the entryway to the New Light sanctuary and put it on my head before going inside. A man I presumed to be the rabbi was leading some preliminaries. I could not follow them. President Cohen was inside and waved to me welcomingly. After I had taken a seat in the very last row of pews and the service had gotten underway, he approached me and asked if I wouldn't mind wearing tallit. I was abashed. Cohen led me into a vestibule where communal *tallitot* were kept. I put one on for the first time in my life, returned to my seat, and felt at once deeply comforted and deeply fraudulent.

The next two hours resembled that type of dream in which everyone knows what is happening and what to do except you. Perhaps you recognize fragments, as I recognized refrains like *Baruch atah Adonai*, but these familiar words and sounds were cautionary signposts that marked off long stretches of incomprehension.

At one point, my attention wandering, my eyes fell on the door behind the rabbi's right shoulder. The EXIT sign above it was an urgent red, as though to override all other instruction. I was suddenly aware that an exit was also an entrance and that anyone at all might burst through it at any moment.

I was called to attention when the man I had thought was the rabbi, but was instead some sort of leader or elder, came down the aisle, leaned over me, and whispered a question: Are you a Cohen or a Levy? The priestly castes. I replied that I was neither. "Will you take the third aliyah, then?" the man asked me. I did not know the meaning of this word or how his second question followed from my answer. I managed to say that I was merely here to observe today. "Okay," he said, with no sign of judgment or affect, a sort of breezy unconcern, almost as though, at the instant I declined to take the third aliyah, I had simply ceased to exist. At least he had not ordered me out.

Later, I looked up *aliyah*. It is Hebrew for "rise" or "ascent" and connotes the return to the Holy Land, the going-back-up to Israel. In its more quotidian usage, *aliyah* refers to congregation members going up to recite Torah verses during service. The first and second aliyot are strictly reserved for Cohanim and Levites, the remainder for non-priestly members of the tribe. I now understood the elder's offer to have been a form of welcome and felt just as I had many years earlier in the mall when the store clerk correctly guessed that I was Jewish, and I was dismayed to have lost the game.

New Light congregation members went up and took the aliyot in turn. Soon there were several people gathered around the Torah, piecing it together like it was a large puzzle for which they did not have the box cover.

Occasionally one of them would stumble and be gently corrected or self-correct with a chagrined chuckle or mumbled apology. I felt relieved that I had known just enough to avoid stepping into the worst kind of actor's nightmare, in which you walk onstage into a play you have not rehearsed and indeed have never seen the script. Yet I also longed to be up there with them, sounding out Hebrew with those elderly Jews, watchful and wise over their scroll as a parliament of owls, heedless of the EXIT sign behind them.

There followed the rabbi's homily. He took sober note of the conflict in Gaza and read from a letter or an editorial written many years earlier by another rabbi, perhaps a Pittsburgher, arguing for the necessity of a Jewish state. After this reading, congregants were invited to invoke the names of Jewish souls they knew who were at that moment living in Israel and send up prayers to them.

In the lobby after the service, the congregation socialized lightly over juice and cookies to which I did not feel I should help myself even though I was quite thirsty and hungry. President Cohen introduced me to the rabbi, explaining that my family had once been members of New Light. The rabbi misunderstood and thought I lived in Pittsburgh. After I clarified that I was in fact visiting from North Carolina, he was quick to volunteer the coincidence that his previous rabbinate was with a synagogue in North Carolina just a half hour's drive from where I live. I invoked the name of the synagogue nearest me there and said I had gone to it long ago. "For your bar mitzvah," the rabbi said, presumptively, as though completing my sentence.

I merely nodded, not daring to tell him I never was bar mitzvah'd. In fact it seemed best not to divulge anything at all about myself, either for fear of being further misunderstood or, worse, too well understood and consequently dismissed. The rabbi repeated his misapprehension that I lived in Pittsburgh and remained perplexed by my purpose and presence at New Light. All at once, I did, too. I felt alien, groundless, inadequate, imprudent, intrusive, foolish, lost, and terribly lonely, and suddenly on the point of an attack of the missy feeling. To try to stave it off, I asked the rabbi questions about his rabbinate in North Carolina, to which he gave fluid and full answers, none of which I now remember. After a few of these questions and answers, an ancient member of the New Light congregation approached and began speaking to him as if I was not there at all. I took the interruption as an opportunity to excuse myself, bid President Cohen goodbye, thanking him for inviting me, went outside Beth Shalom, took out my phone, and immediately emailed the only living relative I have in Pittsburgh: the father of my second cousin who died young and is buried on the declivity of New Light cemetery. I barely know this man. I have not seen or communicated with him since my Uncle Larry's funeral just days after his own son's death at age thirty-six. He is in the habit of sending mass emails on Fridays wishing the recipient a good Shabbos and adding a politically charged image or strident quote that is invariably in stark contrast with my own worldviews. I have never responded to these emails. Before I went to Pittsburgh, I had briefly considered contacting him but resolved not to. Now I found myself letting him know I was in town on business and would like to see him if he had time. He responded within minutes: he would like to see me, too, but had recently had a triple-bypass heart operation, was suffering from debilitating post-surgery leg pain, and in any case was in Florida.

About the New Light rabbi I later discovered what I ought to have foreknown. He had, of course, been conducting Sabbath services in New Light's sanctuary within Tree of Life on October 27, 2018. When the armed man entered and began shooting, the rabbi had led members of his congregation out of the sanctuary and into a storeroom he had discovered just a few weeks earlier, the New Light congregation having only recently moved into Tree of Life, still unfamiliar with the building. The rabbi then managed to escape unharmed through a rear door and seek help. One of the people in the storeroom, Melvin Wax, hearing no more gunfire and thinking the attack over, opened the door onto the corridor to reveal the assailant, who shot him to death. For many months afterwards, the rabbi found it difficult to lead services and suffered from insomnia, anxiety, depression, episodes of disorientation and bouts of forgetfulness, once committing the error of neglecting to put on his tallit until his wife reminded him. Exactly one year after the attack, October 27, 2019, he was among the speakers at a public commemoration.

Hundreds of people from all walks of Pittsburgh life attended, and the event planners had agreed in advance that politics should be kept out of the proceedings. During the rabbi's speech, however, he stunned everyone and offended many by pleading for gun control. Some time later, he was forced to issue a public apology.

The vast reading room of the Rauh Jewish Archive was dark wood and library quiet. I was the only visitor. I requested the boxes that had already been identified for me by the archive's director and took a seat at one of the long dark wood tables, where there was a supply of latex gloves to ensure preservation of materials. My heart began to pound, even harder when the boxes arrived.

The New Light archive was mostly limited to the decade of the 1960s. I had been hoping to find records from New Light's earliest days at the turn of the twentieth century. Little had been preserved. I did find a handful of old photographs in which my Grape Zaidie appeared—his name appeared in the captions—and others depicting relatives of the next generation: my Boiby and Zaidie, their siblings and siblings' spouses. These images were as inert to me as the names on the graves and memorial plaque in the New Light cemetery.

I found lists of fund drive donors and the amounts of their individual contributions. All forty-four of them were either $1 or $2. There were rabbi and cantor contracts, work invoices, building estimates, income and expense ledgers, a 1934 promissory note from the congregation's treasurer vowing to pay back $562.20 for which he could not account. Had he lost the money or stolen it? Which would have been worse?

A large portion of the archive was taken up by the minutes of the monthly meetings of the New Light Sisterhood. The Sisterhood's chairwoman was a great aunt of mine. She was the mother of the relative I had contacted who regretted that he was in poor health and in Florida. I thought of the large amount of time this great aunt must have devoted to her duties as chair of the Sisterhood. I thought of the constancy and dailiness of the Sisterhood whose members, relegated to the congregation's administrative balcony, so to speak, nonetheless organized and oversaw the congregation's busy calendar of functions; fed its financial current with fundraising drives; planned its banquet dinners, parties and indeed nearly all its nonceremonial events; and wrote New Light's voluble quantity of quotidian communication: announcements, death condolences, even Chanukah skits. Song and dance women. Everything haimish issued from the Sisterhood.

My initial disappointment at finding little in the way of very old materials gave way to a delight in the archive's sheer abundance of life: the simple but practical evidence of my ancestral congregation's ordinary world. When I had first learned of the existence of the archive from the congregation's vice-president, and for many weeks after I visited it and returned home from Pittsburgh, I persisted in misreading and mispronouncing the archive's name as *Ruah*, not *Rauh*, transposing the vowels. I had taken an interest in the Hebrew word *ru'ah*, which appears often in the Hebrew Bible, usually translated as "breath" or "spirit"—the lifegiving force both within and without, for which nearly every culture around the world has its own word. It was this breath, spirit, life, *ru'ah*, that I found in the archive. Not the preservation of the dead, but the record of life.

I drove from the Heinz Center to the Hill District. This was where my great-grandparents and in fact most immigrant Eastern-European Jews settled when they arrived in Pittsburgh, and where Ohel Jacob and New Light, among numerous other synagogues, were originally chartered and located. By the early twentieth century, Pittsburgh was home to fifty thousand Jews, who formed one-tenth of the city's overall population, a proportion fifty times greater than that which obtained in the rest of world. When the Sigels came to Pittsburgh, it was one of the most Jewish places on earth. If Salonika was the Jerusalem of the Balkans, Pittsburgh was the Jerusalem of the United States.

The Hill was its heart. The swelling community was "most picturesque," a journalist of the era wrote, "lined with shops, groceries, bottle dealers, Kosher meat shops, fish marts, clothing shops, stogy factories, and in summer teeming with hundreds of women, frolicking children, quaint men with ill-fitting clothes and high hats, push carts, street pianos, peddlers, hucksters, and in fact a kaleidoscope of color, life, and activity to be seen nowhere else in this city." Yet there was another litany of words attached to the Hill: overcrowded, odoriferous, quarrelsome, fetid, sweaty, dirty; a place of filth, sewer rats, poverty, nakedness, vice. "At nighttime it looks very poetic and picturesque," a reporter warned, "but when the light of day breaks forth, what a disenchantment! The Jewish people are furnishing more, alas, a good deal more, than the average rate of immorality in this community."

The Hill District was not strictly Jewish. It was a diverse slum. The Black population on the Hill exploded from a mere two hundred souls in 1900 to more than six thousand just a decade later, and to ten thousand by 1920. Crime was high. My cousin sent me a news story he had found in a 1928 edition of the *Jewish Criterion*—the era's widely-read Jewish paper of record in Pittsburgh—in which gun-wielding thugs, "believed by the police to be raw amateurs," were reported to have walked into "the store of Mrs. M. Sigel," my Great Boiby, who foiled their threat to rob her with four mere words: "Come around next week." The bandits, shamed, or merely confused, fled.

The store and the Jews are long gone from the Hill. By the middle of the twentieth century, they had moved to Squirrel Hill and the neighborhood where I was staying. The Hill fell into a deep decline from which it has never recovered. I passed row after row of crumbling houses, some burnt black, a large, abandoned church in an advanced state of collapse, and many other signs of poverty, degeneration, and dereliction, all somehow intensified by the extreme steepness of the Hill. Cresting the grade at a complicated six-way intersection, I had two or three minutes' wait for the traffic light to change. Off to my right, the view was of the top of the verdigris cupola and steeple of a church. I thought of Gjirokastra, Albania, where I had been just before going to Berat and its Solomon Museum.

Gjirokastra is even steeper than Pittsburgh, and it seems to be constructed almost entirely of heavy, rough stone. It is a former stronghold of Ali Pasha Tepelena and the birthplace of Ismail Kadare, the great Albanian novelist whose magnum opus *The Concert* was among the few surplus objects I took with me on our trip in 2019. A number of his novels are set in Gjirokastra, which he calls "a very strange city indeed. In some places you could walk down the street, stretch out your arm, and hang your hat on a minaret. Many things in it were simply bizarre, and others seemed to belong in a dream."

I felt a little dizzy. Perhaps I was just very hungry. I drove to Ritter's. It was not far from the Hill.

I took a seat at the counter directly across from the kitchen window, watching the waitresses glide over to gather plates at the bark of the cook in the window, ladle syrup or soup, and pour coffee. Years of restaurant work have made this traffic familiar to me, stabilizing, comforting—haimish. Doubly so at Ritter's, which has been in business since 1951 and owned by the same family since 1966. The gruff cook was the presiding doyen, along with the man at the register, his brother, like the pair of brother mechanics at Bruno's. Ritter's is the kind of place where a regular finishes his lunch, rises from his stool, drops a mound of small bills onto the counter next to his place—Ritter's accepts only cash—and announces, "I'll be back tonight for the mashed potatoes."

I was tempted by CHICKEN MARSALA 2 SIDES $12.95 on the list of specials but decided to make a safer choice. I ordered the Ritter's Club, fries, and coffee. My order arrived promptly—it was well after the lunch rush on a Tuesday afternoon and there were only a few tickets hanging in the kitchen window. I ate half my sandwich, deeply absorbed. As I was preparing to pay and leave, an elderly couple sat down on the stools directly to my right. There were empty stools up and down both sides of the counter. The woman's face and body were just inches from mine. She looked like the great aunts I grew up visiting in Pittsburgh and was probably about eighty years old.

They were Jews. In fact they were Cohens. Our discourse flowed easily, and soon we were talking about Jews, about being Jewish. "There's a trait," Mrs. Cohen said. "I'm not sure if it's here," she said, touching her head—"or here," touching her heart—"but there's a trait."

I explained my purpose in Pittsburgh and mentioned B'Nai Israel. Mr. Cohen replied that he had grown up a member of that synagogue. He quickly added that it was very near the Margaretta Street Shul. Mrs. Cohen grew up attending Rodef Shalom, which was one of several synagogues in Squirrel Hill, although it had originally been located downtown in a stately and expensive shul built by its congregation. Rodef Shalom is the oldest continuously active congregation in Pittsburgh. It was founded before the Civil War by the first significant wave of European Jews to arrive in the city, the generally affluent German-speaking class: families such as the Kaufmanns, whose famed namesake department store empire made them one of the most powerful forces in Pittsburgh during the first half of the twentieth century, when the eleven-story flagship emporium ranked among the ten largest department stores on earth. Rodef Shalom was an early proponent of American Reform Judaism and, in 1885, hosted the formal promulgation of the first major document calling for a Reformist American Jewry. The document was called the Pittsburgh Platform. It was not long, however, before some of the congregation's members, preferring more traditional practices, left Rodef Shalom and founded their own synagogue: Tree of Life.

The Cohens allowed that their differing upbringings, Reform and Conservative, had made their marriage not always comfortable, but they both came down firmly on the same side of the conflict in Gaza. Mrs. Cohen put her fork down and explained her opinion succinctly: "We must have Israel."

Whether we must or mustn't have Israel never occurred to me until this moment. In my lifetime there had always been Israel. She had been born before its founding. To her it was a fragile nation. But I could only regard the violence in Gaza as the latest outburst of tribal hatreds, territorial zealotry that had endured for thousands of years and could only end when one tribe wiped the other off the face of the earth, total destruction, put under the ban, pogrom, *herem*.

Soon we were discussing the Tree of Life slaughter. It had recently been in the news. Three months before I arrived in Pittsburgh, five years after the attack, the assailant had been sentenced to death. Mrs. Cohen gave a resigned but disappointed shrug and said, "It won't stick."

I asked the Cohens about Jewish life in Pittsburgh today. They were quick to lament that the city's Jewish population was shrinking. I replied that, compared to where I lived and in fact everywhere I had ever been, Jewry seemed alive and well, especially in Squirrel Hill. This they conceded, "but it's not what it was," Mrs. Cohen insisted. A better example, she said, was Bloomfield, Michigan, outside Detroit, where one of her daughters lived with her own child and grandchild—she now told me with some little pride that she was a great-grandmother, to which I supplied the obligatory response that she looked as though she could not possibly be that old. The Cohens were about to go to Bloomfield for Thanksgiving. Mrs. Cohen was very excited. Bloomfield had twenty-five Jewish delis, she said, as opposed to just one remaining in Squirrel Hill. I thought of Domnul David telling Patrick Leigh Fermor, in 1934, that if he wanted to see thriving communities of Jews he must go to Moldavia, where virtually entire towns were Jewish, like his own, Dorohoi. Evidently, in 2023, I should go to Michigan.

The Cohens and I sat talking for so long that they had time to order, eat, box up their leftovers, and pay. They had been warmly doted on by the entire staff, clearly longstanding regulars of the most welcome kind. When they got up to leave, Mrs. Cohen and I embraced. I watched them amble back into the rear dining room, she pert and put-together, he shuffling in gray sweats. They disappeared like actors into the wings. After they were gone,

one of the waitresses—around my age, tattooed, a sculptress by calling, as she had told me—refilled my coffee yet again and said: "It's so refreshing to hear people having an intelligent conversation."

There's a trait.

She then vouchsafed the information that Mr. Cohen, despite his humble appearance and generally quiet presence—his wife had done most of the talking—had recently retired from his position as head of a surgical department at the nearby hospital. Doctor Cohen, not Mister.

Bloomfield, Michigan, is indeed a largely Jewish enclave. The top recent news story I found described an incident that had occurred during Bloomfield High School's Diversity Day in the spring of 2023. The guest speaker was a Palestinian-American who had recently run unsuccessfully for a Michigan congressional seat. She went off-topic to deliver a screed in which she called Zionists "occupiers" and accused Israel of genocide in the Gaza Strip. This was half a year before the armed conflict began. All 1,700 students were in mandatory attendance. According to the story, "some Jewish students abruptly left the assembly in tears."

Heather flew up to join me for my last two nights in Pittsburgh. From the airport, I took her straight to the Hill and then to lunch at Ritter's, where I could not help feeling disappointed that the Cohens were not there. Then we took a long walk. We went past Tree of Life, Beth Shalom, and into a store that sold nothing but Judaica. Heather bought candles for Chanukah, which was upcoming. We walked back to Highland Park by way of B'Nai Israel and, finally, the green-and-white house, Bruno's garage, and the Margaretta Street Shul. I felt as though I was showing her around my hometown.

I also wanted to solve two related puzzles. When Dr. Cohen had told me that he had grown up attending B'Nai Israel and volunteered that it was near the Margaretta Street Shul, his way of referring to my great-grandparents' synagogue made it clear that the term "Margaretta Street Shul" wasn't limited to my family's usage, as I had assumed. Was this really its name? It was only scarcely less colloquial than "Big Romanian Shul." And if it was the name, why "Margaretta Street"? The shul was not on Margaretta Street and in fact there did not seem to be a street by that name at all. The entrance faced East Liberty Boulevard. The alley where the women lined up to enter was called Mathews Way.

When I had first found the house, garage, and shul, I became so absorbed in conversation with the mechanic that I neglected to go all the way around the building.

Heather is always disposed to see a thing from all sides. We went to East Liberty Boulevard and saw on the building façade the words ADATH JESHURUN. Our phones told us that *Adath* meant congregation, community. *Jeshurun* is an archaism that appears in the Bible only four times, three of them in Deuteronomy. It is a sort of fond epithet for Israel, as the United States is sometimes poeticized as Columbia and Albania as Illyria. *Adath Jeshurun*: Community of Israel. *B'Nai Israel*: Children of Israel.

We walked along East Liberty Boulevard. It ended one block away at Negley Avenue, on which stood B'Nai Israel just three hundred meters to the south. There was a small lane on the other side of Negley Avenue. It was signposted Margaretta Street. It extended only one short, upward-sloping block until it ended in the parking lot of an apartment complex. East Liberty Boulevard had apparently replaced Margaretta across Negley Avenue, leaving only this vestige, appendage, appendix.

Heather suggested we drive home by way of Falling-water. Like anyone else who has once seen a picture of the iconic Frank Lloyd Wright house, I could imme-diately call its precipitously cantilevered exterior to my mind's eye. I knew what it looked like and who designed it, but nothing else. I did not even know where it was, only seventy miles from Pittsburgh.

I certainly did not know that Fallingwater was the home of Jews.

It pleases me that I did not know this. It pleases me that, just as there is an endless amount of Jewish liter-ature I will never have time to read, there is also a deep Jewish force behind more history than I will live long enough to learn.

Edgar and Liliane Kaufmann were the second genera-tion of the same Pittsburgh Kaufmann family who helped found Rodef Shalom, from which came the Pittsburgh Platform, its promulgation of American Reform Judaism, and Mrs. Cohen. Edgar and Liliane—her given name was Lillian, the same as my paternal great-grandmother, al-tered to appear more sophisticated, less Jewish—were not only spouses but also first cousins. They had to be married in New York because Pennsylvania law prohib-ited the union of cousins. The marriage was an apparent consolidation of family forces as much as a consecration of love. It seems plausible, in fact, that Edgar was meant to wed a different cousin, but she committed suicide in her early adulthood.

By the time of the Great Depression, Edgar and Liliane had used their partnership to take complete control of Kaufmann's department store, whose success they took to almost unimaginable heights—literally, in the case of Liliane's eleventh-floor luxury boutique, which she named Place Vendôme in homage to the haute epicenter of style in Paris. The couple parlayed their wealth into lofty status among the Pittsburgh elite, their social capital limited only by being Jews. Among their holdings was a parcel of land in southwestern Pennsylvania's Laurel Highlands, a former campsite for millworkers whose extant cabins the Kaufmanns used for both personal and company retreats. In the mid-1930s, they decided to build a proper weekend home, insisting on this term to distinguish it from a country home or a summer home. "What we wanted at Fallingwater," wrote the Kaufmanns' only child, Edgar Jr., "was neither lordly stateliness nor a mimicry of frontier hardihood, but a good place for city people to renew themselves in nature."

The emblematic source of this renewal was a waterfall on Bear Run, the tributary that ran through the Kaufmanns' property. The view of the cascade was restorative and its roar invigorating, as was swimming in the pool at its base, which was bracingly cold even at the height of summer. The family envisioned building a dreamhouse that would give them this view. Frank Lloyd Wright disregarded his commissioners' vision. Instead, he situated the structure directly atop the falls, thereby making the home part of the view itself, and placing his Jews in a position at once exalted and precarious.

Fallingwater is dazzling from outside. Inside, it must be one of the least haimish estates ever built, from its cold concrete walls and floors down to the furniture and the fireplace utensils, nearly all of which Wright designed or selected. Immediately upon entering the cramped and dank vestibule, my reaction matched that of the many visitors who, as Fallingwater's biographer Franklin Toker puts it, "find its interior too dark, or too cold, or too rough, its hallways too narrow, its ceilings too low, its walls too barren of ornament, its view too restricted, [deploring] the confining proportions, the harshness of the materials, and the cavelike environment." I did not ask myself, as Toker laments of visitors like me, "whether Wright might have *wanted* Fallingwater to be dark."

If he did, it may be for the reason Toker suggests: "It would be hard to find a house plan that better charted the dynamics of a dysfunctional family." It is not quite correct to say Edgar and Liliane were unhappily married. They created a glittering life together, genuinely adored one another—an adoration that was most alive at Fallingwater, the lodestar of their passion—and they shared a bloodline, of course. But Edgar was "the biggest playboy in Pittsburgh," Fallingwater's longtime cook recalled. "Make that the Western world." He did not hide his philandering from Liliane or indeed from anyone at all. She asked for a divorce in 1928 but changed her mind and devoted her heart and mind to Place Vendôme. By the early 1950s, Edgar was openly consorting with one of his business associate's administrators. Lonely, despondent, borderline anorexic, and dependent on alcohol and pills, Liliane died at Fallingwater in 1952 at age sixty-three, overdosing on Seconal in her bedroom. It is not clear whether her death was a suicide, like the Kaufmann cousin Edgar might otherwise have married. He died three years later, in 1955.

The bodies of Edgar and Liliane are in a crypt on the Fallingwater grounds. Its Giacometti-designed door attracted so many tourists that their son, Edgar Jr., to whom stewardship of the estate fell, instructed the staff to stop landscaping the area around the crypt. Eventually it became so overgrown that it could no longer be found. Another derelict Jewish cemetery. *Vegetation. Not maintained.*

Edgar Jr.'s passions were nothing like his father's. He was born in 1910, two months before my great-grandparents emigrated from Europe. He quit the family department store business as soon as he came of age and devoted himself instead to the arts, and to a single, lifelong partner, who was himself an esteemed designer. Edgar Jr. eventually became a curator at New York's Museum of Modern Art, an art history lecturer at Columbia, and an astute collector whose holdings were sold for hundreds of millions of dollars after his death. But the jewel of his collection was Fallingwater, and he doted on this inheritance. He also altered its interior, largely to remove any trace of the family who lived in it. His removal, for example, of the oil portraits of his Orthodox great-grandparents, which had been commissioned by his father, was part of his effort to "de-Judaeize the house," Franklin Toker writes. "Today's visitors see nothing in the house to suggest that the

Kaufmanns were Jews. Edgar Jr. made sure Fallingwater was free of anything Jewish because so was his life." He was what was called at the time *déraciné*. Uprooted.

In addition to de-Judaeizing Fallingwater, Edgar Jr. arranged for its transfer, during his lifetime, along with thousands of acres around it, to the Western Pennsylvania Conservancy. The bequest ensured the home's survival in perpetuity, and it included funds to keep the building not only upright but habitable. The beds are still made, as though the Kaufmanns might return at any time. "Conservation is not preservation," Edgar Jr. wrote. "Preservation is stopping life to serve a future contingency; conservation is keeping life going."

He kept more life going than he knew. After his death in 1989, it was discovered that Frank Lloyd Wright had so mis-engineered the building's cantilevering and his builders had taken such shortcuts in erecting it that it was on the verge of collapse. An arduous labor of years and a fortune were required to shore it up. Edgar Jr.'s bequest had provided for the rescue of America's greatest house from ruin, and, not incidentally, enduring proof of Wright's still unrivalled status as the greatest of all American architects. For this prescience, Toker bestows on Edgar Jr., whom he knew and who eventually shunned him over a petty complaint, the honorific "Lord of Fallingwater." But perhaps it was never really the Kaufmanns' from the start. I could not help noticing that their architect not only gave Fallingwater its name, but had built that name around the consonant cluster of his own initials, FLW.

The day of our visit was cold and rainy. The house was damp and cold inside. I could not shake a chill in my bones and spirit, which was deepened by the grief and gloom which seemed to exude from every room.

After reading Toker, I wondered whether the sorrow I felt had nothing to do with the house. "Fallingwater is architectural manna," he writes, "because it allows us to be reminded of whatever we are carrying inside us."

After our visit, we continued southeast through the Appalachians toward Heather's family home in rural Virginia, where we would spend the night before returning to North Carolina. The rain and fog were so dense and unrelenting that I could barely see the road after nightfall. I felt just as I had felt when I first drove past Tree of Life: every cell of my body braced, my hands gripping the wheel, pulse surging with adrenaline, my heart pounding nearly as hard as it had pounded while I was climbing Kazbegi in Georgia. But unlike the momentary jolt by Tree of Life, the throes lasted the entire four-hour drive. Later that night, drained, exhausted, protected under warm covers as I drifted into heavy sleep, I understood that I had not gone to Pittsburgh to visit archives or graves or congregations. I had not gone in search of my roots or in service to this book. I went to Pittsburgh under the question of home. Perhaps that is also why I went to Romania.

It is just as the Lord of Fallingwater wrote: not preservation, stopping life, but conservation, keeping life going. Another Jew writes that Jewish stories don't end. They merely stop. Endings are Christian. Epiphanies, Revelations. Jewish life is not about finding ourselves. Our Sunday will never end. Jewish life is about creating ourselves out of our own inadequacies, writing ourselves out of our own appendices, in permanent revolt against resignation, permanent danger of rupture and expulsion. I shall go on becoming another man. You hold my life in your hands. And I am still alive.

ACKNOWLEDGMENTS

Spuyten Duyvil Publishing, like my tribe, is comparatively small, but also resilient, faithful to itself, and long-lived—an exemplar of Jewish qualities and spirit. I'm grateful to be part of their tribe, to which I was led by two people: my close friend Ari Berenbaum, an ally of my book, introduced me to his friend Kylan Rice, whose wonderful *Incryptions* Spuyten Duyvil also publishes. Both Kylan and Ari read an early draft of *A Jewish Appendix* and gave me valuable feedback.

I wrote the first draft in one of the most haimish dwellings I have ever called home, situated in one of the most beautiful places I have ever been. Heather and I rented a cabin on House Mountain in Virginia's Blue Ridge range from Philip Clayton and his wife Ava Tucker, whose stewardship and sharing of their extraordinary acreage, sense of home and place, generous spirits, and loving example as a couple I will never forget. It's doubtful that I would have been able to write this book anywhere else.

For friendship, encouragement, counsel, wisdom, draft-reading, advocacy, refuge, and more, I'm indebted to Julie Tetel Andresen, Quincy Beard, Christine Council, Dan D'Allaird, Heidi Johnson, Richard Krawiec, Nayeon Lee, Amanda Rouse, and Stephanie Whetstone. I'm grateful to every person who appears in this book.

In Pittsburgh, I was graciously welcomed and guided by New Light President Steve Cohen and Vice-President Barbara Caplan. My understanding, experience, and appreciation of the city were deepened by Barbara S. Burstin's *Steel City Jews*, her indispensable two-volume history, and by Mark Oppenheimer's outstanding *Squirrel Hill*, which chronicles the Tree of Life attack and its surrounding community's response. Franklin Toker's *Fallingwater Rising* is not only the home's definitive biography but also a keen study of the Kaufmanns. Toker is also one of the great historians of Pittsburgh. I'm sorry I can give him only posthumous acknowledgment. He passed away in 2021.

Other writers, both living and dead, to whom I am indebted include Gillian Gloyer, Ismail Kadare, Robert Kaplan, Frances Stonor Saunders, and of course Patrick Leigh Fermor.

It may seem almost redundant to thank one's immediate family in a book that is partly an homage to them, but their names do not appear. Love and gratitude to my mother Linda Belans and her partner Jim Lee, my father Mark Sobsey and his wife Edie Alfano-Sobsey. I also thank my sister Leah Sobsey, her husband Scott Howell, and their twin sons Lucas and Simon Sobsey Howell. My nephews are the familial heirs of this book. My first cousin Stephen Belans was a sustaining resource, guide, and mensch.

The word *Acknowledgment* doesn't begin to describe how I feel about my wife Heather Mallory. She kept me (barely) upright and functional during one of the most soul- and body-rending times of my life, and she is equally present in moments joyous or ordinary. In her love of justice and truth and her instincts for compassion and mercy; her restless and questioning body and spirit; her penetrating awareness of self and surroundings; her belief in a higher power whose shifting form and ineffable essence she never leaves off seeking; her practice of a heroic tradition of learning; and above all her deep and ineradicable devotion to family, which encompasses not only her own blood but wider circles of friendship, community, and need wherever she finds them—in all this she so fully embodies everything that is best about Jews and Jewishness that it amazes me she is not Jewish herself. She is the heart of my heart, trust of my trust, my wife and my tribe.